# Teaching with Digital Badges

# Innovations in Information Literacy

## ABOUT THE SERIES

This series for librarians and information literacy instructors provides information on the newest ideas and findings emerging from the field of information literacy, from teaching methods to emerging technologies to promising collaborations.

Books in the series engage in dialogues surrounding matters that are both conceptual and practical to librarians and instructors who are interested in teaching information literacy with local, cross-cultural, and international appeal.

The books are aimed at librarians at all types of institutions, from academic to public libraries, and also to non-library faculty members and teachers who are interested and invested in the conversations and advancements in information literacy.

## ABOUT THE SERIES EDITOR

The Innovations in Information Literacy series was conceived by and is edited by Trudi E. Jacobson, MLS, MA, Distinguished Librarian and Head of the Information Literacy Department, University at Albany Libraries.

Trudi Jacobson co-chaired the ACRL Information Literacy Competency Standards for Higher Education Task Force that created the ACRL Framework for Information Literacy for Higher Education. She received the Miriam Dudley Instruction Librarian of the Year award in 2009. Her current research involves metaliteracy, including digital badging for metaliteracy abilities. Her latest books are *Metaliteracy: Reinventing Information Literacies to Empower Learners* (2014), written with Thomas P. Mackey; and *Metaliteracy in Practice* (2016), edited with Thomas P. Mackey. Previously they co-edited four volumes on collaborative endeavors in library/faculty information literacy.

## TITLES IN THE SERIES

*Developing Dynamic Intersections between Collection Development and Information Literacy Instruction* by Amanda Scull
*Teaching with Digital Badges: Best Practices for Libraries* by Kelsey L. O'Brien and Trudi E. Jacobson

# Teaching with Digital Badges

## Best Practices for Libraries

Edited by Kelsey L. O'Brien and Trudi E. Jacobson

ROWMAN & LITTLEFIELD
*Lanham • Boulder • New York • London*

Published by Rowman & Littlefield
An imprint of The Rowman & Littlefield Publishing Group, Inc.
4501 Forbes Boulevard, Suite 200, Lanham, Maryland 20706
www.rowman.com

Unit A, Whitacre Mews, 26-34 Stannary Street, London SE11 4AB

Copyright © 2018 by The Rowman & Littlefield Publishing Group, Inc.

*All rights reserved.* No part of this book may be reproduced in any form or by any electronic or mechanical means, including information storage and retrieval systems, without written permission from the publisher, except by a reviewer who may quote passages in a review.

British Library Cataloguing in Publication Information Available

**Library of Congress Cataloging-in-Publication Data**

Names: Jacobson, Trudi E., 1957– editor. | O'Brien, Kelsey, 1986– editor.
Title: Teaching with digital badges : best practices for libraries / edited by Kelsey O'Brien and Trudi E. Jacobson.
Description: Lanham, Maryland : Rowman & Littlefield, [2018] | Series: Innovations in information literacy | Includes bibliographical references and index.
Identifiers: LCCN 2018018753 (print) | LCCN 2018039417 (ebook) | ISBN 9781538104187 (electronic) | ISBN 9781538104163 | ISBN 9781538104163 (hardcover : alk. paper) | ISBN 9781538104170 (paperback : alk. paper)
Subjects: LCSH: Information literacy—Study and teaching (Higher) | Digital badges.
Classification: LCC ZA3075 (ebook) | LCC ZA3075 .T45 2018 (print) | DDC 028.7071/173—dc23
LC record available at https://lccn.loc.gov/2018018753

∞™ The paper used in this publication meets the minimum requirements of American National Standard for Information Sciences—Permanence of Paper for Printed Library Materials, ANSI/NISO Z39.48-1992.

Printed in the United States of America

To our patient and persevering colleagues and
collaborators, and to the fearless educators who first
embarked on this journey with us
—Kelsey L. O'Brien and Trudi E. Jacobson

And to Mike, for fueling me forward
with encouragement and tea
—Kelsey

And to John, as always
—Trudi

Creativity is intelligence having fun.
>	—Joey Reiman, *Thinking for a Living*

# Contents

| | |
|---|---|
| List of Tables and Figures | ix |
| Foreword<br>    *Carla Casilli* | xi |
| Preface | xv |
| Acknowledgments | xix |

## Part I: The Badging Environment

**1** History of Micro-Credentialing     3
*Cinthya Ippoliti*

**2** Forces of Change for Higher Education: Opening Gates for Digital Badging     15
*Trudi E. Jacobson*

**3** Addressing Stakeholder Needs to Establish Meaningful Digital Badging in Higher Education     31
*Laureen P. Cantwell and Kristyn K. Rose*

**4** Digital Badges in Action     61
*Amanda Rose Fuller*

**5** Badges Can Do That: Ideas for Using Badges to Enhance
Information Literacy Instruction          81
*Allison Hosier*

**6** Badging Best Practices          91
*Kelsey L. O'Brien*

## Part II: Badging and Information Literacy: Case Studies

**7** Pollak Library Spark Tutorials          113
*Lindsay O'Neill*

**8** Competency-Based Education, Badging, and the Library          131
*Michael Fosmire and Amy S. Van Epps*

**9** Hot Neoliberal Commodities or Tools for Empowerment?
A Badges Case Study and Conversation          147
*Emily Ford, Jost Lottes, Betty Izumi, and Dawn M. Richardson*

**10** Badging and Workplace Information Literacy:
Helping Students Prepare for the Professional World          165
*Megan Blauvelt Heuer*

**11** Failing Better: Scaffolding Learning with the Metaliteracy
Badging System          183
*Kelsey L. O'Brien*

Index          199

About the Editors and Contributors          221

# List of Tables and Figures

## TABLES

| | | |
|---|---|---|
| **2.1** | Congruencies between educational forces and needs and the role of digital badging | 20 |
| **4.1** | Aurora Public Schools' digital badging system for all grades and subjects | 68 |
| **4.2** | Flexible two-tier badging system | 72 |
| **5.1** | Outline of information literacy skills from the ACRL standards and threshold concepts from the ACRL framework | 82 |
| **5.2** | Definitions of information literacy | 83 |
| **6.1** | Badge applications aligned with backward design stages | 109 |
| **7.1** | Badges issued for Spark Tutorial completion, 2016–2017 | 125 |
| **9.1** | Core badge matrix, Social Gerontology | 150 |
| **9.2** | Supplemental badges | 151 |
| **10.1** | Temerlin Information Literacy Program objectives aligned with ACRL framework concepts | 173 |

| | | |
|---|---|---|
| **10.2** | Rubric for Level 1 Badge | 176 |
| **10.3** | Learning modules and associated student learning outcomes | 178 |
| **11.1** | Metaliteracy badges aligned with learning goals (2014) | 189 |

## FIGURES

| | | |
|---|---|---|
| **4.1** | Aurora Public Schools' badge program logo | 62 |
| **4.2** | Aurora Public Schools' badge program's 21st Century Credentials | 67 |
| **8.1** | TST degree competencies, grouped into families | 140 |
| **8.2** | TST degree competencies for incoming students in fall 2017 | 142 |
| **11.1** | The Metaliteracy badges | 187 |
| **11.2** | The Metaliterate Learner badge | 188 |
| **11.3** | Master Evaluator badge constellation | 190 |

# Foreword

*Carla Casilli*

In these pages you'll find considerations of badges as tools, as a movement, as a philosophical approach, as answers, and as questions themselves.

The beauty of badges is that they encourage their creators to ask "what if" questions, such as

- What if we had a new world of learning recognition where we could begin anew?
- What if we could acknowledge learning and experiences in ways that were co-created with the individuals who earn them, use them, teach with them?
- What if the tool for learning recognition allowed for self-reflexivity where the builders learned as much about themselves as the earners did?
- What if personal learning trajectories could be traced into meaningful constellations and then spun out into new and even more useful constellations?

This is what badges can do: alter how we recognize learning, shift how we acknowledge accomplishments and each other, and change the world around us.

The 2010 Mozilla Drumbeat Festival—Learning, Freedom and the Web—marked the germinal year of Mozilla's Open Badges initiative. A simple idea at its inception, it grew to become a technical specification, a philosophy, and a movement. How far it's come in such a short time! As one of the founding architects of the open badges movement, I'm thrilled to see the years of commitment to learning about, with and through badges and badge systems represented in this welcome and essential compendium—a true state of the art of open badges.

While the tech world is now abuzz with blockchain and distributed technologies, open badges continue to evolve, mutate, and thrive. The basic DNA of badges, issuers, earners, criteria, and dates of experience are strong and sturdy. Like Mendel and his pea experiments, from small variations in basic components, badges have cross-pollinated, resulting in a variety of forms, shapes, and uses. This book offers critical insight into those variations, as well as the techniques that can provide similar results.

The ethos of the original open badges initiative offered the power of networked thinking. Not simply digital badges, open badges are imbued with an ethos of openness, transparency, and sharing. As compelling communication media, badges afford the capacity for feedback and improvement through iteration. Throughout these chapters we learn that open badges and digital credentials can be giant leaps into new worlds of learning recognition—and these authors are at the forefront of that exploration.

Badge systems are crucibles for meaning and value. At the heart of the open badges initiative is a stalwart commitment to transparency: transparency in pedagogy, transparency in development, transparency in assessment. To the uninitiated or unfamiliar, this may not sound particularly revolutionary, but the authors of these chapters can attest—as can I—that the thorough exploration and development of a badge system will call into question nearly every aspect of a learning environment. Badges can represent knowledge acquisition and touch upon learner motivation. They can represent small achievements and cumulative gains—or act as tools of social and economic justice, righting the scales of learning inequity. Badges are protean in the broadest sense of the word.

Contested, questioned, jeered, cheered, and feared, badge acolytes have had to explain themselves, defend their pedagogies, justify their decisions, back up their rationales, and repeatedly demonstrate results. Here in these pages you'll find laudable badge system successes, hard-won experience, and meaningful areas of consideration. Within these eleven chapters, you'll read about questions of authenticity, discuss issues of privacy, address concerns about validity, visit the ever-changing world of assessment, and explore the efficacy of endorsement. Use this content as a primer, a series of examples, a notebook to share with your professional communities (and learners!) in the co-development and co-creation of badge systems that advance toward a new and enhanced world of learning recognition possibilities.

The chapters in this book operate in a manner similar to badges: by offering many possibilities, interpretations, and opportunities for reflection, consideration, and improvement, they provide a view into a changed and improved future of learning. I invite you to read each chapter with an open mind, to offer yourself up to possibility, and then to dive in. Why? Because the explorations here reveal badges to be more important and complex tools than simplistic carrots or sticks. Indeed, they are collectively more powerful than mere grades and transcripts, although the authors note that badges also function quite effectively alongside those culturally acceptable but blunt learning recognition tools, too.

One of the extraordinary aspects of this work is its wide-ranging approach. You will find discussions that will excite you, encourage you, caution you, and ultimately inform you about the apparently boundless possibilities of badges. With a variety of opinions and approaches, some are bound to chafe. And while the reader may not agree with all that is written on these pages, I applaud each author for their scholarship and commitment to examining and interrogating badges. It is a truism that not everything about badges is simple or pretty. And an exploration of badges that revealed only their benefits without noting their challenges or examining the myriad interpretations of their development, use, and effectiveness would make for a far less interesting book.

Badges enter into existing systems of educational representation. As such they are a system level intervention and consequently operate as independent structures that can be linked to other independent structures, creating new experiences and outcomes and gaining power as they interact. They interconnect in ways and result in generative combinations that mere letter grades can never do. They encourage comparison across environments, including classes, labs, schools, and industries. They reveal where an institution or an organization places their values. They provide an ability to acknowledge learning and experiences not previously possible. They open up pathway possibilities, and act as a way to codify them, to understand and test them as never before.

At their essence, badges are a way to acknowledge and build community. They begin the complicated process of connecting the vast, powerful, and often hidden world of informal learning with the opaque, established, and expected world of formal education. They can act as the bridge between these two vital worlds of learning. What other learning tool can do that?

For the readers who are contemplating badges, you'll find recommendations for consideration, ideas for effective development approaches, and explorations of learning pathways illuminated by badges. You'll discover the potential for connective tissue between competency-based education and badge design.

For the readers who have dismissed badges as the latest educational fad, you'll find new reason to reconsider these multifaceted tools in chapters replete with research indicating where they might be more effective and how they're being used across various environments.

For the readers who have embraced badges, here you'll find your compatriots in the struggle to improve learning recognition. Within case studies, you'll hear echoes of your own explorations, considerations, challenges, and successes.

Finally, for readers like myself, who have helped to construct, support, and encourage the open badges community, you'll experience deep appreciation for the impressive variety of approaches, gratification in the profound consideration of their educational and learning possibilities, respect for the ongoing work of the community continuing to build this important movement, and exhilaration in the hope for the future that badges continue to engender.

# Preface

This volume focuses on digital badging, a specific form of micro-credentialing that can serve as an innovative teaching and assessment tool. First popularized through video games and mobile applications, digital badges are increasingly prevalent in education, lending themselves as granular representations of student achievements. When thoughtfully implemented, digital badges have the potential to significantly disrupt the education landscape. Traditional credentialing methods, with transcripts as a primary example, provide insufficient detail to permit close analysis of acquired knowledge and competencies. While a course title alludes to associated content, a transcript provides neither specific information about the course nor the details of a student's performance and understanding of individual learning outcomes.

Many are familiar with badges from experience as Boy or Girl Scouts, where earning a badge is a mark of distinction shared when proudly worn on a sash. This merit badge represents mastery of a particular topic or skill. Digital badges have many of the same hallmarks, enhanced by the affordances of the online environment. Yet misconceptions about badging abound, in part fueled by the over-awarding of badges for trivial accomplishments.

Digital badges, when created appropriately and used judiciously, offer great potential. Among their advantages, digital badges make learning more transparent, recognize discrete competencies and abilities, acknowledge non-traditional learning, and empower learners to showcase their skills and accomplishments. Providing opportunities to earn substantive badges can be especially valuable in connection with information literacy, to enhance or extend classroom instruction.

While many librarians have likely heard about badging or gamification trends, few resources provide guidance about how to develop an effective badging initiative or how to align badging to meet particular learning goals. Practical advice on how to leverage this innovative learning tool, how to avoid potential pitfalls, and how to create and implement appropriate badges can best be learned from those who have implemented badging within their instructional programs.

We have witnessed firsthand the potential of badges both as vehicles for and indicators of substantial learning. Together with other members of the Metaliteracy Learning Collaborative, we created and are using a robust badging system with students. Its use in information literacy courses and in a broad swath of courses across campus, taught by faculty and teaching assistants, has provided a great deal of feedback. Our positive experiences with badging encouraged us to share what we have learned and to seek out others who have created and used information literacy badging projects in order to represent a range of settings and applications.

Before describing the core of the volume, we would like to encourage all readers to dive into Carla Casilli's energizing foreword. Carla is a key player in the development of the open badges movement, and her foreword captures and illuminates much of the pioneering nature, and the distinct value and potential, of digital badges through the eyes of someone who has been intimately involved since their beginnings. It is not to be missed.

Following the front matter of the book, the chapters are divided into two parts. Part I explores the environment in which badges are being developed, in particular situating them within the current educational setting, and provides guidelines on how best to create a badging program. After an introduction to the nature and potential application of digital badges in the first chapter, "Overview of Micro-credentialing," the second chapter, "Forces of Change for Higher Education: Opening Gates for Digital Badging," examines key social and economic trends that impact education. These forces, such as globalization, online learning, and employment, all provide potential opportunities for badging. The third chapter addresses issues connected to the implementation of digital badges within higher education. This comprehensive chapter, "Addressing Stakeholder Needs to Establish Meaningful Digital Badging in Higher Education," examines issues that affect institutions, students, and employers. Chapter 4, "Digital Badges in Action," examines badging applications in a K–12 school setting. An overview of "Using Badges to Enhance Information Literacy Instruction" is found in chapter 5. Part I of the book concludes with a chapter on best practices aligned with the backward design model. For those who are considering developing badging in their information literacy programs (and beyond), this chapter is a must read.

Librarians have been some of the leading pioneers at the forefront of this exciting new micro-credentialing frontier. Part II of this book details their firsthand experiences, in some cases collaborating with teachers and faculty to create, use, and refine digital badges and digital badging systems. These chapters provide a wealth of ideas about using digital badges in academic and school libraries to engage and motivate students. Chapter 7 describes the first stage of the "Pollak Library Spark Tutorials," a suite of tutorials and digital badges designed to provide foundational information literacy instruction to a campus of 40,000 students. Chapter 8, "Competency-Based Education, Badging, and the Library," explores digital badging as a component of a competency-based degree program at a university where information literacy is a part of the core curriculum. Chapter 9, "A Badges Case Study and Conversation," looks at badging as part of a curriculum mapping and instructional design project undertaken by three faculty members, a librarian, and an instructional designer. Chapter 10, "Badging and Workplace Information Literacy," describes the development of a rigorous, two-level badge initiative that prepares students for the workplace. And chapter 11, "Scaffolding Learning with the Metaliteracy Badging System," explores a robust badging system for metaliteracy that has been used in a wide variety of courses across a university campus.

This plethora of case studies will help you visualize potential applications of this exciting new trend for your setting while gaining valuable insights from the experiences of others. The chapters will provide inspiration if you are interested in

- providing an engaging learning experience for students
- exploring how badges can motivate, support, and celebrate learning achievements
- discovering how badges might enhance your teaching
- using badging to form meaningful collaborations with faculty and teachers
- developing your knowledge about badge system design and badging platforms
- launching a badging project of your own

If you would like to learn more about a particular project mentioned in one of the book's chapters, you will find the authors' e-mail addresses in their biographical statements located at the end of the book. As you explore the guidelines and examples in this book, we hope that you will feel the same enthusiasm for the potential of well-designed badges for information literacy instruction that we do.

Our experiences conceptualizing, developing, implementing, and promoting digital badges have called upon the gamut of knowledge we have about teaching and learning, instructional design, collaborations with faculty, and more, all while we were learning about badges and badging platforms. This opportunity has challenged and re-energized our teaching practices; we encourage you to dive in and consider the possibilities for the learners you work with.

# Acknowledgments

We would like to acknowledge the vision, drive, dedication, and creativity of our chapter authors. Their pioneering work developing badging programs and content provides valuable models to inform and inspire the readers of this book.

We owe our heartfelt thanks to Carla Casilli, a renowned expert and valued scholar in the open badging community, and to Lucas Blair, co-founder of Little Bird Games, both of whom have been generous with their time and have had a profound influence on our conceptualization and implementation of badges. Special thanks to Carla for writing the foreword to this book.

In a badging-related project focused on graduate students and digital literacy, we had the good fortune to work with Stephanie Affinito, Michele Forte, Karen Gardner-Athey, and Donna Mahar. It was a pleasure. Even when we were most confused!

The Metaliteracy badging system is very much a communal effort. Several students, both undergraduate and graduate, provided a welcome students' perspective to our badging system. We appreciate their dedicated work in developing quests and their willingness to make them openly available. Many others, notably Thomas Mackey, Allison Hosier, Michele Forte, Kathleen Stone, Jenna Pitera, and Allyson Kaczmarek, have contributed significantly by writing creative and effective learning materials. We also owe a debt of gratitude to the many instructors and graduate assistants with whom we have worked over the last several years on badging. They played the role of guinea pig in a most accommodating manner and provided helpful feedback in the development of our badging system.

Dean Rebecca Mugridge of the University at Albany Libraries believed in our badging project—so much that she helped to fund it. It literally wouldn't have been possible to sustain the program without her support for its redesign on a new platform. We thank the Innovative Instruction Technology Grant program, in particular Lisa Stephens, Senior Strategist for Academic Innovation at the Office of the SUNY Provost, the powerhouse behind the grant program. IIT grants gave our metaliteracy badging project and its offshoots their chance at seeing daylight.

The epigraph is taken from Joey Reiman, *Thinking for a Living: Creating Ideas That Revitalize Your Business, Career and Life* (Atlanta: Longstreet Press, 1998), 49.

# 1

THE BADGING ENVIRONMENT

# 1

# History of Micro-Credentialing

*Cinthya Ippoliti*

Awards, badges, certificates: these concepts are not new in our cultures; nor are they new to the academy. But they are now being implemented and utilized in previously unanticipated ways. According to Cynthia Durley (2005) of the Institute for Credentialing Excellence's National Commission for Certifying Agencies, credentialing is a process whereby "an entity, authorized and qualified to do so, grants formal recognition to, or records the recognition status of, individuals, organizations, institutions, programs, processes, services, or products that meet predetermined and standardized criteria" (4). Digital credentials emerged as early as the 1990s as the Internet began to change the ways in which existing processes and paradigms functioned. Digital records, as well as more social forces such as gaming cultures, gave way to a new kind of thinking about how these certificates were awarded and functioned as part of this digital environment. Starting in the early 2000s, the focus on gaming has shifted with the emergence of the "knowledge economy," in which employers are seeking skills that are not being provided via typical degree programs (Casilli and Hickey 2016). Enter micro-credentials as alternative ways to earn and showcase these types of skills and knowledge that are at once both elusive yet also in need of clear and authoritative documentation and verification.

Joseph Fanfarelli, Stephanie Vie, and Rudy McDaniel (2015) provide a three-pronged context in which badges serve as rewards, feedback, and narratives, offering the validity and rigor needed to render them a viable means of signaling mastery of certain skill sets or competencies. As rewards, badges can "encourage users to enact certain behaviors or meet particular goals" (57). Applied correctly, badges are awarded for activities that extend beyond simple tasks, such as attendance at an event, and include meaningful engagement with the content via the creation of a learning product or artifact. As feedback, badges offer constructive information to help improve the learning process itself. While badges are not methods of assessment per se, they can act as milestones along a completion trajectory that culminates with the achievement of a goal or task. Badges provide signals to the learner as they advance from one step to the next, indicating progress and completion in the form of a new set of accomplishments. Finally, as narratives, badges can frame success "within the context of a larger environment" (58), thereby empowering the recipient to write their own story about the new knowledge or skills gained and what they mean for that person's academic, professional, or even personal character.

While the potential benefits of badges have been well documented, serious questions remain regarding authenticity, privacy, and validity. These questions exert pressures on credentialing systems to evolve in order to keep up with employer demands. They also call on these credentials to provide concrete evidence of mastery via strategies (outlined in 2007 by then-president of the American Educational Research Association, Eva Baker), such as multiple assessment measures, measures of opportunity to learn, performance assessment, formative assessment, limiting the number of standards, and technology-based assessment (Casilli and Hickey 2016, 121). It is beyond the scope of this chapter to provide an in-depth look at the history of micro-credentials and badges. However, editors Dirk Ifenthaler, Nicole Bellin-Mularski, and Dana-Kristin Mah do a masterful job of laying out all of the issues related to badges and micro-credentials in their 2016 book, *Foundation of Digital Badges and Micro-credentials: Demonstrating and Recognizing Knowledge and Competencies*, which covers everything from the history of badges to their implementation on an international scale and beyond.

## WHY MICRO-CREDENTIALS ARE IMPORTANT

James Willis (with Strunk and Hardtner; 2016) describes micro-credentials as a concept rather than a specific "technology, protocol, or practice" (2) and provides an interesting take on what has become a widespread discussion regarding alternative credentials as supplements for more formal degrees and coursework. Willis proposes that micro-credentials can help those who might be disenfranchised from more traditional opportunities by being deployed "in informal learning environments like extra- and co-curricular activities" outside the "bounds of traditional accreditation" (3). Furthermore, he argues that micro-credentials can serve as important indicators of interdisciplinary skill sets that encourage creativity and re-mixing to highlight individualized learning pathways.

In this context, micro-credentials take the form of a social movement, with power dynamics shifting so that alternative pathways toward achieving goals are just as valuable as their more traditional and formal counterparts. Drawing upon intrinsic motivation, this shift allows individuals to aspire to achieve their fullest potential, which exceeds immediate accomplishment of a specific goal. Thus digital badges could have significant and lasting implications for the development of workforce capacity and self-improvement as a good not just for the individual but also for society at large.

A white paper co-written by the Mozilla Foundation and Peer 2 Peer University, with the MacArthur Foundation, "Open Badges for Lifelong Learning," set the precedent for what has become known as the open badge movement, in which badges are purposefully both open and decentralized. The authors describe how badges provide "portable and sustainable value" for each learner to control how and when they are earned and distributed (2012, 6). Consequently the surrounding infrastructure must support badges from a wide variety of sources, enabling them to be shared and displayed across platforms (and with different viewing options depending on the context). It must also ensure a robust endorsement arrangement providing adequate customization and flexibility to allow learners to determine badge integration into workflows and experiences. Open badges converge as object and ideology, providing learners with opportunities to share their achievements in a variety of contexts.

## DIGITAL BADGES AS A FORM OF MICRO-CREDENTIALING

Micro-credentials tend to represent more discrete skills and achievements and can be thought of as interrelated mini-certificates that can be combined and stacked toward a larger certificate or earned as separate entities. Micro-credentials work on a smaller scale than a traditional transcript, which shows an overall summary of degree work, and tend to provide a snapshot of a particular set of skills. They can be earned in addition to transcripts and can also be combined with each other, giving them more flexible application options. Digital badges are a specific form of micro-credentialing and are defined as a "representation of an accomplishment, interest, or affiliation that is visual [and] available online and contains metadata, including links that help explain the context, meaning, process, and result of an activity" (Gibson et al. 2015, 404). As will be discussed in further detail later in this chapter, badges and badging systems incentivize learners to engage in positive habits and behaviors and encourage individualized pathways to learning that indicate progress and achievement. Most badges also require some form of validation from an organization or entity verifying that the badge is authentic and that the skills or knowledge earned are both accurate and meet certain criteria for quality. The validations are usually set by that same organization.

According to Cameron Wills and Ying Xie (2016), the advantage of using badges is that they represent "varying degrees of mastery and specialization" that can have an impact on learners' values and expectations for success (262). The authors argue that there is still a need for a framework for integrating badges into instructional design and pedagogy that draws from such concepts as self-efficacy, game motivation, and learning regulation and scaffolding in order to truly lay the foundation for the design and implementation of badges within an educational setting (263–64). It is therefore important to note that badges themselves are not the focus for the learner but, rather, the experiences and actions behind them. Care must be taken that the learner understands the implications of following a certain progression to achieve the desired goal. For example, if there is an opportunity for a badge to be earned by attending workshops, it behooves the learner to focus on the value of a particular skill set such as communication that is important to the their long-term goals as opposed to simply picking those workshops that are easiest to attend. As well, the designer needs to ensure that the path contains the necessary elements for success packaged in a trajectory that is flexible and customizable and that provides opportunities for reflection and synthesis along the way.

## DIGITAL BADGES AS TEACHING, LEARNING, AND ASSESSMENT TOOLS

Digital badges are more than virtual tokens awarded for skill completion, however. They serve in several ways as learning catalysts. According to Andrea Rehak, Daniel Hickey, and Christine Chow (2014, 6–7), badges

1. recognize diverse learning by bringing attention to skills and knowledge that might otherwise go unnoticed
2. help to map learning trajectories by offering levels of learning and charting a path for an overall learning plan
3. allow for external endorsements that increase their validity and usefulness in a variety of contexts, including gaining employer recognition
4. and differentiate between the role of the educator and the learner within the same learning ecosystem.

Rehak, Hickey, and Chow's model specifically allows badges to play an active role in both the learning and the assessment aspects of the broader context of curriculum design. Badges facilitate the process of gaining new skills and knowledge as well as define their breadth and depth via progressive levels and meta-badges. Badges can also serve as important teaching tools because they enable learning outcomes and success indicators to be made much more transparent by virtue of their awarding. It is important that learners clearly understand not only how they can earn the badge itself but also the measures of achievement required to demonstrate mastery of that particular skill set.

Badges can also be utilized for assessment purposes. Assessment is usually comprised of learning outcomes and the measures of the outcomes, both in terms of whether the outcome is met and also to what degree. Peter Janzow (2014) solidifies this concept by stating that badges are "a digital representation of a learning outcome" that allows for that outcome to become part of an assessment methodology that can take many forms, dealing with a snapshot or summative approach versus a longer-term view, or a formative one (9). Both types of foci employ different methodologies that range from surveys for a faster, more indirect view of what the learner knows to rubrics that are applied to learning artifacts to determine if there is evidence of learning within an authentic product.

A badge can therefore be awarded as part of a binary function: either the learners performed the appropriate action, or they did not. In this case, the meaningfulness of the badge can vary, because it does not indicate how well that action was performed, simply that it was achieved. Much like a gamer reaching the next stage of the game, in this instance it does not matter how the gamer got there but simply that it happened. On the other hand, badges that contain metadata or attached evidence of completion provide a much richer, almost portfolio-like view into the work that occurred in order for that badge to be earned.

The inclusion of this more detailed information raises the validity of that badge, enhancing it from a visual token of completion to a complete story about the learner's journey. When combined with the broader learning outcomes of the specific badge program, a much more holistic picture of the learning scenario emerges, clarifying what the learner's goals were, how they were achieved, and to what extent they were successful. The combination of embedded evidence and descriptive metadata is especially important, as one of the main criticisms of badges is that it can be difficult to ascertain their reliability and validity. Indications of learner mastery can vary depending on the credibility of the issuing agency or organization, their awarding criteria, and the overall environment in which the badge activities occurred.

## WHY BADGES PLAY AN IMPORTANT ROLE IN TEACHING AND LEARNING

Badges play two significant roles in teaching and learning, both in terms of (1) knowledge acquisition and learner motivation and (2) engagement with the learning process itself. Kyle Bowen and Andrea Thomas (2014) state that "badges can provide insight related to how students learn, which institutions can apply to the way they deliver instruction" (22). This works well for those areas that are much more nebulous in terms of skills and knowledge, such as critical thinking and research skills. Measuring how well a student thinks critically is not a simple task. Badges, however, can provide evidence of a student's ability to analyze and synthesize information and develop a finished product that cuts across curricula, helping educators make a correlation between specific learning experiences and an expected or desired outcome.

In addition, Bowen and Thomas quote Erin Knight, Mozilla's senior director of learning, who states that "we're not talking about throwing out the existing system but moving away from the abstract credential, which is more like a rubber stamp that loses evidence of the pathways people took while learning" (Knight quoted in Bowen and Thomas 2014, 22). Badges can bring to light those hidden pathways and illuminate both the skill set that is being earned as well as the way in which it is being achieved. This provides a transparent view of the learning process itself, thus documenting not simply the end result but also the learner's intellectual work when completing a task or assignment.

The second significant role that badges play in teaching and learning is the shaping of and influence on learner motivation and engagement, especially within a digital environment where the badge may not be earned in a face-to-face situation. Jelena Jovanovic and Vladan Devedzic (2014) take this concept even further as they discuss various important elements of badges as alternative forms of assessment, integrating elements of peer and self-reflection, and charting the learning course (117). They contend that in the digital environment badges not only become mechanisms to assess outcomes and skills but also offer alternative forms of sharing and engagement by allowing peer review and shared commenting, something that is often not possible in more formal assessment activities. The individual's ability to think about the chosen path toward accomplishing a learning goal helps to develop metacognitive, organizational, planning, and development skills during the process of earning the badge itself. The path toward earning a badge is not necessarily predetermined but can be shaped and changed depending on the broader goal, which forces a learner to plan ahead and think through those actions precisely.

This role is deeply embedded in achievement goal theory, which examines the balance between desiring mastery of a certain set of concepts versus simply performing better (Elliot 1999). If badges are considered as a way to scale up knowledge (whether for improvement or mastery), it becomes clear that they are intrinsically tied into the processes learners might use in order to accomplish their desired levels of achievement. In addition, motivation is also related to personal interest; the more a learner views the topic as personally meaningful, the greater the chances that they will devote more time to understanding that topic in depth (Eccles and Wigfield 2000, 68). Eccles et al. (1983) define specific characteristics of this interest: importance of doing well on the task, interest in the task itself, or interest in a goal that is tangentially related to the task itself (89–90). Collectively these elements help paint a picture of motivation and engagement that goes far beyond the superficial need to check a box or earn a grade to indicate a particular requirement has been met. They speak to the learner's most personal motives and goals, some of which may not be directly related to badge activities but are part of that broader set of achievements ultimately driving the learner to earn them.

This reveals an aspect of motivation that is not often addressed in discussions surrounding badges and that can influence how a badging system is designed and implemented on two levels. If the learner is already self-aware of these motivations and consciously working toward them, that system can then support this process much more effectively. If, on the other hand, the learner is more interested in simply moving on to the next step, having a badging model that can uncover the deeper reasons behind those activities would help individualize the process and perhaps even bring out these deeper elements, producing a richer, more robust experience than anticipated.

A cornerstone of the badges movement is that badges provide learners with alternative pathways toward success, permitting engaged, self-directed learners to forge their own learning pathways. The methods and concepts behind instructional design can be used to examine the advantages of user involvement and the dynamics within the learning process itself. Alison Carr-Chellman and Michael Savoy (2004) make a small, but vital distinction between user-centered design, where "something [is] being done to rather than with the learner," and user design, which "brings this conflict into clear relief by engaging users in empowered decision-making through design" (702; emphasis original).

Amy Cox and Zoe Szajnfarber support the idea of active learner involvement: "In considering the innovation literature, it is clear that users are capable of a broader role in the design process" (2015, 1). Likewise,

Carr-Chellman and Savoy discuss the varying levels of user participation, ranging from instructional design in which the teacher defines what the learner will learn, to user-centered and user design in which the focus is on "learning and pedagogy rather than tool use" (ibid., 704). They describe the most inclusive form of design as "emancipatory," defined by Gretchen Rossman and Sharon Rallis as design in which participants "are collaboratively producing knowledge to improve their work and their lives" (2003, 15). When implemented to facilitate user engagement, badges can help transform the learning experience of the individual who in turn may apply that newfound knowledge in the employment sector, helping to further this model for themselves and the workforce.

Granting learners control over their learning experiences engages, motivates, and empowers them to achieve the goals they aspire to. The Carr-Chellman and Savoy continuum of user involvement provides a potential model for a library or institution interested in implementing a pilot badging system. This model would entail collaborating with learners and bringing in representatives from the user community as consultants throughout the development process. The organizing institutions could go beyond the focus groups described by Carr-Chellman and Savoy by incorporating collaborative models such as design thinking, a highly iterative and interactive process that approaches a problem from the user's perspective. This model involves the user both in the design and feedback phases. The methods utilized would depend on the scope of the badging system, its level of complexity, and its overall purpose.

It might appear that more pedagogically oriented models such as backward design are being dismissed here as not having a role to play within this user-designer relationship. Although these models are certainly important in ensuring that the activities in which learners engage are instructionally sound, they represent the end, rather than the beginning, of the journey, and this is where the more user-centered flavor of engagement can thrive. Although the badging schematic might be co-developed by learners in concert with the designers, some of the activities required to complete the journey might be less user-driven due to factors such as specific expertise or access to resources. For example, one would not necessarily expect students to design a lesson around the *Framework for Information Literacy* (ACRL 2015). However, student feedback might be utilized regarding its effectiveness in helping them understand the concepts presented via assessment and some evaluative questions such as "To what extent did the session help you understand x?" Stepping outside of the design process to at least consider, if not directly solicit, user input is a much-needed step in badging system design and planning.

## DIGITAL BADGE APPLICATIONS IN . . .

### Transformational Teaching

Thus far, the discussion has centered on general notions of learning and learner motivation as they relate to digital badges without delving too deeply into teaching and learning theories. The "transformational teaching" framework provides a compelling case for application to the structure and design of digital badges and ultimately their use. George Slavich and Philip Zimbardo coined *transformational teaching* as instruction that increases student "mastery of key course concepts while enhancing students' learning-related attitudes, values, beliefs, and skills" (2012, 576). They go on to describe theories of learning and change management ranging from social cognitive theory to intentional change theory and to examine three results associated with transformational teaching and, by association, learning:

1. promoting personal efficacy (social cognitive theory)
2. changing frames of reference and habits (transformational learning)
3. realizing the ideal self (intentional change theory)

Badges and badge programs can encourage learners to take control of their experiences in two ways: by giving them agency in what skills or knowledge to focus on, as well as providing them with a flexible path to get there. The learner has to make conscious decisions about what badges to earn and then invest enough time and effort into the process in order to earn them. The iterative and often non-linear process of learning via badges challenges the learner's existing habits of mind and points of view because of the new knowledge and/or skills gained. Badged content has the potential to become integrated into learners' mental schema in the course of achieving a desired broader goal, possibly leading to a shift in worldview.

The realization of the ideal self as explained by intentional change theory is another important element within the context of badges; unlike in the gaming world, learners seldom earn badges for so-called bragging rights. Within the context of education, the badge itself is simply a means to a more distant end, one of personal betterment. Whether the badge is meant to assist the learner in scaling up to a better job, developing more robust credentials, or simply providing evidence of specialized knowledge, it is designed to improve upon the learning within a context such as a class, which may have been insufficient to propel the individual to that next stage of their life or career.

**Digital Pedagogy**

As mentioned previously in this chapter, the digital badge itself is meaningless without quality instructional activities and learning experiences surrounding it. Without a solid pedagogical framework, even the most well-designed badge becomes nothing more than something to be checked off the list as opposed to a representation of the learning that has occurred. Ideally badges should help clarify outcomes and outline a path for success. As with any other technology tool it is important to consider when to apply badges and how they might positively or negatively impact the learning process. For example, will tying the badge into a class assignment merely force students to complete it simply to get the grade? Alternatively, if the badge is simply part of the larger course, what value will it have once students have finished the class, and how will they be able to articulate that value later?

Digital pedagogy also takes into account how technology enhances engagement and how it shapes learning. Engagement has already been discussed as a key factor when analyzing badges, but enhancing the learning experience through technology is an essential component of this context. The focus again is not on the badges themselves but, rather, on how they are applied within a learning context. To say that earning a badge has changed an individual may be an accurate statement by virtue of the knowledge gained, but it is also dependent on the type of instruction received, whether it was face-to-face or virtual, what the ultimate goal of the learner might be, and how the pathway for receiving the badge has been constructed. The meta-level process described earlier in the chapter is doubly at play here, especially within a virtual environment where success is highly dependent on self-motivation and interactivity with various systems. The badging experience should be able to harness the technology at hand to tap into the self-reflective aspect of the learning process so that the learner is transformed not only by the knowledge itself but by the experience of earning the badge as well.

## CONCLUDING THOUGHTS

The implementation of digital badges will most likely continue to evoke mixed feelings. It is the goal of this chapter to position badges as transformative opportunities for all those who champion them and to provide thoughtful ideas for those who remain skeptical. It is easy to get lost in the gloss of appealing images and graphics and forget that badges are only as powerful as the learning experiences and opportunities they provide. It is up to educators to help shape the role they will play on an individual level as well as a societal level. On this larger scale, educators can create learning opportunities for those who have no other recourse to see their dreams and goals realized on another, perhaps far more meaningful and personal, stage.

## REFERENCES

ACRL (Association of College and Research Libraries). 2015. *Framework for Information Literacy for Higher Education*. Chicago: ACRL. http://www.ala.org/acrl/standards/ilframework.

Bowen, Kyle, and Andrea Thomas. 2014. "Badges: A Common Currency for Learning." *Change: The Magazine of Higher Learning* 46 (1): 21–25.

Carr-Chellman, Alison, and Michael Savoy. 2004. "User-Design Research." In *Handbook of Research on Educational Communications and Technology*, edited by J. Michael Spector, M. David Merrill, Jan Elen, and M. J. Bishop, 701–15. London: Springer International.

Casilli, Carla, and Daniel Hickey. 2016. "Transcending Conventional Credentialing and Assessment Paradigms with Information-Rich Digital Badges." *The Information Society* 32 (2): 117–29.

Cox, Amy, and Zoe Szajnfarber. 2015. "Case Study Research of User Design Methods." Presentation at the International Annual Conference of the American Society for Engineering Management, Indianapolis, October. Retrieved from https://www.researchgate.net/publication/298212768_CASE_STUDY_RESEARCH_OF_USER_DESIGN_METHODS.

Durley, Cynthia. 2005. *The ICE Guide to Understanding Credentialing Concepts*. Washington, DC: Institute for Credentialing Excellence.

Eccles, Jacquelynne S., Terry F. Adler, Robert Futterman, Susan B. Goff, Caroline M. Kaczala, Judith I. Meece, and Carol Midgley. 1983. "Expectancies, Values, and Academic Behaviors." In *Achievement and Achievement Motives: Psychological and Sociological Approaches*, edited by Janet Taylor Spence, 75–146. San Francisco: W. H. Freeman.

Eccles, Jacquelynne S., and Allan Wigfield. 2000. "Expectancy-Value Theory of Achievement Motivation." *Contemporary Educational Psychology* 25 (1): 68–81.

Elliot, Andrew J. 1999. "Approach and Avoidance Motivation and Achievement Goals." *Educational Psychologist* 34 (3): 169–89.

Fanfarelli, Joseph, Stephanie Vie, and Rudy McDaniel. 2015. "Understanding Digital Badges through Feedback, Reward, and Narrative: A Multidisciplinary Approach to Building Better Badges in Social Environments." *Communication Design Quarterly Review* 3 (3): 56–60. Retrieved from https://www.researchgate.net/publication/281359104_Understanding_digital_badges_through_feedback_reward_and_narrative.

Gibson, David, Nathaniel Ostashewski, Kim Flintoff, Sheryl Grant, and Erin Knight. 2015. "Digital Badges in Education." *Education and Information Technologies* 20 (2): 403–10.

Ifenthaler, Dirk, Nicole Bellin-Mularski, Dana-Kristin Mah, eds. 2016. *Foundations of Digital Badges and Micro-credentials: Demonstrating and Recognizing Knowledge and Competencies*. Cham, Switzerland: Springer International.

Janzow, Peter. 2014. "Connecting Learning to Jobs through Digital Badges." *The Catalyst* 42 (2): 9–11.

Jovanovic, Jelena, and Vladan Devedzic. 2014. "Open Badges: Challenges and Opportunities." In *Advances in Web-Based Learning—ICWL 2014: 13th International Conference, Talinn, Estonia, August 14–17, 2014; Proceedings*, edited by Elvira Popescu, Rynson W. H. Lau, Kai Pata, Howard Leung, Mart Laanpere, 56–65. Cham, Switzerland: Springer International.

Mozilla Foundation and Peer 2 Peer University. 2012. "Open Badges for Lifelong Learning: Exploring and Open Badge Ecosystem to Support Skill Development and Lifelong Learning for Real Results Such as Jobs and Advancement." Working document. With the MacArthur Foundation. Last modified January 23. https://wiki.mozilla.org/images/b/b1/OpenBadges-Working-Paper_092011.pdf.

Rehak, Andrea M., Daniel T. Hickey, and Christine Chow. 2014. "Design Principles and Enacted Practices for Recognizing Learning with Digital Badges: A Collective Case Study." Presentation at The Power of Education Research for Innovation in Practice and Policy, the 2014 Annual Meeting of the American Educational Research Association, Philadelphia, April 6.

Rossman, Gretchen B., and Sharon F. Rallis. 2003. *Learning in the Field: An Introduction to Qualitative Research*. 2nd ed. Thousand Oaks, CA: Sage.

Slavich, George M., and Philip G. Zimbardo. 2012. "Transformational Teaching: Theoretical Underpinnings, Basic Principles, and Core Methods." *Educational Psychology Review* 24 (4): 569–608. Retrieved from https://www.ncbi.nlm.nih.gov/pmc/articles/PMC3498956/.

Willis III, James, Viktoria Strunk, and Tasha Hardtner. 2016. "Microcredentials and Educational Technology: A Proposed Ethical Taxonomy." *Educause Review*, April 18. https://er.educause.edu/articles/2016/4/microcredentials-and-educational-technology-a-proposed-ethical-taxonomy.

Wills, Cameron, and Ying Xie. 2016. "Toward a Comprehensive Theoretical Framework for Designing Digital Badges." In *Foundation of Digital Badges and Microcredentials: Demonstrating and Recognizing Knowledge and Competencies*, edited by Dirk Ifenthaler, Nicole Bellin-Mularski, and Dana-Kristin Mah, 261–72. Cham, Switzerland: Springer International.

# 2

## Forces of Change for Higher Education
### Opening Gates for Digital Badging

*Trudi E. Jacobson*

While higher education is not known for adapting to major changes quickly, digital badges are steadily making their way into the academic landscape. Given the potentially disruptive nature of badging, the lack of familiarity with or suspicion about it, the number of stakeholders involved, and the complexity of making major changes to curricula, the fact that digital badging is happening at all, albeit at a slow pace, is worthy of note.

Badging as a concept leads to the interrogation of long-established traditions in higher education: faculty as content experts, the primacy of the lecture-based method of teaching, the transcript as evidence of learning, and disciplines and majors as the core cohesive unit. While some of this foundation is shifting—teachers moving from the traditional sage on the stage model to a guide on the side, for example, and increasing opportunities for team-based and experiential learning—much is still firmly in place, including transcripts as the currency of the realm and the importance of faculty-shaped and institution- and state-approved majors.

For change to happen, many key players need to be involved in conversations surrounding digital badging, including colleges or schools within an institution, faculty senate and governance councils, academic administrators, academic departments, accrediting organizations, and other outside regulatory and government bodies. Some of these stakeholders may have little or no familiarity with digital badging or may view it with skepticism or wariness, seeing it as certifying basic skills and suitable only for children or job training.

Yet digital badges have the potential to be used in a wide variety of ways in higher education, and the aforementioned hurdles may affect some uses of digital badging more than others. Digital badges may serve to replace or to supplement course work, or they may be co-curricular, an enhancement to a student's academic accomplishments. They may be seen as complementing other evidence-based pedagogical approaches, such as digital portfolios. They may also be a component of assessing prior learning experiences. Each potential application of badges will have its own roadblocks or concerns to overcome, yet some will face an easier path to acceptance than others. Co-curricular badges, it is evident, are far easier to implement than replacing a major's entire set of courses with badges (Glover 2016).

Many of the forces that work to advance the implementation of badges, or oppose their introduction, are on the macro level, so this chapter will focus on examining some of the societal, economic, and technological changes affecting higher education that are relevant to conversations about badges. The impact of globalization; increased expectations of a college education, including the employability of graduates; and the clear importance of engaging in lifelong learning, all buttressed by new opportunities provided by technology, factor into the reception that digital badges may receive.

Chapter 3 includes additional analysis of higher education stakeholders and the roles they might play in the implementation of a digital badging program. When reading these chapters, it should be noted that research studies examining the use of digital badges in higher education are, at the time of writing, scarce. A number of the programs have only been in place a short while or are still under development. Research results will increase as digital badges are successfully integrated in different institutions. I encourage readers to extend their investigation into the most recent literature from the field of education and beyond to learn of new research on the efficacy of badges.

The question might arise as to the applicability of this chapter to digital badging for information literacy. In conjunction with the co-editor of this volume, I have worked to introduce digital badging to the University at Albany and its library. The background information from this chapter was acquired piecemeal during this initiative but would have been beneficial from the start for conversations with key administrators on campus and within the library.

## THE NEED FOR LIFELONG LEARNING

Both the importance of and the opportunities for lifelong learning are having a significant effect on individuals, higher education institutions, and employers. Learning can take a wide range of forms, and the idea that knowledge gained during one's time as a degree-earning student is sufficient is lamentably out of date—if it was ever true.

The New Media Consortium's *Horizon Report* identifies the integration of informal learning as one of six significant challenges currently facing higher education. "Lifelong learning is the lifeblood of higher education. Institutions must prioritize and recognize ongoing learning—both formal and informal—for their faculty, staff, and students" (Adams Becker et al. 2017, 2). The report characterizes this challenge as solvable, rather than placing it in the "difficult" or "wicked" categories. The goal is to encourage an interest in lifelong learning on the part of students and faculty and to recognize prior learning by awarding credit for it. Yet currently "there is a lack of salable methods of formally documenting and assessing skills mastered outside of the classroom" (ibid., 26).

A 2016 Pew study, Lifelong Learning and Technology, found that 73 percent of American adults consider themselves lifelong learners, 74 percent have pursued learning about personal interests, and 63 percent of working adults have engaged in learning to enhance their job skills or to gain experience toward career advancement (Horrigan 2016).

These statistics align with an analysis of labor markets, based on online vacancy notices, which found that a preponderance might be considered "hybrid jobs" that require "new combinations of skills." With increasing career spans, and employers less inclined to invest in employee training, lifelong learning becomes imperative (*The Economist* 2017a).

Individuals increasingly realize that there is a plethora of educational venues to choose from in order to pursue lifelong learning, many of which are not connected to traditional colleges and universities. Beyond established and emerging online opportunities, in-person learning options of all flavors also exist; high schools, libraries, and places of worship are common locations for personal learning, while work-related venues are frequently cited for professional development (Horrigan 2016).

However, although many Americans view themselves as either personal or professional lifelong learners, a number of them do not consider or are not able to access online learning opportunities, according to the Pew survey:

> The survey clearly shows that information technology plays a role for many as they learn things that are personally or professionally helpful. Still, those who already have high levels of education and easy access to technology are the most likely to take advantage of the Internet. For significant minorities of Americans with less education and lower incomes, the Internet is more on the periphery of their learning activities. Fewer of the people in those groups are professional or personal learners, and fewer of them use the Internet for these purposes. Overall, the Internet does not seem to exert as strong a pull toward adult learning among those who are poorer or less educated as it does for those in other groups (Horrigan 2016).

This situation may present opportunities for higher education institutions, from helping to provide access to making local learning options available. Lifelong learning is a disruptive educational trend that can be supported and addressed by alternative credentialing, particularly digital badges. Yet first these institutions must recognize the need and be willing to try new models.

Universities have an advantage over other types of issuers when the reputation of the learning agency is considered. When assessing digital badges there are bound to be questions regarding the education gained and the legitimacy of the credential. Philip DiSalvio (2016), dean of the College of Advancing and Professional Studies at the University of Massachusetts Boston, says that "colleges and universities are in a unique position to be the gatekeepers of many of those credentials"—credentials other than a transcript. According to the *Horizon Report*,

> A key to integrating informal and formal learning is finding a unified manner to support assessment and certification of knowledge and skills gained through a variety of ventures. With the right infrastructure, students might easily display proof of aptitudes and accomplishments in a more transparent and comprehensive manner than traditional degrees allow. . . . Creative partnerships between universities, online learning providers, and industry leaders will be vital in advancing recognition of a broader array of competencies (Adams Becker et al. 2017, 26).

While badging is just one way to certify knowledge and skills, it is potentially a strong component in a unified display of learning. Universities and colleges would be wise to embrace the possibilities set out in the *Horizon Report* as a way to address this solvable challenge.

## ADDITIONAL FACTORS AFFECTING HIGHER EDUCATION

Institutions of higher education are being buffeted by a host of other far-reaching factors that have the potential to dramatically change centuries of tradition (Matkin 2012). Among the most significant are the changing demographics and expectations for higher education, employability and preparation for the workforce, globalization, and transformations made possible by technology.

### Expectations for Higher Education

Obtaining a college degree is a goal that spans both social and economic domains. Economic success is inextricably viewed as intertwined with earning a college degree, yet the costs associated with higher education have increased substantially (Grant 2014, 26). Colleges and universities are committed to making higher education possible for a broad range of students, including those who previously would not have had such an opportunity. These students include some whose preparation for college may be inadequate and non-traditional students whose availability and needs may differ from those of traditional college age students (West and Thompson 2015, 45). Another category of targeted students includes those who met their initial goal of an associate's degree. Initiatives promoting seamless transfer between more affordable and accessible community colleges and four-year schools are one example of a commitment to make higher education more feasible for a broader swath of the population (State University of New York, n.d.).

Governments also see the need for a more educated populace. Australia's Bradley Report, officially named *Transforming Australia's Higher Education System*, says that "the nation will need more well-qualified people if it is to anticipate and meet the demands of a rapidly moving global economy" (as cited in West and Lockley 2016, 468). However, paying for the traditional model of higher education, even with assistance from the school itself, often exceeds the capabilities of prospective students and their families. These prospective learners may turn to other educational options, such as digital badges and massive open online courses (MOOCs).

The expectations of students who do proceed to a college education are changing, and this has a very direct impact on higher education, particularly due to the technological advances discussed later in this chapter. These students may be looking for flexible and shorter education options to accommodate busier schedules, to incur less debt, or to provide evidence of mastery of specific abilities and knowledge. They may also seek "more autonomy and agency in demonstrating what they have learned and where they have learned it" (Lockley, Derryberry, and West 2016, 58). Institutions have had to make significant changes to address their clientele's wishes, ones that raise "questions on what the education process should look like" (West and Thompson 2015, 45). These changes range from experiential education to increased numbers of traditional courses taught online to student-led decisions about compiling a compelling educational portfolio.

This urgent need for change is reflected in one of the *Horizon Report*'s underlying themes: advancing cultures of innovation. It is imperative that higher education recognize the importance of fueling innovation and "finding ways to replicate it across a span of diverse and unique learning institutions" (Adams Becker et al. 2017). This far-reaching theme encompasses an institutional mindset alteration that would actively seek ways to meet the needs of a changing student population, while equipping students and faculty "with the tools needed to spark real progress" (ibid.). Change would radiate from its origins within institutions to affect society much more broadly.

## The Potential for Badges in Higher Education

Badges, and competency-based education more broadly, provide affordances that have the potential to address "some of the dogged issues associated with higher education outcomes and return on investment for students" (Grant 2014, 27).

Digital badges are well-placed to meet all of the parameters mentioned by Matkin (2012) and West and Lockley (2016), in that they can be

- selected to meet a learner's need
- accessed on demand
- used to document prior learning experiences
- offered by reputable organizations and institutions
- and issued in discrete units.

Table 2.1 lays out the congruencies between societal needs, educational needs, and the role of digital badging in addressing these factors. Digital badges, when

Table 2.1. Congruencies between Educational Forces and Needs and the Role of Digital Badging

| Educational Forces and Needs | Horizon Report Meta-Categories | Affordances of Digital Badging |
| --- | --- | --- |
| Online, anytime learning options | Expanding educational access and convenience | Online, with wide availability from a number of institutions/organizations |
| Discrete learning units (modularization and customization) | | Flexible, opportunities to customize one's own learning pathway |
| Well-prepared workers | Need for real-world skills | Vast in range, offering numerous real-world opportunities |
| Value of prior learning | Asses nuanced skills on a personal level | Often evidence-based, may be linked to digital portfolios providing learners' work |
| Importance of lifelong learning | Lifelong learning critical | A convenient method for lifelong learning |
| | Advancing progressive, student-centered learning approaches | Have the potential to be innovative and student-centered if designed thoughtfully |
| Credentials important | | Offer credibility if from established educational institutions |

offered in conjunction with online learning opportunities, greatly increase access to credentialing of specific abilities and skills. They can be selected and pursued according to a chosen personal learning pathway, can be used to recognize prior learning, and may be accompanied by evidence of new learning.

It should be noted that digital badges vary greatly in function. This is to be expected, given the range of issuing organizations. But even with our selective focus on institutions of higher education, badges may range from those attesting to co-curricular accomplishments to those replacing credit-bearing courses, in design and in content. Therefore the affordances enumerated in column three of table 2.1 may show great variation.

One common feature is that shareable badges issued by colleges and universities benefit from the institution's credentials, and such badges will have the advantage of credibility due to name recognition. A more varied component is the availability of the products a learner has created to earn a badge. Some badge systems incorporate access to these learning artifacts, while others do not. For those that do not, digital portfolios may provide easy access. Yet only some institutions promote or require students' use of digital portfolios.

Without standardization across institutions and badging systems, the variability will continue. While this may be the cause for confusion among badge earners and those assessing the value of earned badges, it is not surprising given the recent appearance of this form of micro-credentialing. New models are being developed, and best practices are being identified. It is likely that the badging environment will look rather different five years from now. At that point, common badging affordances might be easier to identify.

## Employability and Preparation for the Workforce

One of the primary concerns of students, parents, and administrators at higher education institutions is whether graduates will find jobs. Increasingly, elected officials are also interested in the employability of students graduating from public colleges and universities. Significantly, this issue is addressed in one of the *Horizon Report* themes. "Real-world skills," says the report, "are needed to bolster employability and workplace development. Students expect to graduate into gainful employment. Institutions have a responsibility to deliver deeper, active learning experiences and skills-based training that integrate technology in meaningful ways" (Adams Becker et al. 2017, 2).

While many jobs require applicants to possess a college degree, employers often want the assurance that their new hires will be able to perform well. They look for experience to provide that assurance (*The Economist* 2017a). If employers were able to assess the knowledge and skills of potential employees at a micro level, they would be able to make better informed decisions than those based solely on a college degree. Digital badges offer employers evidence of mastery of discrete abilities, providing information more finely tuned than course grades on a transcript. "The use of badging technology offers businesses worldwide the opportunity to evaluate a potential employee in terms not only of the résumé or the cover letter but also based on a more objective and thorough method of identifying skill sets and experiences" (Ellis, Nunn, and Avella 2016, 11). Ellis, Nunn, and Avella make the point that rather than "test, evaluate, and monitor employees," employers are able to obtain this knowledge prior to hiring. IBM, Microsoft, Ernst & Young, and other companies recognize the value of competency-based recruitment and hiring (Education Design Lab 2017a). Indeed, IBM provides robust opportunities for interested individuals to earn many of their badges (IBM 2017).

Digital badging is a way to document a range of abilities beyond subject expertise—such as communication and leadership abilities—that employers look for in potential hires. A national survey conducted by Wonderlic's National Soft Skills Consortium found that the 260 hiring managers and business owners surveyed recognized the value of badges for documenting these soft skills. Sixty percent "said they would be more inclined to interview graduates that had job-specific skills badges on their résumés" (Opperman 2016). The Education Design Lab (n.d.), whose mission is to "design, test, and implement new education models," is developing a suite of 21st Century Skills badges to better document soft skills, based on their work with administrators, faculty, students, employers, entrepreneurs, and more. The resulting badges, such as Catalyst, Collaborator, Cross Cultural Competency, and Empathy, assess competencies deemed to be meaningful when hiring decisions are made. In their conversations since 2014, they have found that "employers have become more articulate about what they are not getting from traditional résumés and cover letters. The incumbent self-reported résumé is a blunt instrument filled with lists of activities but few ways to gauge competency about the skills you really have" (Education Design Lab 2017b). Particularly pertinent to this volume, a survey of employers found that they value information literacy and metaliteracy skills, appreciate the ability to examine representations of these abilities, and would be open to doing so through digital badges (Raish and Rimland 2016).

## Globalization

Globalization is another factor having a strong impact on higher education. Teams of individuals from a number of countries may work together to tackle common problems (Ellis, Nunn, and Avella 2016, 12), or workers may find their abilities in demand in countries other than their own. In order for such collaborations or transpositions to work effectively, there needs to be common educational ground from which participants start. The European Union is addressing the issue of comparable and transparent higher education between countries through its Tuning Project. Two of the project goals are to promote mobility of graduates from country to country and to adopt a system of easily understandable and comparable degrees between countries (González and Wagenaar 2003, 1).

In order for the degrees to be comparable, the Tuning Project is also addressing course units. "Learning outcomes," they write, "are described in terms of competencies: what a learner knows or is able to demonstrate after the completion of a learning process. This concerns both subject specific competences and generic competences, like communication skills and leadership" (ibid., 2). However, across regions of the world not participating in the Tuning Project, there may be little standardization or common starting ground. Digital badges have the potential to fill the gaps in these geographic areas. While they would not be standardized, they would provide information about, or the actual documentation of, mastery of specific knowledge areas. This information would help to provide transparency and document competencies outside of the structure provided by the Tuning Project.

West and Thompson (2015) include two additional high impact changes to society that intersect with globalization: the information revolution and the knowledge economy. The wide availability of information allows for the widespread creation and sharing of information, which challenges the role that colleges and universities have held for many centuries (43–44). They state starkly, "As a new interconnected and information rich environment develops, the role and function of higher education institutions is being challenged at the most basic level" (ibid., 44). Online access to information and to education has dramatically altered traditional boundaries that defined the authority and prestige of colleges and universities.

## Educational Transformation through Technology

Technology has a profound impact on the factors discussed in this chapter, and a seminal document that pinpoints changes identified as affecting higher education through the lens of technology is the already-cited New Media Consortium's *Horizon Report: 2017 Higher Education Edition* (Adams Becker et al. 2017). Issued each year, the collaboratively produced *Horizon Report* is a bellwether for key trends, challenges, and developments impacting the educational landscape. While the focus is on technology, the elements identified in this report affect the ways colleges and universities operate. As noted in the introduction, "Technology alone cannot cultivate education transformation; better pedagogies and more inclusive education models are vital solutions, while digital tools and platforms are enablers and accelerators. Further, the way that society is evolving inherently impacts how technology is used as well as the programming institutions offer" (ibid., 6).

A number of the items identified in the 2017 *Horizon Report*'s sections on key trends accelerating technology adoption in higher education, significant challenges impeding technology adoption in higher education, and important developments in educational technology for higher education relate to the broader canvas on which badges are beginning to make their mark. But the *Horizon Report* also extracts ten core themes underlying the trends, challenges, and developments highlighted for 2017. Six of these themes are clearly connected to the ecosystem that is giving rise to digital badging and range from changes in cultural approaches to learning, workplace needs, access to educational opportunities, the demand for personalized learning experiences, the proliferation of online, mobile, and blended learning, and the need and demand for lifelong learning. The integration of findings from the *Horizon Report* in this chapter reflects the underlying impact of technology on higher education's identity.

## Knowledge-Empowering Technologies

Technology has made possible revolutionary changes that impact higher education institutions in diverse ways. These phenomena are Janus-faced, with potentially unsettling and disruptive effects on traditional educational models balanced by new opportunities for institutions and their students.

Three *Horizon Report* themes pertain to the development fueling these changes:

1. Advancing progressive learning approaches requires cultural transformation. Institutions must be structured in ways that promote the exchange of fresh ideas, identify successful models within and outside of the campus, and reward teaching innovation—with student success at the center.
2. Online, mobile, and blended learning are foregone conclusions. If institutions do not already have robust strategies for integrating these now pervasive approaches, then they simply will not survive. An important step is tracking how these models are actively enriching learning outcomes.
3. Despite the proliferation of technology and online learning materials, access is still unequal. Gaps persist across the world that are hampering college completion for student groups by socioeconomic status, race,

ethnicity, and gender. Further, sufficient Internet access remains uneven (Adams Becker et al. 2017, 2).

An example of online learning that requires cultural transformation is the *massive online open course*. Many MOOCs emanate from instructors at colleges and universities. MOOCs take full advantage of and also promote globalization. They provide access to higher education courses for many individuals from around the world who do not have the opportunity to attend college; thus they help, but do not solve, the unequal access issue addressed in the *Horizon Report*. These courses may be free or have a small associated cost for credentialing. Coursera, edX, Canvas Network, and Udacity are all platforms that broaden the educational playing field, though those without sufficient Internet access or who face social, cultural, or economic barriers may still be restricted.

MOOCs can be advantageous for older learners or others who do not have the opportunity to commit the years required by a traditional higher education experience. For these individuals, who may have more responsibilities than traditional college age students, the time cost of learning may be of more concern than the financial cost (*The Economist* 2017b).

For higher education administrators, learners' ability to earn certificates of completion may signal a detrimental impact on traditional enrollments. Yet it can be argued that some colleges and universities offering such courses may be able to attract enrollment to their programs as MOOC learners become familiar with their brand. Another option is for universities to follow the MOOC model and offer modular content. Examples exist, such as the Micro-Masters in supply-chain management offered by edX that can stand alone or count toward a full masters offered by MIT (ibid.).

However, the positive situation in which established colleges and universities offer content through MOOCs has a corresponding challenge. Technology-enabled competition has arisen in the form of a full MOOC–based degree. The accredited online University of the People offers low-cost degrees in the fields of business administration, health science, and computer science. The courses are free; students only have to pay for application and exam processing fees. Their course materials are also free of charge.

Key themes discussed in this chapter—access to higher education, the impact of globalization, and a transformed learning approach incorporating online learning—are all components of the University of the People's vision statement (n.d.), which posits that

> access to higher education is a key ingredient in the promotion of world peace and global economic development. [University of the People] views higher education as a basic right and believes that it can both transform the lives of individuals and

be an important force for societal change. UoPeople believes that education plays a fundamental role in strengthening respect for human rights and fundamental freedoms and in promoting understanding and tolerance.

The school's goals include maintaining high academic standards through continual assessment, fostering critical thinking and lifelong learning, focusing on the "competencies and skills required for success in the global economy," and promoting shared learning through collaboration (ibid.). Depending on the value that employers accord to the degrees they award, the model presented by the University of the People provides a potentially dangerous threat to traditional institutions of higher education.

Another dramatic change to the education landscape wrought by technology is the increasing availability of open educational resources (OERs), which allow motivated individuals to learn without the guidance of professors or the structure and costs connected with traditional textbooks (West and Lockley 2016). Universities would be wise to reflect on the implications, for "the acceptance of the concept of lifelong and life-wide learning has become fairly commonplace, meaning that society places greater value on experience and knowledge gained from a variety of place, spaces, and experiences" (ibid., 470).

Not only are non-traditional institutions of higher education, such as the University of the People, using OERs, but there is also increasing pressure for their use on traditional campuses, to assist with reducing college costs. One example is provided by the State University of New York system, which offers a robust catalog of OER textbooks. In addition, eight million dollars in funding from the 2017–2018 New York state budget is targeted to implement OERs in high enrollment general education courses, half of which is designated for SUNY, the other half for the City University of New York system (Open NYS n.d.).

Both technology and globalization can be seen in the open borders of online education, which "has virtually erased geographical boundaries" (Matkin 2012, 8). The availability of educational resources created anywhere means that almost any option might be available for those learners who target specific needs. These are more likely to be packaged in discrete units rather than an entire higher education degree. This allows learners to select distinct areas of interest to pursue. Matkin calls this *modularization* and says that, "While the four-year degree will not disappear anytime soon, there is increasing pressure for just-in-time education. This requires shorter sequences and certifications" (ibid., 9).

West and Lockley (2016) focus on many of the same factors: a globalized economy's need for well-prepared workers, technology, and an increased emphasis on lifelong learning and the value of prior learning experiences. They note the importance of earning credentials and raise the issue that technology "can provide opportunities for real transition in models and approaches, or it can be used to support existing paradigms" (470).

Beuth University of Applied Sciences Berlin has a digital badging program that assesses skills in information technology, teamwork, and communication. It has been of great value to migrants coming to Germany who have degrees that don't translate to a European degree or whose educational documentation is missing. The ability to demonstrate their competencies is valuable to helping them integrate into the German work force (Ruff 2016).

Using technology to design these new approaches aligns with another of the *Horizon Report* trends that addresses the importance of assessing the knowledge and skills an individual has gained in a variety of ways. "Processes for assessing nuanced skills at a personal level are needed," the report says. "Adaptive technologies and a focus on measuring learning are driving institutional decision-making while personalizing student learning experiences; leaders must now consider how to evaluate the acquisition of vocational skills, competencies, creativity, and critical thinking" (Adams Becker et al. 2017, 2). Higher education must consider how to integrate these personal learning pathways with established and evolving disciplinary domains of knowledge. How might they complement one another, and how are they differentiated (Matkin 2012, 11)?

## MOVING FORWARD

Cultural changes that respond to and build upon the broader open education movement are crucial for the continued prominence of higher education institutions. This movement, facilitated by technological changes and frequently fueled by the need for continued learning, is also affected by globalization and factors connected to employment and return on investment. This complex mix of potent change agents demands an open mind-set on the part of administrators, regulators, instructors, and others who will need to respond in new and creative ways. Digital badges may well be one of the proposed responses, given their suitability for attesting to learning outside of standard structures.

Daniel Hickey (2017), an expert in digital badging in higher education, visualizes a robust future for alternative credentialing. He says,

> Today e-credentials are at a similar juncture as e-commerce in 1997. Most educators and administrators are aware of efforts to extend traditional credentials with innovations such as digital badges, e-portfolios, and "extended" transcripts. Unlike traditional grades and transcripts, e-credentials can contain specific claims of competency and Web-based evidence of those competencies.

They can be curated, annotated, and distributed over digital networks under the earner's control. Rather than relying on vague reputations and opaque accreditations, e-credentials speak for themselves.

Later chapters in this volume will provide examples of the range of badge programs to be found within the area of information literacy. Some of these programs are connected to larger institutional programs, while others are free-standing. The differences in scope and implementation mirror the flexibility of badges in general and their appeal to lifelong learners.

## REFERENCES

Adams Becker, S., M. Cummins, A. Davis, A. Freeman, C. Hall Giesinger, and V. Ananthanarayanan. 2017. *NMC Horizon Report: 2017 Higher Education Edition*. Austin, Texas: The New Media Consortium. http://academedia.org/2017_NMC_horizon.pdf.

DiSalvio, Philip. 2016. "New Pathways to Credentialing: The Digital Badge." *New England Journal of Higher Education*, May 3. http://www.nebhe.org/thejournal/new-pathways-to-credentialing-the-digital-badge/.

The Economist. 2017a. "Lifelong Learning Is Becoming an Economic Imperative." *The Economist*. January 12. https://www.economist.com/news/special-report/21714169-technological-change-demands-stronger-and-more-continuous-connections-between-education.

———. 2017b. "The Return of the MOOC; Upstarts and Incumbents." *The Economist*, January 14.

Education Design Lab. 2017a. "Badges about to 'Change the Game' on Hiring at IBM." *Education Design Lab* (blog). September 26. http://eddesignlab.org/2017/09/badges-change-game-hiring-ibm/.

———. 2017b. "June 20, 2017, News." Education Design Lab (blog). June 20. http://eddesignlab.org/2017/06/10-things-weve-learned-badging/.

———. N.d. "The Lab's 21st Century Skills Badges." *Education Design Lab* (blog). https://eddesignlab.org/21st-century-skills-badges/.

Ellis, Larry E., Sandra G. Nunn, and John T. Avella. 2016. "Digital Badges and Micro-credentials: Historical Overview, Motivational Aspects, Issues, and Challenges." In *Foundation of Digital Badges and Micro-credentials: Demonstrating and Recognizing Knowledge and Competencies*, edited by Dirk Ifenthaler, Nicole Bellin-Mularski, and Dana-Kristin Mah, 3–21. Cham, Switzerland: Springer.

Glover, Ian. 2016. "Student Perceptions of Digital Badges as Recognition of Achievement and Engagement in Co-curricular Activities." In *Foundation of Digital Badges and Micro-credentials*, edited by Dirk Ifenthaler, Nicole Bellin-Mularski, and Dana-Kristin Mah, 443–55. Cham, Switzerland: Springer.

González, Julia, and Robert Wagenaar. 2003. "Tuning Educational Structures in Europe." Tuning Project. December. http://media.ehea.info/file/Tuning_project/89/3/Tuning-Educational-Structures-Europe-executive-summary_575893.pdf.

Grant, Sheryl. 2014. *What Counts as Learning: Open Digital Badges for New Opportunities*. Cork: BookBaby.

Hickey, Daniel T. 2017. "How Open Credentials Will Transform Higher Education." *Chronicle of Higher Education* 63 (32): 13.

Horrigan, John B. 2016. "Lifelong Learning and Technology." Pew Research Center. March 22. http://www.pewinternet.org/2016/03/22/lifelong-learning-and-technology/.

IBM. 2017. "What Is an IBM Digital Badge?" IBM Skills Gateway (website). June 2. http://www.ibm.com/services/learning/badges.

Lockley, Alison, Anne Derryberry, and Deborah West. 2016. "Drivers, Affordances and Challenges of Digital Badges." In *Foundation of Digital Badges and Micro-credentials*, edited by Dirk Ifenthaler, Nicole Bellin-Mularski, and Dana-Kristin Mah, 55–70. Cham, Switzerland: Springer.

Matkin, Gary W. 2012. "The Opening of Higher Education." *Change: The Magazine of Higher Learning* 44 (3): 6–13.

Open NYS. N.d. "What is OER?" https://open-nys.org.

Opperman, Amanda. 2016. "How Competency-Based Programs Can Bridge the Skills Gap." Forbes BrandVoice. *Forbes*. October 17. https://www.forbes.com/sites/gradsoflife/2016/10/17/how-competency-based-programs-can-bridge-the-skills-gap/.

Raish, Victoria, and Emily Rimland. 2016. "Employer Perceptions of Critical Information Literacy Skills and Digital Badges." *College & Research Libraries* 77 (1): 87–113.

Ruff, Corinne. 2016. "Online Badges Help Refugees Prove Their Academic Achievements." *Chronicle of Higher Education*. April 28.

State University of New York. N.d. "SUNY Transfer Policies." The State University of New York (website). https://www.suny.edu/attend/get-started/transfer-students/suny-transfer-policies/.

University of the People. N.d. "Mission & Values." University of the People (website). http://www.uopeople.edu/about/uopeople/mission-values/.

West, Deborah, and Alison Lockley. 2016. "Implementing Digital Badges in Australia: The Importance of Institutional Context." In *Foundation of Digital Badges and Micro-credentials*, edited by Dirk Ifenthaler, Nicole Bellin-Mularski, and Dana-Kristin Mah, 467–82. Cham, Switzerland: Springer.

West, Deborah, and Samantha Thompson. 2015. "Mobile Knowledge: Driving a Paradigm Shift." *Journal of Applied Research in Higher Education* 7 (1): 43–54.

# 3

# Addressing Stakeholder Needs to Establish Meaningful Digital Badging in Higher Education

*Laureen P. Cantwell and Kristyn K. Rose*

The use of badges to denote accomplishments or proficiencies, status or rank, authority or skills, dates back centuries (Ellis, Nunn, and Avella 2016; Glover 2013). Perhaps most familiar, the Boy Scouts of America and the Girl Scouts of the USA use badges as indicators of educational experiences and credentials to attain leadership roles within an organization. But what are *digital* badges? Gibson et al. (2013) define a digital badge as "a representation of an accomplishment, interest, or affiliation that is visual, [is] available online, and contains metadata including links that help explain the context, meaning, process, and result of an activity" (404). The distinction, then, between the digital badge and its more literal counterpart lies in the Internet-accessible components of the badge that help to define its meaning. In "A History and Frameworks of Digital Badges in Education," Ostashewski and Reid (2015) frame badges in several ways. Their definitions have a foundation in the original purposes and goals of badging programs. They variously define digital badges as "information- and evidence-based credentials complete with a set of data that explains and vets that badge," "tools for getting jobs, credit, additional learning, reputation, and other opportunities," and "digital identity and reputation currency" (188). For those with limited understanding of and experience with digital badges in higher education, these contextualized meanings may help readers envision the role badges could play and the conversations that might take place about them.

Ostashewski and Reid also describe digital badge collections as "distributed portfolios in that they are skill first, with the evidence linked behind them, instead of the traditional evidence/artifact first without an indication of aligned or assessed skills" (2015, 189). Unlike their physical counterparts, emblazoned on the shirts of police officers and scouts, digital badges afford viewers the opportunity to verify the authenticity of the badge and to gain confidence in the effort underlying the attainment of the badge.

Several large universities, corporations, and organizations have created extensive badging programs and initiatives, including Khan Academy (Crotty 2012), Purdue University, the University of California–Davis, Penn State University, the University of Michigan (Jovanović and Devedžić 2015), and Educause in conjunction with the University of Central Florida (Diaz, Finkelstein, and Manning 2015). Beyond traditional educational settings, Fedock et al. (2016) note that employers such as NASA, Disney Pixar, and the Smithsonian Institution "use badges for honoring and commending learners' or employees' improved skills, knowledge, and accomplishments in education and in workplace development" (273). The presence of such learning opportunities and their acceptance within these prominent organizations indicates an interest in digital badging among employers, educational bodies, and learners.

Despite these examples, the creation and adoption of digital badging programs and initiatives remains limited and contentious throughout higher education. In his 2015 LinkedIn article, Senior Strategic Consultant for Blackboard Andy Ramsden (2015) notes the mixed emotions that surround digital badging and the impact those sentiments might have on whether and how higher education institutions engage with badging. Descriptors like *uncertainty*, *irrelevance*, and *questionable* stand alongside *potential*, *excitement*, and *learner centered*. Ramsden highlights the fact that societal acceptance of digital badges is an important factor for their success. New ventures bring a certain element of the unknown, which can lead to the mixed feelings identified in his article.

Higher education environments often oscillate between risk aversion and risk management (Strikwerda 2014). Ramsden goes on to note a piece of commentary by Kevin Carey (2012), published in the *Chronicle of Higher Education*, which highlights the likelihood of failure for many badge systems developed in higher education, due to either design issues or problems connecting with "communities of interest." Ellis, Nunn, and Avella (2016) contend that the success of a digital badging initiative depends on three key factors: motivation, pedagogy, and credentialing. Devedžić and Jovanović (2015) identify a variety of stakeholders—"learners, teachers, schools, employers, and other institutions and associations" (603). For the purposes of this chapter, higher education involves three primary populations: college university faculty and administrators, college students, and the employers and industries at large who rely on the tertiary education system for employees—or "the earner, the issuer, and the observer" (Finkelstein, Knight, and Manning 2013, 17). This chapter focuses on each of these stakeholder populations and considers factors of motivation, pedagogy, and credentialing that affect each of these communities and how we can leverage this information to create intentional, meaningful digital badging endeavors for them.

## INSTITUTIONAL STAKEHOLDERS

The demands for digital badging oversight, the realities of working in bigger organizations, the process of the diffusion of information, and the need for digital badging to incorporate assessment present both opportunities and challenges to faculty members and administrators. These stakeholders, as well as students and employers, must understand the motivations, expectations, and needs of the other stakeholders in order for badging ventures to find meaning, value, and success.

### Opportunities and Challenges

Digital badging presents many opportunities for higher education. For instance, colleges and universities can utilize digital badges to invest more deeply in the creation of lifelong learners. Jovanović and Devedžić (2015) describe a role badges can play in the development of lifelong learners, including the "recognition of learning in multiple and diverse environments that go beyond traditional classrooms" and the "recognition of diverse kinds of skills and knowledge, including soft and general skills" (115). They discuss the potential of open badges (OBs) as more than motivational tools. In a separate article, Devedžić and Jovanović (2015) address four value propositions for OBs, concerning the worth of badges as well as the development and design requirements for how they will be delivered, communicated, and acquired. In addition to badges providing avenues for feedback, blueprints for accomplished learning, and recognition of what are often under- or unrecognized learning and skills, Devedžić and Jovanović establish that the badges develop "the sense of community membership" and support "goal setting, planning, and self-reflection" (606). In order for colleges and universities to accomplish these goals, the authors make clear the conditions that must be met: the open badging system must "create some domain-specific community-level badges, to help learners develop the sense of belonging to the community" and must "enable learners' control over and efficient management of badges" (ibid.). These community-level badges need not be tied directly to a course or major.

Digital badges can foster lifelong learning through both curricular and co-curricular engagement and development. The term *co-curricular* denotes "activities that contribute to the academic learning experience, especially activities that provide students with opportunities to learn and develop skills through active participation" (Wu, Whiteley, and Sass 2015, 51). Purdue University created a co-curricular digital badging opportunity designed to engage college students with professional development learning opportunities. Purdue's scaffolded design for LinkedIn Boot Camp Badges (LinkedIn Learner, LinkedIn Leader, and LinkedIn Legend) allows for specificity in tasks and accomplishments for a skill set that, if not structured in tiers, might otherwise be abstractly termed "networking" or "reputation management." Ellis, Nunn, and Avella (2016) call these *meta-badges*, which Beattie (2014) identifies as badges earned through the accrual of other, specific badges. Digital badges provide an opportunity to enhance student co-curricular engagement while increasing students' responsibility and know-how for managing their professional profiles and generating discoverable, employable online identities.

The co-curricular value of digital badges could also be applied to learners studying abroad to enhance the documentation and visibility of their experience (Ellis, Nunn, and Avella 2016). The University of Central Oklahoma (UCO) uses badges to recognize *transformative learning*, which they define as learning that "develops beyond-disciplinary skills" and "expands students' perspectives of their relationships with self, others, community, and environment" (King, Kilbourne, and Walvoord 2015, 3–4). UCO's Student Transformative Learning Record, created using Kuh's (2008) High-Impact Practices, tracks achievements outside the classroom including study abroad experiences, service learning opportunities, internships, and diversity experiences. Co-curricular badge programs allow the university to highlight markers of student development that have deep importance to their campus community and the global community beyond student coursework and provide not just incentives but expectations that students will engage with and attain the established tenets.

Examples such as those described above can benefit institutions planning to implement their own digital badging programs. The "diffusion of innovations" theory, popularized by University of New Mexico communication studies professor Everett Rogers, aims to illuminate why and how new ideas become adopted and includes five steps: knowledge, persuasion, decision, implementation, and confirmation. It also has four critical components: innovation, communication channels, time, and social system (Sahin 2006). The time line for adoption varies among different societies, depending on a variety of factors. Even within higher education, different institutions can be considered different societies. While they share common characteristics, they also have factors that make them unique—particularly with regard to the exploration and implementation of innovative tools, practices, and resources, such as digital badging. Rodgers created a bell-curve shaped distribution for how adopters of innovation can be categorized: innovators (first 2.5 percent), early adopters (next 13.5 percent), early majority (middle 34 percent), late majority (later 34 percent), and laggards (final 16 percent) (ibid., 19). Since the diffusion of innovations is already in-progress for digital badging, an institution considering implementing a badging program can learn from the experiences of earlier adopters.

Institutions must evaluate their existing circumstances when considering engaging with digital badging. These "prior conditions" include any previous practice with the innovation under consideration, the needs and problems the institution is experiencing, the general innovativeness of the institution, and the norms within the social system (the institution itself). Prior conditions feed into the first stage of the diffusion of innovation (knowledge), which in turn must factor in the socioeconomic, personality, and communication variables of the institution. If digital badging continues to be an opportunity under consideration once these factors have been assessed, an institution will enter the persuasion stage of the diffusion of innovation. This stage relies on "perceived characteristics of the innovation," which include relative advantage, compatibility, complexity, trialability, and observability. The knowledge stage allows institutions to consider whether badging will be worth pursuing, awareness building, how-to, and principles-based grounding in the innovation. The persuasion stage of the innovation-decision process should be where institutions make efforts at the individual level to work with the sentiments and opinions of the institution's community.

Concerns about student motivation may rise to the forefront during the knowledge and persuasion stages, in discussion with university faculty, staff, and administrators. Campus faculty may balk at the extent to which students may be extrinsically motivated by digital badging. However, one must realize that higher education already builds in extrinsic motivators, and these factors are not likely to go away. These incentives include grades, praise, scholarships, and opened doors to opportunities, although faculty may not consider these to be extrinsically motivating incentives. Nonetheless, many faculty members and administrators, particularly those with a conventional view of education or in traditional liberal arts settings, worry about crossing a threshold into extrinsic motivators, giving students abundant reasons to learn other than their *desire* to learn (e.g., as noted in Ford 2017). Jovanović and Devedžić (2014) mention two major difficulties in particular:

1. Digital badging initiatives can result in *motivation displacement*. This indicates that improvements to the pedagogy surrounding the badge may be necessary. An example they cite for such an instructional strategy shift is having the badge "award learners certain roles associated

with both privileges and responsibilities in the learning community" rather than using them solely to recognize achievements (59).
2. Opportunities to accrue digital badges can lead to students focusing on the badge rather than the "learning activities/materials associated with [the badge]" (ibid.). They suggest that, in the case of this scenario, revision of badge award requirements may be necessary and that the institution/faculty member might consider "chaining" (or scaffolding) their badges to place students on "learning trajectories" (ibid.).

The two areas of concern identified above are important when creating, marketing, and implementing digital badging initiatives. Further information on student motivation, pilot populations, and additional issues are included in the student stakeholders section.

**Pilot Programs**

As a means of countering the challenges noted by Jovanović and Devedžić (2014), those institutions in the "late majority" might capitalize on the best practices and successes of other institutions for the development of their own less innovative but also less risk-laden program. For example, many institutions of higher education have adopted existing platforms in order to lighten the load in terms of technological developments. This in turn enables the institution to focus on other areas of the implementation process, such as communication and pilot programs.

Digital badge program creation and improvement necessitates potentially time-consuming planning and assessment efforts. Organizers may need to plan a pilot rollout so that the situation is more manageable—and more likely to produce feedback, which will enhance a more comprehensive debut. An example can be found in connection with Purdue's LinkedIn badges. A rubric was created whose values correlated with the three levels of badges students were able to receive. Prior to use in a boot camp with over 150 students, those overseeing the initiative set up a pilot group, sought and received feedback, and made adjustments with boot camp participants in mind.

In order to create meaningful badging programs, organizers must acknowledge and focus on key elements of the diffusion of innovation process:

- They must communicate the advantages of the planned program and aim to minimize the complexity of digital badge adoption and use.
- They must embrace trial-ability and compatibility. They must ask to whom badging might appeal most. Can they be recruited first, as pilots, in highly compatible, specific/well-defined, and assessable ways? This

approach might apply to the business school (e.g. Sheffield Hallam University [Glover 2016]), the IT department (e.g. Harvard [Ostashewski and Reid 2015]), or a series of courses designed to bridge students' transitions into the higher education setting (Law 2015).
- And they must illustrate how the effort fits the community and scale the effort to address the best fit first, only *then* making the effort visible to a wider community.

As others in an institution's community see badging applied in simple, appropriate ways, diffusion and adoption tends to increase. Trial projects in the aforementioned co-curricular elements of the college experience might present convenient, scalable, communicable examples for discussion with broader campus departments, programs, and offices regarding implementation. Evidence can take many forms, including papers, presentations, or video links. A school, program, or department must decide whether badging for skills mastery or accomplishments is appropriate for their goals and how to meet these goals. At the pilot project level, students receiving and faculty allocating digital badges can serve as ambassadors to the broader institutional community.

An additional option for a pilot program might involve the faculty as badge-earners, as in the "Gamify Your Writing Group" article from *The Chronicle of Higher Education* (Prof. Hacker 2016). In this example, an institution initiated a faculty-focused summer writing challenge of thirty minutes per day to help with writing habit formation and increased faculty productivity. While the program initially used participation-based activities for badges (e.g., writing five days in a row), "hidden achievements" were also available (including promotion of the summer writing challenge via social media). At the time of the article's posting, the group had also been discussing how to challenge other writing groups on campus and holding a team-based writing competition. Similar to students, faculty can explore badging as ways to make their own "obligatory tasks" more engaging, which enables faculty to be guinea pigs for digital badging opportunities and to gain insider experience with badging's ability to motivate learners.

Even if broad scale adoption does not occur (or in the case of "late majority" or "laggard" groups), the smart, simple application of digital badging for one, or several, key communities may be enough. On the Educause blog, director of special projects Sondra R. Smith (2015) identified lessons learned from a badging initiative in order to enable others to better craft their own badging programs. Her insights include creating badges for existing opportunities, finding partners with whom you can collaborate, stacking badges carefully,[1] targeting populations and having a marketing plan (internally and externally), and remembering that design[2] *and* metadata *both* matter.[3] Considering badging best practices—such as those identified here by Smith—during the planning stages enables institutions to avoid potential missteps and to be as strategic as possible prior to implementation.

## Learning from Early Adopters

Tools are in development to help institutions working to create (or improve) badging programs and their analysis. For example, the Design Principles Documentation Project—or DPD Project—led by Indiana University's Daniel T. Hickey, analyzed how the 2012 MacArthur/HASTAC Digital Media & Learning grant competition-winning badging systems were developed. From this research, the DPD team developed badge design best practices that fall into four badge function categories: recognizing learning, assessing learning, motivating learning, and studying learning. The DPD Project resources include a badge design card deck (Design Principles Documentation Project 2014) and a worksheet (2016) that can be implemented at the individual level, in workshops, within administrative offices or institutional digital badging committees, and in other scenarios. Assets developed by experienced badging practitioners aid in the resourcing of higher education institutions, which frequently struggle for adequate staffing, funding, and time for the development of new projects and programs.

Because digital badging has quite a number of components, institutions still have many ways to become involved at various stages of the diffusion process. The existence of digital badging programs does not mean that there is no longer room for innovation. Those who take advantage of opportunities to spearhead the integration of badging in transcripts, for example, may be able to enter at the "innovator" or "early adopter" categories.

## Badge Rigor, Workload, and Acceptance

Badges must be not only reliable and valid but also assessable and measurable in order to determine whether a student (or employee) meets the requirements to achieve the badge. This can be difficult, because faculty often like broader objectives (Tally 2012). Successful badging initiatives may require faculty to narrow their outcomes or only assign badge-earning opportunities in very specific ways connected to their learning outcomes. Bill Watson of Purdue University's Passport digital badging program believes badge work's "most constant" challenge "is going to be the load it can put on the person assessing the work . . . figuring out how to create very specific and measurable learning outcomes that the badge is targeting" (Fedock et al. 2016, 278).

Digital badges also allow the higher education community to have a way of approaching competency-based learning rigorously, carefully, and specifically alongside traditional (comfortable) grading practices.

Badges, therefore, should not be based merely on passing or attendance. While grades and attendance are assessable factors of a student's performance in a course, they neither contain competencies nor involve mastery. Ostashewski and Reid (2015) note that the value of digital badges can be granular (skills/achievements) or high-level (mastery/certification), and badges can signal an individual's skill set to relevant stakeholders. Watson claims that, despite best efforts to design sustainable badging programs, "it can be difficult to support learner-mastery approaches when the semester has its deadlines, and they are not flexible" (Fedock et al. 2016, 278). If an institution seeks to develop a successful, sustainable badging program, time and timing will be important factors for the ease with which faculty feel they can implement and administer badges.

Institutions must establish standards for their badges and publish them in a way that is readily available. This will establish credibility with employer stakeholders and will ensure that an institution's badges are reliable and valid. The DPD Project's assessment category for "studying learning," for example, delineates specific goals that encourage designers to contemplate a host of issues: whether they seek to strengthen or broaden skills, how they may gain feedback, what "mastery" looks like (specifically, for a context), what the benefits and drawbacks of rubrics are, and how to go about quality assurance for their program. Diaz, Finkelstein, and Manning (2015) note very similar elements necessary for a successful, measurable badging program: a relational badge constellation; mapped badge meanings; an assessment strategy; a mechanism for tracking how learners progress through badges; provisions of benefits, rewards, and opportunities in the badging system; consideration for technology needs and badge delivery and showcasing; and cohesive visual design.

The workload of these development and management components should not be underestimated, especially in the higher education environment, which is already prone to overwhelming faculty and staff resources with service and administrative needs. The prospect of integrating new responsibilities, roles, oversight, positions, reassignments, committees, assessment expectations, and technology routinely daunts those in higher education. Because higher education is not known for its flexibility or agility, digital badging endeavors must be planned carefully and introduced thoughtfully. A negative experience, involving the time and energy of already-strapped human resources, could impact far more than just the success of a single badging venture.

Even well-designed, best practices–adherent badging programs may not always find success right away. Evidence shows that "undervalued badges routinely fail" (Ellis, Nunn, and Avella 2016, 16). Failure is not necessarily a negative, however. For, as Ellis, Nunn, and Avella add, "what appears to be a failure at the time might be the link needed in a future effort" (17). While there is no guarantee that the reverse is automatically true (or that *valued* badges routinely *succeed*), the documentation of processes and best practices allows institutions to engage with badging thoughtfully and meaningfully—on their terms.

## STUDENT STAKEHOLDERS

Institutions that know what engages and motivates their learners can use this information to build student investment in digital badges as a meaningful form of self-development. Institutions must understand relevant educational perspectives and the motivational opportunities and challenges, as well as specific learner characteristics for current and future generations of college students. Educational psychologist Dale Schunk (1990) says that, "when students perceive satisfactory goal progress, they feel capable of improving their skills; goal attainment coupled with high self-efficacy, leads students to set new challenging goals" (71). It is useful, then, for badging programs to keep in mind that the opportunity to implement digital badging lies not in fully "gamifying" curriculum but in building scaffolding toward goals and progress routes through micro-credentialing systems. Students can then develop and advance in smaller increments as well as gain confidence, retain motivation, and appreciate the accumulation of skills along the way.

Students need to assign value to badges. On a basic level, badges have the ability to indicate what a community values, to motivate or incentivize participation, to connect learners more closely with their learning experience, and to visually display a learners' path to outside communities (Halavais 2012). Further, while students may not anticipate this going into badging, they may find that digital badging engagement increases their autonomy and control of their own behavior—both of which have been shown to be strong indicators for student performance (Pintrich and De Groot 1990). Clayton, Elliott, and Iwata (2014) indicate that badging may also help learners establish a more organic view of their development and successes. Making faculty aware of the potential ways in which their students could develop as the result of a badging initiative not only helps them understand how their courses might benefit from using badging but also helps them communicate the value of badging to students.

### Educational Perspectives

Abstract thinking capabilities such as creative thinking, metacognition, decision-making, and problem solving (Yen and Halili 2015) are "higher order" skills that are often difficult to quantify. Within academic libraries, librarians are frequently engaged in information literacy instruction. This typically involves working with students to increase their critical thinking and information assessment abilities. Through this instruction, students learn to (re) search, develop strategies for information access and evaluation, and discuss ethical access and uses of information (among other topics). While Ford says that information literacy badging "reinforced box-like thinking" in students (2017, 20), Yen and Halili (2015, 41) observe that, to develop abstract skills within students, "teachers should promote student engagement with learning tasks which exceed the second level 'comprehension' in order to encourage [the higher levels of learning:] *application, analysis, synthesis,* and *evaluation* activities in processing information." This emphasizes the criticality of integrating digital badging initiatives with appropriate levels of Bloom's taxonomy, including using badges to encourage students to move toward higher levels of complex thinking and skills development.

Yen and Halili describe a number of challenges in fully addressing higher-order skills, including time, student attitudes and motivations, teacher competence and perception, assessment and its hindrances, the learning environment itself, and resources. Specifically considering the element of student attitude and motivation, the authors state firmly that "some students (even the good ones) have the mentality of taking the easy way out" and that "it will be faster and easier to be given a direct answer instead of being asked to think out of the box and to provide rationales afterwards" (ibid., 43). Understanding that students struggle to think abstractly, particularly early in their college careers, provides ample reasoning for the development of scaffolded or leveled badges, so that students can see and demonstrate their growth from lower-level skills into higher-order skills. This could be done within a course, in conjunction with a scaffolded assignment, and/or within a major, where students grow in subject expertise, discipline-relevant skills, and preparedness for increasingly complex work and engagement.

**Motivation and Empowerment**

Badging succeeds when students are motivated to earn the credentials they represent. To engage learners, badges must have a context: they must be relevant and meaningful. Such badge qualities can result from social engagement, from student interest(s), and from the learning content itself. Additionally, as stated in Sheryl Grant's 2014 report for the Digital Media and Learning Research Hub, "Perhaps most significantly for schools and universities, relevance may be defined by the degree to which students can customize their learning pathways so they are less tethered to more rigid scaffolds" (6). Digital badging programs, therefore, benefit from program administrators learning about their learners and planning (and revising) accordingly, as they refine their understanding of their learner community so that badges can be more targeted, motivating, and effective for all stakeholders.

If digital badging in higher education is to be a success, it is important to understand motivation strategies regarding its student stakeholders. There are a number of positive relationships between student motivation and digital badging. Maslow's hierarchy of needs indicates that the two highest-order human needs are self-actualization and self-esteem (Ellis, Nunn, and Avella 2016). Institutions of higher education provide a setting ripe for developing both.

Fedock et al. (2016) contend that digital badges can motivate both intrinsic and extrinsic learners. Intrinsic learners are motivated by opportunities to gain recognition, internal feelings of satisfaction, and the enjoyment of participation and a job well done. In contrast, extrinsic learners are motivated by their fear of failure. Many millennials fall into the category of extrinsic learners. They will achieve goals in order to avoid punishment, even if they do not perceive a given activity as fun or enjoyable the way that intrinsically motivated students might. For students struggling to assign intrinsic value to intellectual pursuit, to complete coursework, and to achieve passing grades, the extrinsic motivation that accompanies digital badging may create positive momentum, particularly if it is well-structured and attached to concrete activities and concepts.

While former US Secretary of Education Arne Duncan felt digital badging could allow individuals to feel empowered, he also stressed the importance of students constructing a reputation for themselves and branding what learning they have mastered (ibid.). Duncan saw digital badges' potential to act as micro-credentials (Wu, Whitely, and Sass 2015) and strategic game-changers (Waters 2013). Due in part to trends surrounding tertiary education costs, shorter seat time, and any-pace learning (e.g., via massive open online courses, or MOOCs), the attractiveness and utility of micro-credentials grows. As learners make progress, develop skills, and identify knowledge to pursue, badges can indicate milestone achievements leading up to a degree, diploma, or other traditional, larger scale credential (Lowendahl, Thayer, and Morgan 2016). As the higher education industry continues to grow and allows for more micro-achievements (e.g., digital badges, nanodegrees, micro-masters, certificate programs), the efficiency of time and money combined with the opportunity to accumulate, display, and showcase one's learning *as one learns* will likely in itself be a motivator for learners that empowers them to take charge of their educational path.

## Motivating Millennial Learners

Millennials, as previously noted, tend to be externally motivated with regard to direction and approval. Buckner and Strawser (in Morreale and Staley

2016) note that the millennial learner—whom they also refer to as the "Me"llennial—has a significant interest in success and a high level of motivation, as well as an externalized need for approval and direction, but a lower-than-desirable valuation of learning and intellectual curiosity. Students in the millennial generation often need to be taught to embrace the learning process and academic responsibility. Meaningful learner development for millennial students, in the form of badging, should acknowledge and adapt to two key components: their "external locus of control" (partly due to narcissism, partly due to reduced self-reliance) and their orientation with grades as opposed to intellectual stimulation (361).

Faculty members have documented a number of successful ventures employing digital badges with millennial learners in mind. For example, in addition to a variety of strategies for engaging this generation of students (e.g., using narratives to help students with new concepts, multimodal instruction and assignments), Kelly Richmond (2015) includes digital badging as a means of gamifying her accounting courses. Using "tactics such as earning badges, points, or levels throughout the course," she writes, "quickly adds challenge and motivation to students' learning experience. Digital badges recognize students' achievements on a smaller scale than typical academic credentials, giving millennials the feedback and recognition they crave." By working with common millennial characteristics and using intentional strategies, institutions can work to establish values and a sense of educational purpose within this generation of learners.

The granularity and the highly recommended scaffolding of badging programs, identified by Ostashewski and Reid (2015), can work to benefit millennials in terms of increasing their feelings of confidence, the perception of marketable skills, and the positive reinforcement from receiving and sharing markers of accomplishment and achievement. Madsen-Brooks (2013) notes that a history major interested in a public history career (outside of teaching) could focus on badges that support the skill sets for that field—for example, "original research," "digital media production," and "communicating knowledge to the public." As the millennial generation shifts into the "adult learner" or "non-traditional" student population category (Bump 2014), higher education stakeholders will need to understand and work with the needs of the next generation of college-level learners, referred to as Generation Z or Boomlets (Novak n.d.), the Homeland Generation (Williams 2015), and the iGen (Twenge 2017). When these students start to enter college over the next decade, the digital badging programs developed during the higher education reign of millennials will need to be configured to the worldviews, educational desires, and habits of a new learning community.

The way that one generation might use and appreciate badging will be different from another. For iGen-ers, who have been described by the Innovation

Group's Lucie Greene as "conscientious, hard-working, and somewhat anxious and mindful of the future" (in Williams 2015), compelling badging initiatives may need to focus on ways to signify and denote their hard work, to display co-curricular engagement (e.g., activism, volunteer work), and to enable them to plan for their future. While current initiatives, in many ways, already "sell" these components of badging to college students, knowing iGen students will *value* this orientation will be critical when connecting them to potential meaningfulness of digital badging in their academic development and career-readiness.

## Pairing Digital Badging with Other Specific Student Populations

Along with catering to their "traditional" college students, institutions must also understand their nontraditional or adult learner population and what motivates them through learning and through challenges on their path within higher education. Additional student populations that can benefit from the integration of digital badging into their educational setting include adult learners and nontraditional students, developmental and at-risk students, honors students, students excelling outside the curriculum, and students focused on or majoring in professional or applied fields.

Finkelstein, Knight, and Manning (2013) provide substantial guidance for working with adult learners from several perspectives. Recognizing prior learning and experiences functions as "retroactive badge-granting" and provides a means to establishing immediate value to digital badges within an adult learner population while also enabling institutions to acknowledge the full complement of skills and knowledge that adult learners often bring with them (18).

Utilizing badges to recognize prior learning also enables higher education institutions to better acknowledge the skills, knowledge, and accomplishments of unique adult learners, such as veterans, as demonstrated by early badge program Badges for Vets, which showcased skills acquired during military job training (Fain 2012). A study from *U.S. News & World Report* finds that "rusty academic skills, family responsibilities, and a sense of alienation from younger classmates can make it hard for veterans to succeed on campus" (Jacobs 2012).

Similarly, adult learners may increasingly encounter digital badging within continuing education settings and professional development. Glover and Latif (2013) mention that badges in conjunction with professional association membership can help students connect their academic efforts with their career aspirations. The employer stakeholder section of this chapter addresses how professional organizations, on their own and in collaboration with institutions of higher education, can pursue digital badging and includes examples of how this has been approached by existing organizations and fields.

Remedial, developmental, and/or disabled students comprise learner populations that often struggle to adjust to the higher education environment. Patrina (2015) describes the implementation of OpenLearn at the Open University (UK). Based on evaluations, program directors found that their pilot project helped to "provide accessible routes into the university for students who might not otherwise have the opportunity to participate in [higher education]" (301). Learners in this pilot program included a "relatively high percentage of disabled learners" (305). It may be that there is an opportunity to use digital badges as a way to immediately motivate developmental, at-risk, and other students who may otherwise struggle to persist in higher education pursuits.

Digital badges present opportunities for honors-level work as well. At Illinois State University, the Honors Program builds badging into their electronic portfolio efforts (Illinois State University, n.d.a). Badges can be earned for critical thinking, interdisciplinary learning, information literacy, creative productivity, leadership development, and intercultural competency (Illinois State University Honors Program, n.d.b). These badges, created and granted via Credly, have curricular, co-curricular, and community-related ties and enable evidence to be attached to the badge (e.g., a paper) to facilitate review by Honors Program staff and faculty.

Badging can also be successfully deployed to students engaged in professional and applied studies programs. Ian Glover (2016) from Sheffield Hallam University recommends using badges to highlight the "concrete, 'marketable' skills, experience, and knowledge" of university students—which may be particularly well-suited to students pursuing professional or applied studies degrees (452). Such clear, focused, and applicable badges would be more desirable and motivating for these learners than participation-based and/or more abstract badges. Glover worked with students at the Sheffield Business School, a professional program that, as such, has an intentional lean toward concrete, practical, and marketable skills and experience. Additional programs that can benefit from digital badging programs include nursing (e.g., for documenting acquisition of specific clinical skills), mechanical engineering (e.g., evidence of safety training, equipment training, and refresher-style trainings), and computing (e.g., to highlight specialist paths through program electives) (Glover and Latif 2013). Library science programs (Walker, Lee, and Lonn 2015) and medical school education settings (Mehta et al. 2013) may also benefit from this targeted approach to digital badging within postgraduate settings.

Many institutions of higher education are already working with, or in the process of implementing, e-portfolio systems to broaden the concept and documentation of institutional competencies and learning outcomes at the individual student level, as well as more granular and potentially co-curricular experiences during college. Brent Herbert-Copley (2013) of the *Globe and Mail* mentions the growth in the appeal of the "T-shaped" graduate—the learner who demonstrates a depth of subject area or domain-based knowledge (or "vertical" knowledge) as well as broad communication, teamwork, data/technology, cultural understanding and appreciation, and literacy skills (or "horizontal" knowledge). In late October 2016, the Digication Help Desk posted an update that their e-portfolio platform now enables integration with the digital badging platform Credly as a result of a successful pilot with the University of Notre Dame that incorporated digital badges into Notre Dame portfolios (Kelly 2016).

Community-focused engagement provides another badging opportunity outside the traditional college curriculum. Such badges foster and benefit learners as global citizens and community members. Young (2012) notes the University of Southern California's Joint Educational Project, a badging program that has faculty members collaborate with the community to establish service-learning opportunities and provide extra credit for volunteer work. Glover and Latif (2013) also mention student government leadership badges for elected responsibilities (e.g., chairing meetings, event organization, etc.) to be granted *after* students complete their term. In the same article, Glover and Latif state that, through badges, "real value could be offered to students who don't do as well academically but performed well in other areas that aren't formally assessed" (1401). There are a variety of new ways in which institutions of higher education can consider, discuss, and create digital badging programs that motivate and engage learners in their broader university and global community. These are particularly compelling given the need for broader skill sets and interests within our global population, including civic engagement, community awareness, and cultural consciousness.

While it may be attractive to plan for a set of learners based on particular characteristics (like those discussed in this section), badging's appeal, ability to motivate, and role in demonstrating student skills and interest very much lies with the individual learner. Bowen and Thomas (2014) use the phrase *leadership journey* to describe the digital badging profile established by a Purdue University senior whose digital badges allow him to display "the arc of [his] development across classes and other activities from [his] freshman to [his] senior year" (22). The credentials this student earned are less abstract and more evidence-based and individualized, details that cannot be conveyed with a traditional degree (ibid.). Students must understand the extent to which they will need to be a unique and compelling "resource" in the labor market supply and the ways in which digital badging can aid them in developing a singular, specific, and verified demonstration of skills and accomplishments.

While there are clearly a variety of ways to successfully create student-stakeholder-driven digital badging programs, and arguments for their value, the role of employer stakeholders remains a key factor in making sure that student and institutional efforts are marketable and accepted. Digital badging has the capacity to be a highly visible, granular, evidence-based display of learner skills, achievements, and interests. But do employers know about, understand, and trust digital badges as evidence of learning and mastery? And what would convince them to do so?

## EMPLOYER STAKEHOLDERS

In order for digital badges to be marketable to students, faculty, and administrators, the job market needs to have an understanding of what digital badges are, have a way to access and assess those badges, and develop trust in the rigor and reliability of the badges and their issuers. Qualification visibility, badge credibility, and labor concepts like supply and demand are important for the construction of value between the employer, the badge holder, and the badge grantor.

### Seeing Is Believing: Metadata Discoverability

As badge metadata must be discoverable in order for third parties (e.g., employers) to see the rigor and requirements involved with attaining a particular badge, the overt placement of such details could influence how transcripts are viewed and used. The badging world benefits from a system where employers can check these credentials (akin to a badging background check). Employers need assurances, safeguards, and standards, perhaps even at the global level. Mozilla and others are engaged in addressing employers' needs, but a concrete system has yet to be established. This means that at the very least badge credibility remains a persistent concern for employer stakeholders. Further, employers face uncertainty about the utility of badging as well as the realities of supply and demand within the job market.

The digital badging programs within higher education might consider utilizing terms with which employers may have ready mental benchmarks. Alternative terms might include *digital certificate* or *digital credential* and *nanodegree* or *micro-master* (Barabas and Schmidt 2016, 4–5). Further, institutions might pursue awarding a printable badge-attainment certificate (with badge metadata in it) in addition to the digital version. The Badge

Design Principles Documentation Project Interim Report includes a case study in which interest in a printable certificate option is documented. Similarly, Glover's (2016) chapter in *Foundation of Digital Badges and Micro-credentials* describes the potential usefulness of "mechanisms to enable badges to be printed in a certificate-like format [that] could be added to badging platforms to facilitate this use case, thereby enabling the sharing and verification features of the digital badges while also allowing a high-quality printed version to be used during job interviews" (452). These certificates would be helpful for earners and employers alike at least until digital badges are "recognized and credible to both potential earners and those with whom they are likely to be shared" (ibid.) and should help employers adjust to the proliferation of digital badges within their prospective employees' application packets.

Learners can use the agility and transparency of digital badging and e-portfolios to connect education, expertise, and skills with employment opportunities and career prospects. Interviews conducted with staff and students at City, University London identified the sentiment that employer awareness of digital badges and institutional initiatives would benefit everyone involved and that staff could use the digital badging profiles of students to aid in writing references for those students (Glover and Latif 2013). The metadata behind badges, which details the evidence and rigor behind the granted badge, will be powerful when seeking to build employer awareness and craft letters of recommendation for students.

Institutions, however, will want to beware of *carpet badging*—the "mass awarding of badges with little or no assessment of work" (Class Hack, n.d.). If badges are too easy to attain, have little rigor, or are not unique enough to be particularly informative, learners will struggle to market themselves using their earned badges, and institutions will face difficulty gaining employer and industry buy-in for digital badging programs.

## Employment Market Responsiveness and Buy-In

Particularly within community colleges, institutions frequently explore ways to reconfigure how they offer programs, particularly at the certificate and graduate levels. This often has to do with market demands for training and expertise and an institution's interest in supplying resources (potential employees) to fulfill that need. Website *Investopedia* defines the law of supply and demand as "the theory explaining the interaction between the supply of a resource and the demand for that resource" (n.d.b.). Relating this to college degrees, certificates, and skill sets, the employment market has demand for these credentials and skills and pays for them in terms of salary, benefits, and increased job openings. Learning service providers must establish sufficient agility and responsiveness to market needs or else run the risk of ignoring market needs and, as a result, producing graduates who struggle to find gainful employment in the global marketplace.

While employability is not the sole concern of higher education institutions, graduates capable of finding employment are of significant interest to colleges and universities. The skills related to a badge and its metadata must be desirable in the market (whether degree-related or not) and speak to qualifications of the learner (who is both the prospective employee and the market commodity). If market supply is too high, the value of the badge (and the resource/prospective employee it attaches to) may be diminished—the badges and badge holders could flood the market. Should that happen, the "price" would drop: it would be a buyer's market, and resources would be available at the lowest prices possible to be competitive. This is decidedly a poor situation for credential bearers entering the job market and highlights the power that employers have regarding potential employees and market resources. Higher education can use the laws of supply and demand to reinvigorate its relationship with employer stakeholders through the careful and strategic deployment of digital badging and protect the value of its resources at the same time.

One way to gain employer and industry buy-in, of course, is to connect them with higher education institutions that can run digital badging programs for professional development purposes. In addition to the examples and strategies addressed in the student stakeholder section, a digital badging initiative created by Penn State University enabled one hundred science teachers to engage in professional development efforts with badges as evidence of their learning (Raths 2015).

At the professional association level, digital badges can have similar appeal. Davies and West (2015) discuss the ongoing conversation within the American Evaluation Association regarding the certification of evaluators. The authors note that weaknesses exist within traditional certification avenues (specifically for concerns regarding training, assessment, work experience, certification, implementation, and administration) and advocate for the use of open badges to establish an individual's certification credential. Perceived benefits of implementing an open badge–driven certification process include transparency (about credentials—badge evidence versus résumé claims), flexibility and adaptability (e.g., ease of integration into existing technology), rigor (including for initial acquisition and for recertification), and management (e.g., division of labor among issuers, focusing on badge clusters or discrete skills, establishing levels of expertise).

Educational leadership programs are also mentioned as potential homes for digital badging initiatives. Further, a 2016 report from Fong, Janzow, and Peck indicates that the business, education, technology/IT, professional and business services, and healthcare industries are offering certificates and badges more than other industries surveyed. This may indicate a desire for, need for, or value placed upon incremental and continued education within these fields, and digital badges may complement these industry interests in that they can help learners create a path and display their educational accomplishments.

## Locally Relevant Learner-Employer Connections

While colleges and universities should have badges that are broadly applicable and marketable for their students, it can also be worth considering the viability of locally relevant badges, tied to employer needs in the region of the school. Finkelstein, Knight, and Manning (2013) state that local employers might add indications of what badges fulfill specific job requirements for their vacant positions. This could be particularly useful for community colleges, where a badge awarded for skills and knowledge on food sanitation, for example, might be accepted by employers looking for hires fitting that requirement (e.g., in the 2017 *eCampus News* article "Community Colleges Begin Linking Digital Badges, ePortfolios and Recruiting Matches"). Fedock et al. (2016) address the value of badges within the community college, vo-tech, and other non-four-year degrees. They state that when these credentials are "publishable and endorsed by the issuers, employers may find a larger group from which to select qualified employees for technical positions that required a select set of skills. Global business leaders need a wide range of employees with a diversity of skills; however, often the skills do not require four years of college or technical education" (277).

Where workshops or other educational programming can provide the training, skills, and expertise prospective employers need, badge metadata can communicate the rigor, guidelines, and standards of these experiences. By collaborating with local industries and their representatives, badges can be created to meet immediate and predictable needs for the region. Institutions can then market the availability of workforce-approved badges to current and prospective students.

## Building Trust Takes Time and Effort

In addition to valuing the badge credential, employers must also recognize the criteria required for acquiring a badge or cluster of badges. Finkelstein, Knight, and Manning (2013) point out that establishing recognition and credibility takes time, as digital badges could have the same arc as traditional credentials and that status could be driven by professional associations (e.g., the National Council of Professors of Educational Administration, or NCPEA), specific companies (e.g., NASA), or learning services providers (e.g., colleges and universities). Employers can also drive awareness of new areas of skills needed in the workforce.

Institutions of higher education might then use digital badging as an intermediary or supplemental step that supports skills development along with formal courses or programs. Students might acquire digital badges through workshop attendance, independent study, and other learning efforts, and the metadata of the badge would match the needs indicated by the initiating employer or industry. Institutions might then communicate the acquisition of applicable badges to indicate learners' development of the necessary skills. Strong collaboration between employers and universities may aid in employers recognizing badging and gaining increased confidence in applicants with badges as evidence of skills and knowledge.

## THE FUTURE OF DIGITAL BADGING IN HIGHER EDUCATION

In 2014, Bernard Bull, assistant vice president of academics, associate professor of education, and chief innovation officer at Concordia University Wisconsin, published a post on his blog, *Etale*, in which he envisioned the next three to seven years with digital badging and micro-credentialing. At the higher education level, he expected to see

- badges and micro-credentials challenging traditional credentialing bodies
- improvements in the viability of alternative credentialing routes
- granularity of badge and micro-credential metadata enabling this information to serve as a supplement to traditional diplomas and transcripts
- traditional/formal educational environments continuing to experiment with badging
- partnerships and collaborations between traditional education institutions and non-educational institutions continuing to develop, in part thanks to open badging platforms
- entrepreneurship finding a place within digital badging
- the personalization (or curation) of one's portfolio of badges enabling learners to stress specific skills and accomplishments—their strengths and interests—without displaying their weaknesses
- and potential benefits to advising, adaptive learning systems, and other learner touch points as badging entities gather assessment data and analytics.

While Bull's post, which provides the rationale for each item, is several years old already, much of his prognostications are still in development or reside on the horizon. Colleges and universities anticipate challenges from alternative credentialing opportunities (Crotty 2012; Herbert-Copley 2013; Lemoine and Richardson 2015; Ellis, Nunn, and Avella 2016). They also continue to find options for experimentation with badges, like at Eastern Michigan University in collaboration with the NCPEA (Anderson and Staub 2015; Wu, Whiteley, and Sass 2015) and between Penn State, NASA, and the National Science Teachers Association (Gamrat et al. 2014).

Ostashewski and Reid (2015) note that increased functionality may hold the key to increased usefulness and applicability for digital badges,

- from demonstrating one's pathways to learning with increased granularity to demonstrating relevant skills to relevant stakeholders
- from one badge opening up opportunities for additional learning experiences to acknowledging milestones and mastery
- and from motivating further skills acquisition and education to establishing a flexible, innovation-friendly approach to learning within the traditional academic environment.

Technology can play a pivotal role in the development of increased functionality of badges and increase a learner's ability to explore useful applications, such as those noted above.

Standardization of credentialing may also help bridge a current issue in higher education. At the 2016 Parchment Summit on Innovating Academic Credentials, Anthony P. Carnevale (who directs the Center on Education and the Workforce at Georgetown University), said that "our current credentialing system is too fragmented. The many credentials—including certificates, licenses, college degrees, industry-based certifications, even apprenticeships—all have labor market value . . . We need a transparent and comprehensive system for tracking their economic value" (in DiSalvio 2016).

Institutions seeking to establish high buy-in digital badging programs as a means of "unbundling" their learner credentialing options must ask what that would look like. Might it drive the (perhaps necessary) revisions to transcripts, integrating detailed competencies, skill sets, and achievements and their documentation and metadata? How should institutions address privacy issues regarding sharing these acquired, or awarded, skills and honors? Can higher education institutions create and manage an intentional, assessable digital badging initiative that works for both intrinsically and extrinsically motivated learners? And that works for learners interested in both traditional degree and/or micro-credentialing educational opportunities? Can an institution achieve this while establishing and maintaining rigor and validity? How can institutions communicate such shifts in transcript documentation, skills and accomplishment sharing, and learner development to the global employment market and its employers?

## CONCLUSION

In exploring how badging can be meaningful within higher education, this chapter has considered the role of students, faculty, and administrators within higher education institutions and employer stakeholder roles. The needs, opportunities, and challenges for these communities have also been addressed, along with examples and resources to better understand and confront badging pitfalls. Learners of all ages can benefit from the ability of digital badges to connect with learners through goal setting, incentives and motivation, accomplishment signification, and communicating achievements.

Digital badging is a form of disruptive technology, which *Investopedia* (n.d.a.) defines as "a technology that significantly alters the way that businesses operate." Bob Nilsson (2014), director of vertical solutions marketing at Extreme Networks, notes that such technologies "tend to establish themselves just outside the mainstream, before they grow to supplant the established technology or tradition. As a new generation of users takes over, they bring with them the emerging technologies they grew up with." As badges become more popular in elementary and secondary education (e.g., Westminster High School and the Adams 50 public school district, as noted in Waters 2013), students will arrive at colleges and universities with experiences and perhaps even expectations related to badging opportunities. Higher education may begin to see badges as part of student application packets. As digital badges become less disruptive and more broadly understood, accepted, and used, higher education institutions, their students, and employers will be better positioned to implement strategic badging initiatives and high-impact badging practices.

## NOTES

1. *Stackable credentials* can be defined as "part of a sequence of credentials that can be accumulated over time to build up an individual's qualifications and help them to move along a career pathway or up a career ladder to different and potentially higher-paying jobs" (Oates 2010, 6).

2. Smith believes that institutions should consider using a professional graphic designer.

3. Metadata involves a badge description, the award criteria, and evidence for the recipient badge issuance. The metadata provides meaning for both the badge recipient and for individuals looking at the badges an individual has attained.

## REFERENCES

Anderson, David M., and Selva Staub. 2015. "Postgraduate Digital Badges in Higher Education: Transforming Advanced Programs Using Authentic Online Instruction and Assessment to Meet the Demands of a Global Marketplace." *Procedia: Social and Behavioral Sciences* 195 (3): 18–23. https://ac.els-cdn.com/S1877042815036447/1-s2.0-S1877042815036447-main.pdf?_tid=2056196c-7f01-4922-82f9-d2d9e2d9fc18&acdnat=1522806959_03e9a75185d8927a7f4c69518f539966.

Barabas, Chelsea, and J. Philipp Schmidt. 2016. "Transforming Chaos into Clarity: The Promises and Challenges of Digital Credentialing." Roosevelt Institute. August. http://rooseveltinstitute.org/wp-content/uploads/2016/08/The-Promises-and-Challenges-of-Digital-Credentialing.pdf.

Beattie, Scott. 2014. "Types of Digital Learning Badges: Drawing on the XBox Achievement Experience." HASTAC (blog). June 30. https://www.hastac.org/blogs/scott-beattie/2014/06/30/types-digital-learning-badges-drawing-xbox-achievement-experience.

Buckner, Marjorie M., and Michael G. Strawser. 2016. "'Me'lennials and the Paralysis of Choice: Reigniting the Purpose of Higher Education." *Communication Education* 65 (3): 361–63.

Bull, Bernard. 2014. "How Will Badges and Micro-credentialing Change Education?" *Etale—Education, Innovation, Experimentation* (blog). January 27. http://etale.org/main/2014/01/27/how-will-badges-and-micro-credentialing-challenge-formal-education/.

Bump, Philip. 2014. "Here Is When Each Generation Begins and Ends, According to Facts." *The Atlantic*, March 25. https://www.theatlantic.com/national/archive/2014/03/here-is-when-each-generation-begins-and-ends-according-to-facts/359589/.

Bowen, Kyle, and Andrea Thomas. 2014. "Badges: A Common Currency for Learning." *Change: The Magazine of Higher Learning* 46 (1): 21–25.

Carey, Kevin. 2012. "A Future Full of Badges." *The Chronicle of Higher Education*, April 8. http://www.chronicle.com/article/A-Future-Full-of-Badges/131455/.

Class Hack. n.d. "Carpet Badging." *Class Hack* (website). http://classhack.com/post/50915858999/carpetbadging.

Crotty, James Marshall. 2012. "Why Get a Pricey Diploma When a Bleepin' Badge Will Do?" *Forbes*, January 26. https://www.forbes.com/sites/jamesmarshallcrotty/2012/01/26/the-end-of-the-diploma-as-we-know-it/.

Davies, Randall, and Richard E. West. 2015. "Using Open Badges to Certify Practicing Evaluators." *American Journal of Evaluation* 36 (2): 151–63.

Design Principles Documentation Project. 2014. "DPD Project Design Workshop: Building a Badge System for Learning." Design Principles Documentation Project (website). http://dpdproject.info/files/2014/03/DPD-Project-Cards-Handout.pdf.

———. 2016. "DPD card deck frontback." Design Principles Documentation Project (website). http://dpdproject.info/files/2016/04/DPD-card-deck-frontback-draft7.pdf.

Devedžić, Vladan, and Jelena Jovanović. 2015. "Developing Open Badges: A Comprehensive Approach." *Educational Technology Research & Development* 63 (4): 603–20.

Diaz, Veronica, Jonathan Finkelstein, and Susan Manning. 2015. "Developing a Higher Education Badging Initiative." *EDUCAUSE Learning Initiative Brief* (website). August. https://library.educause.edu/~/media/files/library/2015/8/elib1504-pdf.pdf.

DiSalvio, Philip. 2016. "New Pathways to Credentialing: The Digital Badge." *The New England Journal of Higher Education*, May 3. http://www.nebhe.org/thejournal/new-pathways-to-credentialing-the-digital-badge/.

Driscoll, Kelly. 2016. "Digication Now Provides Integration of Credly for Digital Badges." Digication Help Desk (website). October 28. https://support.digication.com/hc/en-us/articles/231579608-Digication-Now-Provides-Integration-of-Credly-for-Digital-Badges.

eCampus News. 2017. "Community Colleges Begin Linking Digital Badges, ePortfolios and Recruiting Matches." *eCampus News*, March 14. http://www.ecampusnews.com/top-news/partnership-badges-eportfolios/ (subscription required).

Clayton, John, Richard Elliott, and Jun Iwata. 2014. "Exploring the Use of Micro-credentialing and Digital Badges in Learning Environments to Encourage Motivation to Learn and Achieve." *Rhetoric and Reality: Critical Perspectives on Educational Technology*, edited by Bronwyn Hegarty, J. McDonald, and Swee-Kin Loke, 703–707. Proceedings of the ASCILite2014 conference. Dunedin, New Zealand, November 23–26.

Ellis, Larry E., Sandra G. Nunn, and John T. Avella. 2016. "Digital Badges and Micro-credentials: Historical Overview, Motivational Aspects, and Challenges." In *Foundation of Digital Badges and Micro-credentials*, edited by Dirk Ifenthaler, Nicole Bellin-Mularski, and Dana-Kristin Mah, 3–21. New York: Springer.

Fain, Paul. 2012. "Digital Badging for Veterans." *Inside Higher Ed*, December 7. https://www.insidehighered.com/news/2012/12/07/website-recognizes-military-skills-digital-badges.

Fedock, Barbara, Mansureh Kebritchi, Rebecca Sanders, and Alicia Holland. 2016. "Digital Badges and Micro-credentials: Digital Age Classroom Practices, Design Strategies, and Issues." In *Foundation of Digital Badges and Micro-credentials*, edited by Dirk Ifenthaler, Nicole Bellin-Mularski, and Dana-Kristin Mah, 273–86. New York: Springer.

Finkelstein, Jonathan, Erin Knight, and Susan Manning. 2013. *The Potential and Value of Using Digital Badges for Adult Learners.* Washington, DC: American Institutes for Research. https://lincs.ed.gov/publications/pdf/AIR_Digital_Badge_Report_508.pdf.

Fong, Jim, Peter Janzow, and Kyle Peck. 2016. *Demographic Shifts in Educational Demand and the Rise of Alternative Credentials.* Pearson Education and UPCEA, June. http://upcea.edu/wp-content/uploads/2017/05/Demographic-Shifts-in-Educational-Demand-and-the-Rise-of-Alternative-Credentials.pdf.

Ford, Emily. 2017. "To Badge or Not to Badge? From 'Yes' to 'Never Again.'" *C&RL News* 78 (1) (January): 20–21. Retrieved from http://crln.acrl.org/index.php/crlnews/article/view/9602/ 10991.

Gamrat, Christopher, Heather Toomey Zimmerman, Jaclyn Dudek, and Kyle Peck. 2014. "Personalized Workplace Learning: An Exploratory Study on Digital Badging within a Teacher Professional Development Program." *British Journal of Educational Technology* 45 (6) (August): 1136–48.

Gibson, David, Nathaniel Ostashewski, Kim Flintoff, Sheryl Grant, and Erin Knight. 2013. "Digital Badges in Education." *Education and Information Technologies* 20 (2): 403–10.

Glover, Ian. 2013. "Open Badges: A Visual Method of Recognizing Achievement and Increasing Learner Motivation." *Student Engagement and Experience Journal* 2 (1): 1–4. doi:10.7190/seej.v1i1.66.

———. 2016. "Student Perceptions of Digital Badges as Recognition of Achievement and Engagement in Co-curricular Activities." In *Foundation of Digital Badges and Micro-credentials*, edited by Dirk Ifenthaler, Nicole Bellin-Mularski, and Dana-Kristin Mah, 443–55. New York: Springer.

Glover, Ian, and Farzana Latif. 2013. "Investigating Perceptions and Potential of Open Badges in Formal Higher Education." In *Proceedings of World Conference on Educational Multimedia, Hypermedia and Telecommunications 2013*, edited by Jan Herrington, Alec Couros, and Valerie Irvine, 1398–1402. Victoria, British Columbia, Canada, June 24–28.

Grant, Sheryl. 2014. *What Counts as Learning: Open Digital Badges for New Opportunities*. Irvine, CA: Digital Media and Learning Research Hub. https://dmlhub.net/wp-content/uploads/files/WhatCountsAsLearning_Grant.pdf.

Halavais, Alexander M. C. 2012. "A Genealogy of Badges: Inherited Meaning and Monstrous Moral Hybrids." *Information, Communication and Society* 15 (3): 354–73. doi:10.1080/1369118X.2011.641992.

Herbert-Copley, Brent. 2013. "Ditch the Resume and Pick Up a Badge, They're Not Just for Boy Scouts." *The Globe and Mail*, May 1. Updated March 26, 2017. https://www.theglobeandmail.com/news/national/education/ditch-the-resume-and-pick-up-a-badge-theyre-not-just-for-boy-scouts/article11639205/.

Illinois State University Honors Program. n.d.a. "Dimensions of Honors Learning." Illinois State University (website). https://honors.illinoisstate.edu/academics/dimensions/.

———. n.d.b. "Digital Badging." Illinois State University (website). https://honors.illinoisstate.edu/opportunities/badging/.

Investopedia. n.d.a. "Disruptive Technology." https://www.investopedia.com/terms/d/disruptive-technology.asp.

———. n.d.b. "Law of Supply and Demand." http://www.investopedia.com/terms/l/law-of-supply-demand.asp.

Jacobs, Joanne. 2012. "Report: Veterans Go to College but Face Challenges." *U.S. News & World Report*, May 18. https://www.usnews.com/education/best-colleges/articles/2012/05/18/report-veterans-go-to-college-but-face-challenges.

Jovanović, Jelena, and Vladan Devedžić. 2014. "Open Badges: Challenges and Opportunities." In *Advances in Web-Based Learning—ICWL 2014*, edited by Elvira Popescu, Rynson W. H. Lau, Kai Pata, Howard Leung, and Mart Laanpere, 56–65. New York: Springer.

———. 2015. "Open Badges: Novel Means to Motivate, Scaffold and Recognize Learning." *Technology, Knowledge and Learning* 20 (1): 115–22. doi:10.1007/s10758-014-9232-6.

King, Jeff, Camille Kilbourne, and Mark Walvoord. 2015. "Student Transformative Learning Record (STLR): Capturing Beyond-Discipline Learning In and Out of the Classroom." Paper presented at the Research to Practice Conference in Early Childhood Education, University of Central Oklahoma, Edmond, Oklahoma, November 15–17. https://sites.uco.edu/central/tl/files/JKingCKilbourneMWalvood_2015_proceedings_R2P.pdf.

Kuh, George D. 2008. *High-Impact Educational Practices: What They Are, Who Has Access to Them, and Why They Matter*. Washington, DC: AAC&U.

Law, Patrina. 2015. "Recognising Informal Elearning with Digital Badging: Evidence for a Sustainable Business Model." *Open Praxis* 7 (4): 299–310. doi:10.5944/openpraxis.7.4.247. https://openpraxis.org/index.php/OpenPraxis/article/view/247/182.

Lemoine, Pamela A., and Michael D. Richardson. 2015. "Micro-credentials, Nano degrees, and Digital Badges: New Credentials for Global Higher Education." *International Journal of Technology and Educational Marketing* 5 (1): 36–49. doi:10.4018/ijtem.2015010104.

Lowendahl, Jan-Martin, Terri-Lynn B. Thayer, and Glenda Morgan. 2016. "Top 10 Business Trends Impacting Higher Education." *Gartner* (website), January 15. https://www.gartner.com/doc/3186325/top--business-trends-impacting (subscription required).

Madsen-Brooks, Leslie. 2013. "Rethinking Digital Badges: Harnessing Badges in Remaking Undergraduate Curriculum." *The Blue Review* (blog), April 24. https://thebluereview.org/rethinking-digital-badges/.

Mehta, Neil B., Alan L. Hull, James B. Young, and James K. Stoller. 2013. "Just Imagine: New Paradigms for Medical Education." *Academic Medicine* 88 (10): 1418–23. doi:10.109/ACM.0b013e3182a36a07.

Morreale, Sherwyn P., and Constance M. Staley. 2016. "Millennials, Teaching and Learning, and the Elephant in the College Classroom." *Communication Education* 65 (3): 356–76. doi:10.1080/03634523.2016.1173715.

Nilsson, Bob. 2014. "Will Digital Badges Replace Resumes . . . and Diplomas?" *Extreme Networks Blog*, March 21. https://content.extremenetworks.com/extreme-networks-blog/will-digital-badges-replace-resumes-and-diplomas.

Novak, Jill. n.d. "The Six Living Generations in America." *Marketing Teacher*. http://www.marketingteacher.com/the-six-living-generations-in-america/.

Oates, Jane. 2010. *Training and Employment Guidance Letter No. 15-10*. United States Department of Labor, Employment and Training Administration (website). December 15. https://wdr.doleta.gov/directives/attach/TEGL15-10.pdf.

Ostashewski, Nathaniel, and Doug Reid. 2015. "A History and Frameworks of Digital Badges in Education." In *Gamification in Education and Business*, edited by Torsten Reiners and Lincoln C. Wood, 187–200. New York: Springer.

Pintrich, Paul R., and Elisabeth V. De Groot. 1990. "Motivational and Self-regulated Learning Components of Classroom Academic Performance." *Journal of Educational Psychology* 82 (1): 33–40. doi:10.1037/0022-0663.82.1.33.

Pope, Kelly Richmond. 2015. "Engaging Millennials through Digital Learning." AICPA (website), July 14. https://www.aicpa.org/interestareas/accountingeducation/newsandpublications/engaging-millennials-through-digital-learning.html.

Prof. Hacker. 2016. "Gamify Your Writing Group." *ProfHacker* (*The Chronicle of Higher Education* blog), August 24. http://www.chronicle.com/blogs/profhacker/gamify-your-writing-group/62656.

Ramsden, Andy. 2015. "Open Badges: Trying to Navigate through the Melting Pot of Ideas." LinkedIn (website), June 18. https://www.linkedin.com/pulse/open-badges-trying-navigate-through-melting-pot-ideas-andy-ramsden/.

Raths, David. 2015. "5 Tech Tools that Help Personalize PD." *THE Journal* 42 (1): 22–24. https://thejournal.com/articles/2015/02/04/5-tech-tools-that-help-personalize-pd.aspx.

Sahin, Ismail. 2006. "Detailed Review of Rogers' Diffusion of Innovations Theory and Educational Technology-Related Studies Based on Rogers' Theory." *The Turkish Online Journal of Educational Technology* 5 (2): 14–23. http://files.eric.ed.gov/fulltext/ED501453.pdf.

Schunk, Dale H. 1990. "Goal Setting and Self-Efficacy during Self-Regulated Learning." *Educational Psychologist* 25 (1): 71–86.

Smith, Sondra R. 2015. "10 Lessons Learned from an Award-Winning Digital Badging Program." *EDUCAUSE Review* (blog), June 29. https://er.educause.edu/blogs/2015/6/10-lessons-learned-from-an-awardwinning-digital-badging-program.

Strikwerda, Carl. J. 2014. "Risk Managing or Risk Averse? Neither Approach Is Fully Suited for Higher Education." *The Chronicle of Higher Education*, November 10. http://www.chronicle.com/article/Risk-Managing-or-Risk-Averse-/149889/.

Tally, Steve. 2012. "Digital Badges Show Students' Skills Along with Degree." Purdue University (website), September 11. http://www.purdue.edu/newsroom/releases/2012/Q3/digital-badges-show-students-skills-along-with-degree.html.

Twenge, Jean. M. 2017. *iGen: Why Today's Super-Connected Kids Are Growing Up Less Rebellious, More Tolerant, Less Happy—and Completely Unprepared for Adulthood*. New York: Atria Books, Simon and Schuster.

Walker, Ashley Marie, Florence Lee, and Steven Lonn. 2015. "Scaffolds: Experimenting with Student-Driven Digital Badging in an iSchool Context." Deep Blue (University of Michigan Library online),, March 24. https://deepblue.lib.umich.edu/bitstream/handle/2027.42/110790/walker_lee_lonn_scaffolds_iConference-2015Submission.pdf;sequence=2.

Waters, John K. 2013. "Everything You Wanted to Know about Badging in the Classroom: Our Definitive Guide." *THE Journal*, May 30. https://thejournal.com/articles/2013/05/30/everything-you-ever-wanted-to-know-about-badging-in-the-classroom-our-definitive-guide.aspx.

Williams, Alex. 2015. "Move Over, Millennials, Here Comes Generation Z." *New York Times*, September 18. https://www.nytimes.com/2015/09/20/fashion/move-over-millennials-here-comes-generation-z.html.

Wu, Margaret, Dan Whiteley, and Margaret Sass. 2015. "From Girl Scout to Grown Up: Emerging Applications of Digital Badges in Higher Education." *The Online Journal of Distance Education and e-Learning* 3 (2): 48–52.

Yen, Tan Shin, and Siti Hajar Halili. 2015. "Effective Teaching of Higher-Order Thinking (HOT) in Education." *The Online Journal of Distance Education and e-Learning* 3 (2): 41–47. https://www.tojdel.net/journals/tojdel/articles/v03i02/v03i02-04.pdf.

Young, Jeffrey R. 2012. "'Badges' Earned Online Pose Challenge to Traditional College Diplomas." *Education Digest: Essential Readings Condensed for Quick Review* 78 (2): 48–52.

# 4

# Digital Badges in Action

*Amanda Rose Fuller*

The sun was shining as Trinell Samuel slowly ascended the steps toward Opera Colorado. She shivered with anticipation, ready to take part in her digital badge experience with an amazing non-profit organization endorsing students' digital badge credentials in Aurora Public Schools (figure 4.1). Trinell first learned about digital badge credentials through an email that explained how the credentials she earned in high school could be "cashed-in" for a career exploration opportunity. After learning more about digital badges and what they meant, she browsed the list of potential companies with which she could have a hands-on, interactive experience. Opera Colorado immediately jumped out to Trinell because of her love of theater.

Ever since her freshman year, Trinell had been enrolled in technical theater classes. She found that the theater was a place of solitude, her safe haven, and the thought of being able to spend time there, immersed in what she loved most, really resonated with her. Shortly after she began taking technical theater classes, Trinell enrolled in a video production class. This was incomparable to anything she had ever pursued. "While technical theater is my first love, video production is my soul mate," says Trinell.

Trinell earned her digital badge credentials in a video production class while working on an assignment for the television network PBS. In this class she created, filmed, and edited a video about women in technical theater. As she completed this project, she developed and demonstrated many different credentials, from creation and innovation to forecast and simulation. Developing these real-world skills helped open a door for Trinell, allowing her to have an experience with a non-profit organization connected to career fields close to her heart and, hopefully, her future.

Figure 4.1. Aurora Public Schools' badge program logo

On the day of the career exploration experience with Opera Colorado, the on-site culmination of her badge earning process, Trinell was feeling very excited. For the first time, she was able to visit with a professional technical theater crew and go behind the stage to see where all the magic happens. "My eyes were probably the size of marbles, and my mouth [was] on the ground when I actually got to see what it looked like backstage!" says Trinell. "There were so many things techies would only dream of having in high school." She asked questions of the crew for the whole day as she explored the ins and outs of Opera Colorado. The experience was more than she ever expected. She was eager to go back to school and share what she had seen and learned with her technical theater class. She knew her friends would be excited to learn about what it was like behind the scenes of a professional theater. She was also excited about the potential to earn more digital badges for other skills she would develop in her future. Trinell's *evidence-based credentials*, or digital badges, allowed her to have an experience within an industry she values. This career exploration opportunity allowed for her to understand the range of her current possibilities. Even though she hopes to someday be working in the film industry, Trinell always wants to keep one foot in the theater door as that is what helped spark her passion and desire.

## EQUITY AND ACCESS

Trinell attends Aurora Public Schools (APS), a district located east of Denver, Colorado, that serves over forty thousand students. Our unique population is made up of students who speak more than 130 different languages and is home to the largest refugee and immigrant population in the state. More than 70 percent of APS students receive free and reduced lunch, and many face difficult, even extreme, economic challenges. In order for these students to be successful in their futures, they need compassionate teachers who care deeply and a safe environment in which to learn. They also need opportunities to develop twenty-first-century skills and ways to communicate these skills with colleges and employers. While it is difficult to predict what types of careers and opportunities will be readily available to them, we do know that if they are armed with twenty-first-century skills, such as self-direction, collaboration, and critical thinking, they will be better prepared for successful futures.

In 2013, newly appointed superintendent Rico Munn began reshaping the district's College and Career Success (CCS) department. Munn believed that the district's CCS framework of preparing students for college and careers (with university credits, industry certificates, and associate degrees) and engaging students through career exploration and relevant core academics was strong but was not appropriately scaled throughout the district. The framework provided insufficient access to students most in need, raised questions around sustainability and student impact, and encouraged deficit-focused practices. By fall of 2014, Munn's vision that students would determine their own futures led the APS board of education to approve a strategic plan, APS 2020: Shaping the Future, which includes three main components:

1. Goal 1 is that *every student will have a plan for his or her future*. Students will think critically about their future and develop an Individualized Career and Academic Plan (ICAP) that will guide them as they excel in school. The CCS team supports school leaders to help students in the creation of their plans, which begin in third grade and are continually reviewed and revised throughout the subsequent years.
2. Goal 2 of the strategic plan is that *every student will have a set of skills to implement his or her plan*. Following Colorado's state standards, teachers will help students develop the skills that will enable them to achieve the goals written in their plan.

3. Goal 3 of the strategic plan is that *every student will have credentials that open doors*. While some schools in the district already had access to credentials for their students (such as work-based certificates, International Baccalaureate diplomas, advanced placement credits, and career and technical education certification courses), other schools were left without sufficient opportunities for their learners. Digital badging is strongly emphasized in this aspect of the plan as a means for providing equitable access for every student in the APS district to earn credentials.

Superintendent Munn's passionate advocacy for meaningful credentials that open doors is rooted in his own experiences. He grew up in Colorado Springs, and his family is well known around the area. His father was a minister in a local church, and this familial calling card allowed him to make many connections in the community. Throughout his professional life Munn has held various prestigious roles and titles. When he travels back to Colorado Springs, however, he is known as Deacon Munn's son. This is his door opener, and that, according to Mr. Munn, is exactly what our forty thousand students in APS need. "Digital badges are a tool for social and economic justice," he says. "A company has vouched for your skills, and that digital badge, that credential, can open doors for our students. It's so incredibly important that they have that door opener for them."

## THE BEGINNING

In spring of 2014, a diverse team was created to help implement a Digital Badge Initiative as a way to expand access to postsecondary and workforce readiness credentials to all students. The right people needed to be at the table to ensure the work was strong and that we were putting our best foot forward breaking ground in the P–12 digital badge world. Charles Dukes, director of the CCS team, assembled the badge leadership team:

- *Project manager:* As all team members already fulfilled many other roles in the district, it was imperative that we hire someone to help guide our work and keep us focused and timely. This was an essential factor in our quick success and continued growth. Creating a communications plan, assisting in strategic planning and resource allocations (including staff time) for our program, organizing and running team meetings, and keeping general records to ensure next steps are being followed are among the regular tasks.

- *Digital badging consultant:* Implementing a quality program that meets both industry and student needs has been crucial for the success of the team. The consultant also needs to stay current on all the broader "digital badge happenings." This outsider perspective helps ensure that we are reflective about the quality of the program and employ a continuous improvement mindset.
- *Information technology specialists:* Supporting the technology needs of forty thousand–plus students and three thousand staff members, once the program was opened up district wide, was going to be a huge challenge. We had yet to land on a technology application; however, once we did we wanted to ensure it ran smoothly.
- *Teachers:* Seasoned teachers with pertinent experience are essential members of the team. In order to get that perspective on what program implementation might look like in the classroom, we need guidance from those who are there. This led to the development of a *digital badge partner* role, which is described below.
- *Educational technology experts:* Digital Badging within the classroom adds another layer to teaching and instruction, and teachers utilizing our program need to understand the technology behind badging as well as how best to help guide their students on this path. Educational technology experts bring this crucial insight.
- *External relations liaison:* It was essential that our digital badges mean something to our community and to the world beyond APS. We needed to provide validation for the skills that students are learning and use the credentials to open doors of opportunity. This team member's role is to bridge the connection between community and school district.

Once the team of experts was up and running, the pilot began, which included about forty teachers at fourteen different schools. Throughout this pilot, the digital badge system architecture was being developed, and teachers received one-on-one and small group training with our team members. Teachers collected and saved badge evidence using whatever method worked best for them, whether through a Google sheet, Google Doc, or Word doc. The Badge Leadership Team then began researching different platforms to house and manage data online, with the goal of finding a company that ensured data privacy while also allowing student digital badges to be portable, or open. During this semester we followed a crucial user-centered approach to help guide our work. We continuously gathered feedback from teachers and students throughout the pilot to ensure program improvement.

By the fall of 2015, after researching several platforms, the team ultimately decided to use the badging platform Credly, since it adheres to the Open

Badges Infrastructure (OBI) standard and has the ability to handle the volume of our district. Using Credly's Enterprise account, student accounts are automatically created for all students and APS employees once they join the district. In order for this program to be successful, a full-time educator dedicated to the work was also hired. The CCS director hired me, the district's first ever Digital Badge Partner, to provide exclusive support and to help address the needs of the program and the requests of our users. The Badge Leadership Team began creating online training materials, including a user toolkit. The digital badge architecture was also simplified and tweaked in order to meet the needs of the initiative. Finally, in January of 2016, the pilot ended, and the Digital Badge Initiative was successfully rolled out to each and every school in the district.

## WHAT ARE DIGITAL BADGES IN APS?

In APS, we define a *digital badge* as a credential that validates students' twenty-first-century skills. Digital badges provide students with a platform to share both the skills for which they have been credentialed and the evidence they have provided in order to receive their credentials. Digital badges help develop a better narrative of who our students are as learners and provide students with a language for describing their strengths. Badges also provide credentials that will enhance access and open doors for APS's forty thousand students, aligning directly with goal 3 of the strategic plan.

After several iterations, we ultimately created a two-tiered badging system that would allow teachers flexibility in proving how students demonstrate skills (figure 4.2).

The top tier of our system is comprised of what we call *summit badges*, and the lower tier is comprised of *journey badges*. The hope was that students would go on a *journey* throughout their academic career, developing skills and earning the digital badge credentials in order to reach their *summit*. APS summit badges represent the twenty-first-century skills that are woven into the Colorado Academic Standards. Adopted in 2009, the Colorado Department of Education published an outline describing the twenty-first-century skills related to each content area. The program aims to draw out the twenty-first-century skills in each of these content areas, along with after school programs and clubs, so that we can acknowledge and name them in the form of a digital credential.

It was important that the digital badge system didn't feel like something extra burdening our teachers. The system was intentionally designed to synthesize

Figure 4.2. Aurora Public Schools' Badge Program 21st Century Credentials

with teachers' existing standards-based work. The goal is for teachers to badge their students for the skills they are already helping them develop. In order to break down those skills into a more granular level, the badge leadership team engaged in research, which included using International Society for Technology in Education (ISTE) standards to help determine the smaller components that comprise the summit badges. The APS digital badges are deliberately not content specific. By developing a one-sentence definition for each badge, we created a system in which students could earn digital badges in any grade and subject area as long as they were meeting that one-sentence criterion (table 4.1).

**Table 4.1. Aurora Public Schools' Digital Badging System for All Grades and Subjects**

| | |
|---|---|
|  | **Summit Badge: COLLABORATION**<br>*Students communicate and work collaboratively to support individual learning and contribute to the learning of others.*<br>**AWARENESS:** Develop cultural understanding and global awareness by engaging with learners of other cultures<br>**COMMUNICATION:** Communicate information and ideas effectively to multiple audiences using a variety of media and formats<br>**CONTRIBUTION:** Contribute to project teams to produce original works or solve problems<br>**INTERACTION:** Interact and actively collaborate with peers, experts or others |
|  | **Summit Badge: CRITICAL THINKING**<br>*Students use critical thinking skills to plan and conduct research, manage projects, solve problems, and make informed decisions using appropriate digital tools and resources.*<br>**ANALYSIS:** Collect and analyze data to identify solutions and/or make informed decisions<br>**INVESTIGATION:** Identify and define authentic problems and significant questions for investigation<br>**EXPLORATION:** Use multiple processes and diverse perspectives to explore alternative solutions<br>**ORGANIZATION:** Plan and manage activities to develop a solution or complete a project |
|  | **Summit Badge: INFORMATION LITERACY**<br>*Students apply digital tools to gather, evaluate, and use information. Students demonstrate a sound understanding of technology concepts, systems, and operations.*<br>**RECOGNITION:** Develop an understanding of the various tools and applications of a digital workspace<br>**RESEARCH:** Locate, organize, analyze, evaluate, synthesize and ethically use information from a variety of sources and media<br>**SYSTEMS:** Understand and use technology systems to plan strategies, guide inquiry, and solve problems<br>**TRANSFER:** Transfer current knowledge to learn new technologies<br>**TROUBLESHOOTING:** Effectively troubleshoot systems and applications using available tools and knowledge |

**Table 4.1.** *(Continued)*

| | |
|---|---|
|  | **Summit Badge: INVENTION**<br>*Students demonstrate creative thinking, construct knowledge, and develop innovative products and processes.*<br>**CREATION**: Create original works as a means of personal or group expression<br>**FORECAST**: Identify trends and forecast possibilities<br>**INNOVATION**: Apply existing knowledge to generate new ideas, products or processes<br>**SIMULATION**: Use models and simulations to explore complex systems and issues |
|  | **Summit Badge: SELF-DIRECTION**<br>*Students understand human, cultural, and societal issues related to technology, and practice legal and ethical behavior.*<br>**ADVOCACY**: Advocate and practice safe, legal, and responsible behaviors<br>**ATTITUDE**: Exhibit a positive attitude that supports collaboration, learning, and productivity<br>**LEADERSHIP**: Exhibit leadership abilities in a variety of settings<br>**LIFELONG LEARNER**: The on-going, self-motivated pursuit of knowledge and experiences for personal joy and improvement |

In order to earn a summit badge, a student must earn all of the journey badges below it. Once a student earns a summit badge, the Badge Leadership Team will reach out to the student or their teacher (for younger grades) to help organize their career exploration opportunity.

Additionally, in order to promote continuous development of twenty-first-century skills and have our students take part in appropriate career exploration opportunities, we have divided our badge system into four grade bands: P–2, 3–5, 6–8, and 9–12. Each time a student moves from one grade band to the next, their opportunity to earn a summit badge restarts. Earned digital badge credentials are never deleted from a student's Credly account; instead, their opportunity to earn each summit badge and take part in their career exploration opportunity restarts as students advance in grade level. As students continue to develop and move from grade to grade, they might earn many of the same badges. This information is valuable for the teachers, as it creates a better narrative of who students are as learners and lets students know where their strengths lie. For example, a student might earn three Creation badges while in fourth grade and yet another in fifth; however, in order to earn the Invention summit badge, that student would still need to acquire the remaining three journey badges.

## Digital Badges Endorsed by the Community

Partnering with the community was always a key aspect of the APS badging program. External partners provide validation for the digital badges and help give them meaning outside of APS. We want students to learn what the world has to offer and where their education could possibly take them. For years employers have been saying that there is a disconnect between students' transcripts and their workplace performance. Many of us know individuals who may not have been straight-A students but are now excelling in the workplace. To ensure that all students are prepared for workforce success, the Badge Leadership Team knew from the beginning of the project that we needed industry input on what those twenty-first-century skills look like in the workplace. For digital badges to hold their value with employers, those employers need to validate the badges and more importantly the skills that students are developing. APS has built a growing network of digital badge endorsers who provide input on our badge system and definitions. Endorsers also provide feedback on students' abilities to showcase their skill development through various career exploration opportunities.

Once a student has earned a summit badge, a door is opened for them to take part in a career exploration opportunity with one of the APS endorsers. They are able to learn about various professions they might be unaware of, which will help inform their individual learning and career plans. They will also hear directly from industry professionals about how skills are used within their workplace environment, allowing students to more easily transfer what they are learning in the classroom to the workplace.

The experiences are tailored to be engaging and effective for learners of all ages. For the youngest students, preschool through fifth grade, endorsing partners visit the schools to speak with students and provide interactive and hands-on demonstrations of their work settings. As students get older, they have the opportunity to visit endorser workplaces to begin to visualize themselves in various work settings. Students can also use their digital badges to access job shadows, where they will follow an employee at their place of business to learn about their career, internship opportunities, and even interviews for entry-level jobs with the badge endorsers. For endorsing companies that have entry-level positions available for high school students, the program provides multiple opportunities to meet with students. We also encourage endorsers to speak with elementary students so that, by the time students begin job searching, they are aware of the many employment opportunities available. Additionally, these partners know from the moment an application is received that the students they are interviewing have been credentialed for the skills that are important in their workplace. After the career exploration opportunity, endorsements then validate whether or not that student has demonstrated skills. Our team receives feedback from the endorser to learn if the students were able to demonstrate the skills and then awards the student their endorsed digital badge credential on Credly. Students can then take their open badge and use that as a currency within the community to help them get an internship or job, add it to their résumé or college application, or even post it to their LinkedIn profile or to other social media.

## IMPLEMENTATION

These career exploration opportunities have also improved teacher buy-in for the program. Rather than viewing the program as one more redundant task, teachers frequently provide feedback that digital badge credentials are good for their students. Teachers credit these types of credentials with helping them look beyond grades and test scores to a more high-definition picture of their students as learners and achievers.

An important aspect of the APS Digital Badge Program is that it is not a top-down mandate. Teachers who issue digital badge credentials to students have all opted in voluntarily. Once they have done so, teachers have access through myriad touch points to gather the information they need about the program so they can help their students receive recognition for skill development. Supportive resources include school-wide professional development, small-group training, online-learning modules, Google Hangouts, and even one-on-one training.

When teachers are planning to implement badges, they begin by connecting these twenty-first-century skills to their instruction. The badge leadership team has collaborated with teachers to create (through multiple iterations) a helpful planning document that makes it easier to identify these connections. By examining the learning tasks being offered, teachers can cross-walk the skill development that occurs in each learning task directly to our badge system. Using the one-sentence badge definition as a guide, teachers are able to identify how that specific skill might be demonstrated in the lesson they are planning. After teachers have chosen the learning task that will help elicit the skill, they then determine what piece of evidence will most clearly convey that the skill has been demonstrated. This might be something as concrete as a Google Doc, a Google Slides presentation, or even an audio file of two students' dialogue along with the teacher's testimony (table 4.2). As the program evolves, the hope is to foster a culture in which *students* recognize and determine different badge-earning opportunities and the potential evidence to be used in order to earn credentials.

Table 4.2. Flexible Two-Tier Badging System

| Summit Badge | Journey Badge | Definition | Grade Band | Learning Opportunity | Evidence |
|---|---|---|---|---|---|
| Information Literacy | Research | Locate, organize, analyze, evaluate, synthesize, and ethically use information from a variety of sources and media | P-2 | After finding credible websites online, students research the history of Halloween and add the information to their graphic organizer. | Graphic organizer |
| Information Literacy | Systems | Understand and use technology systems to plan strategies, guide inquiry, and solve problems | 3-5 | Students develop a Google site, which organizes information from a novel they are reading in their book group. | Link to the website |
| Self-Direction | Leadership | Exhibit leadership abilities in a variety of settings | 6-8 | 8th grade WEB (Where Everybody Belongs) lead 6th grade students through team leadership building activities. | Copy of their lesson plan and pictures or video of their 6th graders collaborating |
| Critical Thinking | Organization | Plan and manage activities to develop a solution or complete a project | 9-12 | Students work during the summer to design, move, and create technology labs. They have to solve multiple problems to create these labs. | Pictures of labs along with testimony around the significant design changes for better teacher/student use. |

After teachers have spent time mapping their instruction to the digital badge system, the next step is for them to learn how to effectively utilize the online badging platform, Credly. Within Credly, issuing badges can either be initiated by teachers or by students. Teachers can issue badges directly to students by attaching evidence within Credly that confirms how a student demonstrated a specific skill. This occurs most often with teachers of students in the younger grades or in schools that have limited access to technology. Since APS has a Credly enterprise account and all students are given accounts upon their arrival in the district, teachers can search for student names using the member search and add the students they wish to badge by typing in their name or adding their email. Once the badge is issued by the teacher, students will receive an email alert prompting them to log in to their Credly account and view their digital badge credential through a secure portal.

Students may also earn a badge by applying for it. This is the most common manner in which badges are issued, as it places ownership and effort of providing evidence with the students who will be earning the badges. After the teacher has decided which digital badge credentials are connected to their lesson, they create a claim code using their personal Credly account. This allows students to claim the badge, or apply for it, by entering a code. After explaining an assignment, the teacher alerts students that it is mapped to a digital badge representing the skill that will be developed. Teachers often share this information through a Google Doc or by writing it on the board so that students know exactly what they need to do in order to earn the badge. This is a best practice for our program. We trust teachers to be the experts in implementing this program into their classroom, as they know what is best for the success of their students. After a student applies for a badge using their teacher-supplied code, the teacher can look in their Credly account to view the evidence that their student submitted. It is then up to the teacher to either accept the badge evidence and issue the badge or decline it if it doesn't meet the expectation set forth. When declining a badge request, teachers are able to attach a message for students explaining why they have not yet met expectations and what they need to do in order to re-apply. Teachers are encouraged to consider the following guiding questions concerning badge quality:

- Does this badge provide rigor for your students?
- Can the student demonstrate this skill independently?
- Has the student had multiple opportunities to show this skill?
- Is the badge evidence-based?
- Is the badge transferable? Can students demonstrate the skill in other settings or subjects?
- Is the badge based on a granular-level skill?

Teaching students about the badge system is the final step for integrating this program into the classroom. Arming students with knowledge about how to log in to their Credly account and teaching them how to apply for badges allows students to be accountable for earning badges. It is important that students write their own personal narratives and develop a digital archive of who they are as learners. A goal for this program is that students will recognize their developing strengths and skills, which will encourage them to apply for a digital badge. In addition to creating resources for teachers to employ when introducing students to digital badging, we have been collecting testimonials from students who have earned badges. We believe that peer voices will be the most convincing when it comes to fostering student buy-in.

## Badging in Younger Grades

When hearing the word *micro-credentials*, an individual may not immediately think about primary grade students as badge earners. However, these students also deserve the chance to be recognized for what their report card or traditional grades may not capture, even as early as preschool. For example, Sofia Vallarte Hernandez wanted her preschool students to earn badges—and even more so wanted to open doors for her students and provide career exploration opportunities for them once they earned a summit badge. Sofia asked the badge leadership team to help support her in mapping digital badges to the work she was already doing with her students. As I sat in the tiny chair reserved for her small students, knees high up to my chest, I glanced around the room and noticed the centers and stations set up around her classroom that promoted twenty-first-century skill development—especially critical thinking. Sofia is very intentional about ensuring that her students have access to materials and lessons that allow them to interact and critically think with each other. Together we planned backward through a unit about sponges, in which students completed the following tasks:

- Students *investigated* various objects and items at a water table during whole and small group lessons. They identified a question to explore more deeply: "Why do some objects sink and some float?"
- After investigating, students graphed their results as a class and shared their findings. They *organized* their results by graphing the different attributes of the sponges, adding their data to chart paper.
- They also *analyzed* as they looked at the different amounts of water that came out of the sponges, compared and contrasted color, size, texture, etc.
- Finally, students *explored* using the sponges in various centers. They used them to create artwork with paint and food coloring and even during dramatic play.

As Sofia's students applied these twenty-first-century skills toward each lesson, she was able to both digitally badge those who demonstrated those skills and also mark their progress on a visual chart hanging on the walls of her classroom. Sofia's students do not have access to their Credly accounts, since they do not have computers in their classroom. As Sofia teaches half day preschool, she also does not have time to support each young student logging in to their Credly account. She did, however, want her students to be able to see which digital badges they earned and how far they needed to go before earning their summit badge. After listening to her needs, I suggested a digital badge tracking poster that could hang in her room. That way all of her students would be able to track their digital badges and would be motived to earn more. Once Sofia's students are in a classroom that has access to technology, they will be able to log in to Credly and see all of their badges; however, for now they will use the chart to mark their progress. Inspired by teachers like Sofia who need physical badge supports for their learners, we have recruited the Print Services Department to help us create many different types of visual supports that are useful for teachers. These include charts and posters for classrooms and hallway walls, as well as passports in which students can keep track of which badges they have earned and why.

Students in Sofia's classroom eagerly eyed the chart and were excited to take part in their career exploration opportunity once they earned their summit badges. When the Aurora History Museum visited this classroom, students were so thrilled they bounced in their chairs, waiting to get their hands on some of the artifacts that were brought in for them to explore. Most of these students had never even been to a museum, so this was their first exposure to not only the reasons behind the museum's preservation of these artifacts but also to the skills necessary for evaluating these different pieces of history. Since these students had earned digital badge credentials, they were able to take part in an experience that they might not have otherwise.

## Badging in the Middle Years

When middle school technology teacher John Portelle first learned about digital badges, he knew this would be a great way to incentivize learning within his classroom. Having a business background helped John understand the community component of the program. He felt that the program became authentic for his students once they knew that the badges they could earn were directly connected to what community members believe are important traits. Students enrolled in John's technology class would be engaging in activities from community-based projects to the production of the school's daily news program, Lobo TV. The project illustrated a clear connection between school and real life.

In order for students to be successful in the creation of each episode, they must be able to

- *research* content online
- efficiently navigate different technology *systems* needed in order to edit each episode
- and learn how to persevere and *troubleshoot* effectively through challenging technology situations.

These skills are embedded into John's lessons, and students are able to develop skills daily as they engage in the hands-on and interactive work completed in class. Once students learned about the digital badge program and the potential to expand their horizons beyond the school walls in order to connect with businesses in the community, they eagerly applied for badges.

One student, Tiyana, planned how she would earn all five summit badges before the end of the year in order to connect with a variety of companies before continuing on to high school. On a sunny spring day, Tiyana was picked up at school and whisked off to McDonald's to have her first career exploration opportunity for earning her Self-Direction summit badge credential. This experience exceeded her expectations, providing an opportunity to learn about the corporate/business side of this multi-million-dollar international company (However, they did let her make a burger and work the drive-through!). "Earning these badges will give me more opportunities in my future," says Tiyana.

> I want to go into engineering, but if I ever want to get a job with McDonald's, I now have their digital badge, which proves I have the skills necessary to be successful, and they will be more likely to hire me. Their manager has encouraged me to come back in a few years once I'm old enough to work and put in an application for employment! I also have knowledge that I didn't previously have: I never thought about the business side of McDonald's and all the opportunities you might have to move up in the corporation. This experience has really given me a different perspective and has opened my eyes about what could be.

Tiyana eagerly awaits her next four career exploration opportunities and is thankful for all the support that has helped her get to this point. "It feels great to be the first middle schooler to earn all five summit badges and accomplish something that nobody else has. So many of my teachers have helped me—especially Mr. Portelle, who is my mentor, and especially my friends; they have given me the mind-set to keep going."

## Badging in High School

High school teacher Randy Mills speaks about the relevance of digital badging for his students.

> My students assemble for the CyberPatriot club meeting as I tell them something about "badges" and how they can earn them through exceptional work and skill development. Most of my students aren't paying much attention and seem to not really care. The more the badge idea is described, the more the students

tune it out, because it sounds like the sticker charts they knew in elementary school. As the CyberPatriot coach at Rangeview High School (RHS), the trick is to connect the digital badges to students' lives. CyberPatriot is the National Youth Cyber Education Program created to inspire students toward careers in cyber security or other types of STEM careers. High school students enrolled in the club can be very demanding around the question, "What's in it for me?" when learning about digital badges. If a teacher doesn't acknowledge that question, they are doomed to fail.

Within the APS Digital Badge Program, the opportunity exists to make the real life connections that students demand. Badges acknowledge skills that students are developing through projects and tasks that are not formally integrated into the curriculum. Students in the CyberPatriot club have done a number of things:

- They have *contributed* toward projects such as assisting the school district with putting together laptop and Chromebook carts for use at other schools.
- They have *communicated* with middle school students during mentoring sessions for computer competitions. The work of a particular student, Matthew, impressed Bryan Westman, the middle school technology teacher at Mrachek Middle School, with whom we collaborate on these mentoring sessions: "We have used Matthew's experience with programs that most people know very little about or have never even heard of. He has taught young students higher order thinking and technology skills that are in demand by high tech companies."
- They have *interacted* with their peers and teachers at RHS as technology support and interns. We have partnered with IT in giving students who earn certain credentials administrative rights that allow them to assist their teachers with technical issues on their computers such as running software updates and connecting to network printers. In a very real way, these students are able to help keep a building of more than 2,000 devices operating at peak efficiency.
- And they have *organized*, moved, and designed layouts of computer labs, as tech interns, to optimize space and reduce wires and clutter.

These are powerful skills for the world beyond high school but are not formally covered or acknowledged in any curriculum. Digital badge credentials have given these students tangible recognition of their hard work and provide them with a meaningful way to share with colleges and future employers. Matthew speaks about the value of digital badges: "The digital badge demonstrates the commitment to helping mentor students, the time and effort that the student spent mentoring, the ability to help prepare students for a challenging competition that portrays aspects of the real world computer field, and the willingness of contributing to the community. The digital badge helps others recognize the value of the accomplishments the individual made."

RHS has seen students use these badges as an added value for getting paid internships as well as jobs in the real world before graduation. As businesses look for twenty-first-century skills that are immediately transferable to the workplace, badges are a tangible demonstration of those skills. Rather than saying to an employer, "I am a hard worker, and I am good with computers," a Rangeview student can show a digital badge credential for the design and execution of a computer lab or the network needed and the team leadership to make it happen. It is powerful and exciting for any employer or college to know exactly what the student is capable of in a business setting.

Although these students have opportunities for skill development and badge earning through the CyberPatriot club, they also have opportunities in their core classes along with other after school activities. The beauty of the APS Digital Badge Program is that students can develop skills in any part of their educational career and earn a credential proving that skill has been developed.

## WHERE ARE WE GOING?

In October 2016 the APS board of education officially transitioned APS from the Digital Badge Initiative to the Digital Badge Program. This not only confirms the value of the work being implemented but also makes the path ahead clearer, allowing equitable access to credentials for every single one of our 40,000 students. To continue to accomplish this, the Badge Leadership Team will need to think through a number of issues.

- How do we ensure the program continuously improves in response to the needs of APS teachers and learners? As the program grows, what systems might be implemented to remain agile and responsive, to iterate, and to continue our user-centered approach?
- As we begin to brainstorm about what the program could look like five years from now, it is exciting to think about the possibility of creating positions that have never existed in our district. Micro-credential Curriculum Designer? Work-Based Learning Coordinator? Application Specialist for Micro-credentials? How could we utilize current APS employees to help meet the needs of these positions?
- How might we expand professional development for our educators and grow our online resources, allowing teachers to become badge experts from the comfort of their computer screens? More importantly, having students and teachers create these resources will make them even more powerful.
- Continuing to build up our base of endorsers will also be the focus of our future work. By identifying career sectors with guidance from the Colorado Career Cluster Model—a model that groups careers and industries based on the common academic and technical knowledge and skills

required of employees in each career—we will ensure equitable access to students, which includes opportunities with endorsers in all possible career pathways.
- It is essential that we never allow our work to be siloed. We must allow others to learn about the success of what we have built and our lessons learned so that digital badge credentials within the P–12 setting continue to develop and grow. All of our work is shared under a Creative Commons license, and team members are available to other districts interested in learning about the work. How can other institutions adopting our system add value to the credentials and increase their transferability?
- Telling the story of APS students is another important component for helping them earn credentials. How might our district capitalize on the students who have already earned credentials and allow them to tell their story to their classmates? Will this encourage other students to take the reins and apply for badges or encourage their teachers to connect digital badges to their curriculum?

Whichever path we take as we continue to expand and improve our program, one APS core value will always be in the forefront of our minds: students first. This program was created for students, and improvements are made based on student feedback. As middle school student Tiyana moves on to high school, she will now have an advantage when applying for internships and jobs. Her backpack full of digital badge credentials will prove to industries that she has the skills necessary to be successful. She is no longer just a face in the crowd as these badges are her door opener. This is what we want for all 40,000 of our students. Superintendent Munn emphasizes, "Every time you think about how cool, how innovative, it is, stop. Stop at that point, and think about how it can impact and change lives."

# 5

## Badges Can Do That

### Ideas for Using Badges to Enhance Information Literacy Instruction

*Allison Hosier*

**W**ith the advent of the *Framework for Information Literacy for Higher Education* (ACRL 2015), information literacy has shifted from the skills-based approach represented by the ACRL *Information Literacy Competency Standards for Information Literacy* (ACRL 2000) to a more concept-based approach.

Before, in order to be considered information literate, the successful student would need to demonstrate mastery of a set of basic skills related to library-based academic research, preferably across a variety of disciplinary contexts. Under the ACRL's new *Framework*, information literacy is no longer presented as a set of skills but instead as a set of frames centered around six threshold concepts (table 5.1). These threshold concepts are all associated in some way with the reflective discovery of information on the path to creating new knowledge. The knowledge practices and dispositions accompanying each concept illustrate some of the ways in which a learner may develop different degrees of expertise in these areas as he or she gains experience in various information-seeking and research contexts.

The shift from the ACRL's *Standards* to their *Framework* opened the door to a number of new possibilities for information literacy instructors who want to move past the limitations of the *Standards*. However, it also led to certain complications.

The first complication is that existing models of information literacy instruction were designed around *Standards*-based notions of information literacy. A short one-shot session or online video tutorial may be sufficient for teaching a basic research skill or two, but by themselves they are not enough to help students develop the expertise described by the *Framework*. Existing models therefore do not fit well with the *Framework*, but change to those

Table 5.1. Outline of Information Literacy Skills from the ACRL Standards and Threshold Concepts from the ACRL Framework

| ACRL Standards (Skills-Based) | ACRL Framework (Concept-Based) |
|---|---|
| An information literate individual is able to<br><br>- determine the extent of information needed<br>- access the needed information effectively and efficiently<br>- evaluate information and its sources critically<br>- incorporate selected information into their knowledge base<br>- use information effectively to accomplish a specific purpose<br>- and understand the economic, legal, and social issues surrounding the use of information and access and use information ethically and legally. | The framework is organized into six frames, each consisting of a concept central to information literacy, a set of knowledge practices, and a set of dispositions. The six concepts that anchor the frames are presented alphabetically:<br><br>1. Authority is constructed and contextual<br>2. Information creation as a process<br>3. Information has value<br>4. Research as inquiry<br>5. Scholarship as conversation<br>6. Searching as strategic exploration |

Sources: ACRL 2000 and 2015.

models cannot happen overnight. Information literacy instructors need to find ways to engage students on a deeper level while still largely working within the confines of these models—at least for the time being.

The second complication is that it has become harder to describe what, exactly, information literacy is to those outside of the library and information science field. The expanded definition provided by the *Framework* (table 5.2) includes the layers needed to properly capture what information literacy means from an expert point of view. However, it is not a definition that lends itself quite as easily to the "elevator speech" style explanations that are sometimes necessary in conversations with outside stakeholders. This poses one problem when those conversations are with administrators and disciplinary faculty. It poses another problem, more relevant to the current discussion, when students who have developed a certain level of expertise in one or more of the *Framework*'s threshold concepts try to communicate what they have learned when presenting themselves as prospective graduate school students or job-seekers.

These complications can be addressed in a number of ways. As a relatively new tool for learning that has captured the attention of institutions of higher education and their students in recent years, badges may represent one potential solution. Badges can be used to enhance information literacy instruction, define clearly what it means to achieve different levels of information lit-

Table 5.2. Definitions of Information Literacy

| Per the ACRL Standards | Per the ACRL Framework |
| --- | --- |
| A set of abilities requiring individuals to recognize when information is needed and have the ability to locate, evaluate, and use effectively the needed information | A set of integrated abilities encompassing the reflective discovery of information, the understanding of how information is produced and valued, and the use of information in creating new knowledge and participating ethically in communities of learning |

*Sources:* ACRL 2000 and 2015.

eracy, and convey this achievement to potential stakeholders in an accessible way. Badges can also have an impact on student motivation, which is often lacking in an information literacy instruction context.

This chapter explores how some of the advantages badges have as an educational tool in general can be applied to information literacy specifically.

## WHY INFORMATION LITERACY IS IMPORTANT

First, it may be helpful to briefly review the significance of information literacy, beyond the short term goals of teaching students the skills they need to complete a specific research project. For librarians and other instructors who teach information literacy, the true value and potential of information literacy is already clear. However, reviewing these points will help frame the argument for the role badging might play in information literacy instruction.

Research has shown that when it comes to the skills and abilities that information literacy encompasses, students' confidence often does not match their proficiency (Molteni and Chan 2015). Specifically, students tend to believe that the experience they have acquired with sorting through the results of searches conducted on popular search engines has made them experts in finding, evaluating, and using information. While it is certainly true that these skills have value, what students fail to realize is that the contextual nature of the information-seeking process means that the strategies and sources they are most familiar with will not be applicable in every situation. As a result, students commonly approach information literacy instruction lacking both an appreciation for how much more there is to learn and the motivation to learn it.

Despite this, the findings of a 2013 study by Head, Van Hoeck, Eschler, and Fullerton make it clear that there is a gap between the research and information competencies that employers value and the ones newly graduated hires typically possess when they first join the workplace. According to the employers who participated in the study, new hires place too much importance on finding quick answers via search engines and fail to demonstrate competencies related to recognizing people as important resources of information, retrieving information in a variety of formats, and taking the time to do a thorough search. This shows that students' skills with search engines, while valuable, are not enough.

Information literacy has also gained importance recently in light of issues such as the proliferation of so-called "fake news." While information literacy itself may not be enough to fully overcome factors such as confirmation bias and filter bubbles that contribute to the spread of misinformation, it can give students an appreciation for the responsibilities that come with being both a consumer and creator of information. Information literacy instruction gives students the crucial practice needed to become more reflective thinkers when it comes to the information they encounter in different contexts.

From this discussion, it becomes clear that students need to better recognize themselves as information-seeking novices—at least in some contexts. Becoming aware of the gaps in their skills and knowledge will help motivate students to develop their expertise in the areas that employers value. It will also help them better navigate the information landscape in a post-truth world. But even if this happens, students still need an accessible way to communicate what they have learned once they move on to graduate school or to the workplace.

These issues of motivation and communication are areas where badges may hold particular value for information literacy.

## BADGES AND MOTIVATION IN INFORMATION LITERACY

Two types of badges exist. The first is confirmatory in nature. It serves as a check in a box to show that a task has been completed. The second is more achievement-based. Both types of badges can inspire motivation in ways that are relevant to information literacy.

An example of a confirmatory badge can be found in the model used by the nonprofit organization Office of Letters and Light as part of their annual online event, National Novel Writing Month. Participants in the event work toward a goal of writing fifty thousand words in thirty days. Along the way, they can earn badges that represent the use of certain strategies to achieve that goal (such as a marathon writing session) as well as milestones (such as ten consecutive days of writing). These badges are displayed to the user on a special profile page in which the badges not yet earned are grayed out. The desire to collect more badges, which can then be displayed on a public profile, motivates the user to keep going. Users who reach the fifty thousand–word goal in the required time frame receive a special badge at the end of the thirty-day period.

What makes these badges confirmatory is that the user's word is generally taken that a task has been completed. Nothing is done to verify whether this is the case, beyond a special "word count checker" that participants are required to use at the end to prove that they aren't trying to game the system by (for example) typing the same word fifty thousand times. There is also no evaluation of the quality of the user's work. The badge is simply a check in a box.

The second type of badge, the achievement-based badge, will be familiar to anyone who has played a video game in recent years. In many games, players can earn achievements, similar to badges, upon demonstrating certain skills or successfully completing challenges along the way. In open universe games, players can earn additional achievements by "wandering away" from the main story to discover story-related secrets through the completion of extra tasks. The achievements a player earns can be displayed to fellow gamers via public profiles. Naturally, more accomplishments mean more bragging rights for the player in question.

Achievements in video games are not verified by an outside evaluator, per se, but, unlike the National Novel Writing Month badges, the achievement in question cannot be unlocked without doing the needed work (barring the use of cheat codes—which are, of course, considered cheating). For example, a player cannot earn an achievement related to a challenge that requires them to successfully demonstrate certain skills related to defeating an enemy within the game without actually using the skills in question. Because of this, the achievement represents something more than a checked box.

Both confirmatory and achievement-based badges can motivate users in ways that are relevant to information literacy. First, badges can be used to represent what the user has accomplished while also making clear that there is still work to be done. National Novel Writing Month participants seeing the grayed-out badges in their profiles may be inspired to take on writing-related challenges they may not have thought of otherwise. Gamers can use badges to show off the skills already attained while working toward developing new skills. In an information literacy context, it is not hard to imagine how badges could be used both to show overconfident students that the skills and experience they already have are both valued and valuable while also displaying areas in which they may have less expertise. Such a display may alert students to their overconfidence and incentivize them to learn more about areas of information literacy about which they may have been previously unaware.

It would also make clear what they are working toward in a manner that is more meaningful to them than a course syllabus or a checklist of the types of sources needed for a research assignment.

## BADGES AND COMMUNICATION IN INFORMATION LITERACY

As jargon, the term *information literacy* does not translate well between contexts, which is why in the past an "elevator speech" style explanation was needed to define information literacy for students and other non-experts. Under the ACRL's *Standards*, information literacy was commonly described as the ability to effectively find, evaluate, and use information as part of the research process. This description was always widely considered to be an oversimplification and is even more so with the advent of the new, expanded definition provided by the ACRL's *Framework*. However, many may still use the old definition if only because the *Framework*'s definition is not quite as compact and readily digestible.

For some, this resistance to reduce information literacy to a sound bite is a welcome change if information literacy is ever to be recognized as something more than a set of basic skills related to library-based academic research. For others, it presents a complication: consider the students who wish to convey their information literacy–related expertise to graduate school admissions officers or potential employers.

Adding to this problem is the fact that a student's experience with information literacy instruction may not be reflected on a transcript, because current models do not often include a separate credit-bearing course on the topic. Even in cases where information literacy instruction does show up on a student's record in some way, employers may not recognize the potential relevance of a course if they are not already familiar with what information literacy is or what students might learn as part of such a course.

A badge displayed as part of an online professional profile can go a long way toward resolving this issue. When a student earns a badge, the badge comes with metadata describing what the student needed to do in order to earn that badge. If used correctly, this metadata can capture exactly what topics the student learned about or what skills were required to earn the badge. This description would be much more meaningful to a non-expert than the vague, oversimplified definition provided above. In this way, students who have done the learning necessary to closing some of the gaps identified by employers like the ones from the Project Information Literacy study can make the details of their expertise more accessible to the people they want to work for. An employer will be able to tell much more easily whether a student possesses the information competencies valued in that particular workplace.

## USING BADGES TO ENHANCE INFORMATION LITERACY INSTRUCTION

Knowing that badges can address issues of motivation and translation when it comes to information literacy is all well and good, but what are some of the ways in which they can actually be used as part of information literacy instruction? There are many possibilities.

Information literacy instruction can take many forms. Ideally an institution will offer either a general or discipline-focused information literacy course that students can take for credit. Such a course offers the opportunity to present students with a mix of skills-based and concept-based instruction that will at the very least give them a good foundation on which to build their information literacy expertise. More commonly, students learn about information literacy through course-related guest lectures given by librarians at the start of a research project or through online tools such as interactive tutorials. These modes of learning may incorporate some concept-based instruction but are often by necessity focused primarily on skills. While any information literacy instruction is better than no information literacy instruction, the shift from the ACRL's *Standards* to their *Framework* has made it clear that changes need to be made to the existing skills-based models, which do not allow for the depth of time and engagement needed for students to develop sufficient information literacy expertise.

Unfortunately, real change can be slow to come. In the meantime, badges can be used as a way to enhance existing models of information literacy instruction without needing to entirely upend them. They can be attached to lessons and tools that are already in use, or they can be used as an additional, separate tool as part of a spectrum of instructional choices.

The most obvious way to make badges part of an information literacy program is to make it possible for students to earn confirmatory badges for completing a course, one-shot session, or tutorial. Unlike credit-bearing courses, one-shot sessions and tutorials are largely invisible to any record of a student's learning while they are in college. A badge that can be displayed on a public profile could make this learning more visible. The metadata for the badge could be used to describe the topic the student learned about as part of the session or the tutorial.

As discussed earlier, confirmatory badges have their value, particularly when it comes to issues of motivation, but they do not generally represent more than a simple confirmation that a task was completed. A different way to use a badge would involve more work but would result in and represent deeper engagement in the learning process on the part of the student.

Consider one-shot course-related sessions as an example. The time allotted for instruction as part of a course-related session is typically short—at most a few hours. Often, this is the only time the information literacy instructor has to teach students what they need to know. As mentioned earlier, these sessions tend to be focused on the application of skills with little or no time to give students the needed conceptual background that makes those skills meaningful.

Badges could be used not just as a marker for completion for students who are present at a one-shot session but also as a supplement for that instruction. In a flipped model, for example, students might be asked to complete an assignment before coming to the session. The assignment may give students the concept-based background they need to get the most out of the skills they will be learning as part of the session, or it may be a pre-test that shows students areas of strengths and weaknesses to keep in mind before coming to the session. Alternatively, a badge could be used to help students continue learning even after the session is over, offering more advanced content that builds on what they learned in the session or a chance to practice further. Students could complete an activity or reflection to show what they have learned. As a result, the badge no longer represents a simple rubber stamp on the student's attendance or participation in a session but instead an actual demonstration of their learning. To earn the badge, students would have to go the extra mile.

The key to effectively using badges in this way is in the evaluation aspect of whatever activity the badge may represent. This would require some effort to develop a rubric against which to evaluate the work as well as a system for helping students whose work may not meet the required standard so they can try again as needed. It would also need to be decided whether the information literacy instructor or the course instructor is the one doing the evaluation or if the evaluation would be done collaboratively. These details would take more time and effort to put in place, but the long-term benefit to the students would almost certainly outweigh the initial costs.

Attaching badges to existing components of an information literacy program is one option for integrating badges into information literacy instruction. Another is to create or use an existing separate, stand-alone badging system that can be used as part of a spectrum of instruction options.

The Metaliteracy Badging System, discussed in more detail later in this book, is an example of such a system. The lessons and activities that can be completed as part of this system require more engagement and reflection than the average tutorial, making room for both concept-based and skills-based learning. Unlike a one-shot session or a credit-bearing course, the activities associated with the system can be completed on one's own time. Students and instructors who are interested in more in-depth learning than what a tutorial may offer but who may not have room on their schedules for a one-shot session or an entire course can use badges like these as a solution. As an additional point, offering a constellation or spectrum of instructional options that speak to different levels of learning and engagement is much more aligned with ACRL's *Framework*-based thinking about information literacy.

One last advantage of badges for enhancing information literacy instruction is in their potential for customization, which makes them different from most interactive tutorials. A librarian working with badges could collaborate with a course instructor to create a customized badge based on content or activities tailored to a specific course or assignment. Some may argue that the goal for badges should be standardization rather than customization, particularly if they are to be used for assessment purposes. This idea is certainly worth debating, especially when taking into consideration some of the ideas discussed earlier about using badges to communicate what exactly information literacy means to non-experts. However, the idea of customization is in line with the ACRL *Framework*'s acknowledgment of the importance of context to the research process.

## CONCLUSION

Ideas about information literacy are ever-changing, as are ideas about how information literacy can or should be taught. The shift from ACRL's *Standards*-based thinking about information literacy to their *Framework*-based thinking has created both opportunities and complications. The ideas discussed here are just a few of the possible ways that badges could be used to take advantage of those opportunities and perhaps mitigate those complications. When thoughtfully integrated, badges have the potential to enhance information literacy instruction by addressing issues related to motivation and communication.

## REFERENCES

ACRL (Association of College and Research Libraries). 2000. "Information Literacy Defined." In *Information Literacy Competency Standards for Higher Education*, 2–3. Chicago: ACRL, American Library Association. https://alair.ala.org/bitstream/handle/11213/7668/ACRL%20Information%20Literacy%20Competency%20Standards%20for%20Higher%20Education.pdf?sequence=1&isAllowed=y.

———. 2015. *Framework for Information Literacy for Higher Education.* Chicago: ACRL. http://www.ala.org/acrl/standards/ilframework.

Head, Allison J., Michele Van Hoeck, Jordan Eschler, and Sean Fullerton. 2013. "What Information Competencies Matter in Today's Workplace?" *Library and Information Research* 37 (114): 75–104. http://www.lirgjournal.org.uk/lir/ojs/index.php/lir/article/view/557/593.

Molteni, Valeria E., and Emily K. Chan. 2015. "Student Confidence/Overconfidence in the Research Process." *The Journal of Academic Librarianship* 41 (1): 2–8.

# 6

# Badging Best Practices

*Kelsey L. O'Brien*

**B**y definition, a digital badge is a symbolic icon. As a visual cue, it signifies importance and prompts the viewer to investigate the full story of a particular achievement. In essence, a badge is a communication mechanism that promotes, tracks, and showcases learning.

As a symbol, however, a badge is only as valuable as the learning experience it represents. This chapter thus aims to prioritize function over form by employing Wiggins and McTighe's (2005) "backward design" model as a guiding framework, envisaging how educators might leverage the unique qualities of badges at each stage of curricular design.

The Understanding by Design (UbD) framework asserts that "the best designs derive backward from the learnings sought" (ibid., 14). Using this method, the educator must begin by considering the desired results and assessments before planning lessons, selecting materials, and determining teaching strategies. Stage 1 of the UbD process establishes expectations for what learners will be able to understand or do, while stage 2 considers the evidence that will be used to assess this understanding, and stage 3 maps out the learning activities that will prepare learners to meet the desired objectives (ibid.).

Viewed through a results-focused lens, the badge represents the learning goal set out by the educator and the driving achievement to which the learner aspires. This approach counteracts the inclination to simply append a badge to the end of an assignment or activity, which wrongfully assumes that the badge itself is inherently motivational or valuable to every learner. The badge should not simply be defined by its associated content but, rather, by the objective of the learning.

While badging in education is still in its infancy and best practices continue to evolve, backward design, or "badges first" design, has emerged as a common approach among badge practitioners, both as an explicitly stated framework (Higashi et al. 2017; Bartoletti, Seitzinger, and Kilgore, 2015; Grant 2013, quoted in Hickey and Willis 2017, 9) and in the application of related pedagogical and instructional design principles (Rimland and Raish 2018). The conceptual badge system prototype presented by Higashi et al. (2017) provides an especially comprehensive model grounded in design theory.

Following the stages of backward design, this chapter begins with guidelines on establishing the purpose of the badge or badge system before considering the supporting evidence that defines the quality of the credential and, finally, the infrastructure that will lead to the culminating achievement. The points of consideration included at each stage seek to highlight ways that librarians and other educators might thoughtfully integrate and thus maximize the unique opportunities offered by digital badging. The key points presented for each of the three stages are outlined in table 6.1, located at the end of the chapter.

## STAGE 1, ESTABLISH YOUR PURPOSE

The *purpose* of the learning, according to UbD, serves as the impetus and touchstone throughout the design process. According to Wiggins and McTighe (2005), "Answering the 'why?' and 'so what?' questions that older students always ask (or want to), and doing so in concrete terms as the focus of curriculum planning, is . . . the essence of understanding by design" (15–16). Maintaining this "transparency of purpose" throughout planning and implementation helps establish, reinforce, and communicate the value of the learning experience for the educator, learners, and ultimately outside evaluators.

At the outset of the design process, the badge designer should envision the badge embedded on an electronic portfolio or a professional online profile such as LinkedIn. What might this badge mean to someone who has earned it, and what does it convey to an observer? Does the badge enable opportunities for the earner? Does it represent a competency that a recent graduate might refer to as a talking point during a job interview?

Imagine where you want the learner to be before planning the pathways they will take to get there. While there is often reluctance to label badges as extrinsic motivators, they nevertheless represent a kind of award system. A badge is akin to a flag waving at the summit or a trophy at the finish line. As an embellishment on an otherwise text-based profile or online résumé, the badge draws attention, which should prompt the badge designer to ask, What is worthy of recognition? To establish a badge's purpose, one must consider its relevance and applicability within various contexts.

### Identifying Needs

A widely circulated illustration by Bryan M. Mathers (https://bryanmmathers.com/credentials-big-and-small/) depicts micro-credentials such as badges as pebbles in a jar, filling in the gaps left by bigger rocks that represent traditional credentials such as college degrees. When determining the purpose of a badge or badge program, consider how badges might fill in existing gaps. This begins with identifying needs in national, community, and institutional settings. Where is there a demand for better representation of learning?

A badge can represent the answer to an established need. Chapters 2 and 3 of this volume situate badges within the broader context of higher education, considering their potential for addressing substantial challenges, pressures, and expectations of various stakeholders in the academic community. Additionally, reports such as those published by Project Information Literacy (http://www.projectinfolit.org/) continue to point to student frustrations and career readiness disparities that librarians can help address. In creating a badge that represents a relevant learning goal, an educator is effectively putting their stake in the ground as a resolution to strive toward solving a given problem.

When considering the potential application of a badging program, librarians need not limit their scope to library-specific initiatives but should rather consider the far-reaching capabilities of information literacy in addressing campus-wide challenges. Exploring strategic planning documents and regional accrediting agency reports may present opportunities to participate in established initiatives. Attending academic department meetings and engaging in conversations with faculty can help establish institutional and disciplinary needs.

Additionally, calls for grant proposals offer an effective gauge of local and national interests on which a badging program might focus. Along with providing start-up funding, grants can help the applicant articulate (and hopefully ultimately demonstrate) the role of the library or department in fulfilling the institution's mission or addressing a broader societal issue. While funding may focus on technological infrastructures, innovation grants often present challenges related to more expansive themes such as student success, social media ethics, and accessibility—all calls that librarians can help answer.

Existing badge programs provide valuable resources that can inspire purposeful implementation in a library setting. Interested readers may refer to case studies from this volume along with other examples from the field documented within the following resources: the Libraries section of HASTAC's annotated research bibliography of digital badges (https://www.hastac.org/digital-badges-bibliography), ACRL's Digital Badges Interest Group (https://acrl.libguides.com/digitalbadgeinterestgroup), volume 29 (4) of the *Journal of Electronic Resources Librarianship* (https://www.tandfonline.com/toc/wacq20/29/4?nav=tocList), and the DPD Project's Badge Systems page (http://dpdproject.info/). Established badge programs can serve as models in the early stages of badge design and as reference points when discussing a potential project with administrators and in some cases may be openly licensed for reuse or adaptation. At the time of writing, current endeavors involving the development of badge repositories (see, for example, https://badgerank.org) suggest promising opportunities in the near future for targeted searching of the open badges ecosystem, which should assist in unearthing additional relevant programs and initiatives.

## Transferability

When considering the purpose of a badge program, the badge designer must continually contextualize the badge, from its initial purpose to its ultimate applicability for the earner, in order to ensure its relevance. McTighe and Wiggins (2012) assert that the true value of learning lies in its applications beyond the classroom. Transferability, or "the ability to effectively use content knowledge and skill" is therefore a foundational tenet of the UbD framework. "The bottom-line goal of education is transfer. The point of school is not to simply excel in each class but to be able to use one's learning in other settings" (2).

If badges are to be utilized as a kind of educational currency endowed upon the learner, they must have value outside of the context in which they are earned. While some might rightfully argue for the merits of learning for personal enrichment or enjoyment, educators should carefully consider whether a learning experience warrants credentialing in the form of a badge (though lightweight badges can play a different role, as will be discussed in stage 3). As a credential, a badge indicates that the acquired ability can be applied to other situations, such as the workplace or graduate school.

Transferable learning is performance-based, and the credibility of badges likewise operates on verified, evidence-based claims. In essence, a badge asserts that, "Using past performances as evidence . . . the earner of this badge possesses the indicated skill, and will be able to apply it appropriately and build upon it in the future" (Higashi et al. 2017, 55). To consider the purpose of the badge is thus to contextualize the potential applications of the associated learning experience.

## Purposeful Badging in Libraries

As epicenters of lifelong learning and discovery, libraries promote inquiry, openness, and innovation—values that are also championed by the open badging movement. Libraries of all types, particularly academic libraries, have long since shifted their focus from knowledge repositories to service-oriented institutions focused largely on teaching vital research and learning strategies. Outside entities, however, are often unaware of the educational opportunities that librarians provide and how they can help meet established needs.

As illustrated by the following examples, there are several ways that academic library programs might meaningfully integrate digital badges to showcase teaching and learning.

### *Promoting Information Literacy Programs*

According to the culminating report of the Design Principles Documentation Project, which followed up on the progress of the thirty pioneering badge programs funded by the MacArthur Foundation's Badges for Lifelong Learning competition in 2012, badges tend to work well as an overlay for existing programs. The report found that "badges work better where educational content already exists," partly due to the considerable workload involved when creating both new content and new technology (i.e., website and badge mechanisms) (Hickey and Willis 2017, 16).

Badge systems can enhance the structure and visibility of existing information literacy programs by illuminating, clarifying, and promoting teaching and learning that is already in practice. This can be especially valuable for librarians whose instruction is distributed across the curriculum as integrated one-shot sessions, as opposed to a designated information literacy course. Digital badges can be created as goal markers that delineate important competencies within an information literacy program; the work required to earn a badge might be assigned in conjunction with face-to-face library instruction for pre- or post-assessment or in place of in-person instruction when carefully coordinated with the instructor assigning the work (Rimland and Raish 2018). Such a badge program can provide a cohesive visualized package to disciplinary faculty members who may be unaware of the instructional opportunities librarians provide, and it can help clarify misunderstandings about what librarians do and teach.

For programs that are more formally integrated into institutional organizations, badge systems can reveal the more granular intricacies of information literacy. Badges might be used to pinpoint critical competencies assessed in an information literacy course, for example. By using more generic titles and descriptors (i.e., critical thinking or problem-solving), badges can also be used to translate unfamiliar terminology for observers who may not fully understand what information literacy is when they read the course title on a transcript.

It is important to note that, while badges are well-utilized as a mechanism for highlighting the finer aspects of an existing course, badge designers should be wary of redundancy. If a credential or clear marker already exists (e.g., a grade or a course designation on a transcript), an accompanying "completion" badge does not necessarily present added value for the learner or an observer. In fact, these types of badges typically do not motivate potential earners who tend to perceive them as redundant with existing assessment indicators (Hickey and Willis 2017, 51). Rather, badge designers should emulate the more successful examples presented in the DPD report, in which "badges contained unique information and evidence that was not easily accessible or available elsewhere" (ibid., 19). In other words, badges can work well when carefully aligned with measurable learning goals in a course, but they should not simply replace course or assignment grades.

As eye-catching visuals, badges can make valuable marketing and branding tools that concisely and attractively communicate the goals and mission of a library or information literacy program. While the lack of a formalized program presents familiar challenges for many academic libraries, there are also advantages to starting with a blank slate, as librarian Nicole Pagowsky pointed out in the early stages of the badging movement. Integrating badges, Pagowsky says, "is difficult for libraries when trying to align with campus curriculum, particularly if information literacy is not formally integrated. However, this could present an opportunity rather than a problem by allowing a means to explicitly map library instruction to campus goals, track progress, and activate clear assessment" (Pagowsky 2013). As promotional tools, badges might accompany the mission statement on the library's webpage, illustrate departmental goals to an administrator, or provide a visual talking point when working with a faculty member.

*Communicating Learning Goals*

As mentioned earlier in this section, maintaining transparency of purpose helps communicate the "why" of learning to various audiences. Along with making teaching practices evident to faculty colleagues and administrators, badges can illuminate learning for students by highlighting goals and expectations, visualizing learning processes, and helping them articulate what they have learned. Badges embedded into a course, such as those described in the section above, can illustrate and reinforce course learning goals and objectives, which, while likely reviewed on the syllabus on the first day of class, are often promptly forgotten.

Using badges to "map learning trajectories" for learners and educators is one of the simplest and most achievable uses of badge systems (Hickey and Willis 2017, 34–35) and is particularly pertinent to information literacy, about which students often do not know what they do not know. Badges can put a label on critical learning processes that may be obscured for students by automated or habitual search behaviors. While students may know how to find resources for a research assignment using Google, for example, in many cases they are unaware of how to find the best resources or why doing so is important. When designed to represent desired outcomes, badges communicate the purpose of the learning to students and signal that the culminating competency is important and worthy of promotion.

Educators can also leverage badges to connect learners to their learning, shifting the focus from knowledge transfer to helping students become better learners. Viewed through a constructivist lens, which "places the focus of design on helping the student to construct their own knowledge through active learning" (Rimland and Raish 2018, 213), badges might be presented as knowledge building blocks to be collected, built upon, and displayed. As personal identifiers, badges can frame the learning as an internal process by which an achievement is *earned* rather than as an external transaction that happens *to* the learner. Akin to its physical counterpart adorned on a sash or uniform, an earned digital badge becomes an extension of the earner's public identity.

When used to enhance awareness and understanding of learning, badges can help learners articulate what they know, doubling the function of a badge not only as a credential on a résumé but as a talking point in a job interview or graduate school application. Likewise, by enabling the ready identification of gaps in learners' knowledge, badges may encourage learners to seek opportunities to fill them.

## *Unlocking Opportunities*

While a badge should primarily represent the learning outcome, the value of badges may be enhanced "when they provide additional opportunities within the environment where the badges are issued" (Hickey and Willis 2017, 55). Depending on the weight of the credential, these opportunities might include internships, jobs, or peer mentor status. Hickey and Willis clarify that external opportunities need not undermine intrinsic motivation when they are tied closely to the learning experience represented by the badge: "Digital badges might be external to the *learner* but intrinsically related to the learning *process*" (ibid., 48). In other words, the opportunity should be related to the competency as opposed to an unrelated prize or privilege (e.g., a gift card for printing or unlimited borrowing privileges).

The story recounted in chapter 4, in which a student eagerly worked toward a badge that would unlock a desired career exploration opportunity, provides an example of how these kinds of badges can facilitate goal setting. Badges can provide a meaningful target for students by encouraging them to strive toward personal learning goals and contextualizing learning activities within real-world applications. By partnering with employers or community organizations, libraries might utilize a badge program to reach students interested in a particular career track and to illustrate the value of information literacy in the workplace.

Librarians reading this volume are likely already doing a great deal in service of students, but these efforts may be hidden to outside observers. Consider how a badging program might be utilized to reveal, clarify, document, and showcase student learning. Once the guiding purpose has been established, the next phase involves authentically assessing and communicating the value of the badge to external audiences.

## STAGE 2, DETERMINE EVIDENCE: HOW WILL LEARNERS DEMONSTRATE WHAT THEY KNOW?

The distinctive value of digital badges as credentials lies in their metadata, descriptive information that is encoded or "baked into" the badge image. Metadata adds dimension, helps establish the quality and validity of the badge, and tells the story of the learning that took place.

While the terms *digital badge* and *Open Badge* are often used interchangeably, Open Badges are distinguished by their metadata standards. The umbrella "digital badge" designation includes the static icons one might encounter in a video game or mobile application; Open Badges, however, adhere to the Open Badges Infrastructure (OBI), an interoperability standard established by Mozilla Foundation in 2011 and transitioned to IMS Global Learning Consortium in 2017 (https://openbadges.org/about/) that enables badges to be implemented and displayed across all compatible environments. OBI–compliant badge-issuing platforms such as Credly and Badgr make it simple for a badge designer, regardless of programming expertise, to create the metadata fields required for an Open Badge, including the badge description, issuer, and earning criteria.

As both a technical specification and a movement, Open Badges support and promote transparency in education. In contrast to cryptic course titles on transcripts and vague college diplomas, Open Badges invite the reviewer to investigate the validity and meaning of the credential. Badges concisely package the competency claim with the assessment, enabling the immediate interrogation of the badge's authenticity. Digital badges thus communicate their own value, and a poorly designed badge will quickly be revealed for what it is. "An attentive evaluator would reject (with prejudice) a badge that claims one thing but measures something else, and no learner would be excited to earn a token thus discredited" (Higashi et al. 2017, 53).

While more detailed metadata strengthens the quality of the credential, however, not all badge observers will investigate beyond the surface level. The badge designer must bear in mind that the hiring manager or admissions officer may not take the time to click on the embedded badge and should accordingly include useful and efficient information at each layer. The badge image should provide a quick "visual summary" for the evaluator (ibid., 56) and avoid ambiguity by including a straightforward title, while the metadata, revealed upon the first click, should provide a thorough yet concise textual description. Links to evidence, program details, and issuer credentials should be included in the metadata fields for those reviewers interested in deeper evaluation.

The following sections present points of consideration for creating metadata that communicates and verifies the quality of the badge.

**Badge Claims**

Higashi et al. (2017) posit that, "In essence, the entire badging enterprise—and, indeed, that of microcredentialing in general—hinges upon the question of why a viewer should believe the badge's claim" (53). The ability of any individual or organization to certify learning outside of conventional credentialing systems presents a liberating but challenging prospect for academics and employers. Detailed metadata about the issuer and supporting evidence is essential in order to validate and solidify a badge's claim.

As information literacy experts, librarians are well poised to teach and assess particular skill sets and competencies that are in high demand, such as critical thinking, media literacy, and creative problem-solving. Potential badge reviewers, however, may be unaware of an issuing library's qualifications or the robustness of an information literacy program. Links to professional credentials and department pages, along with issuer endorsements, such as Credly's verified status, can help assure a badge reviewer of the academic expertise of those developing and issuing badges. Librarians should discuss with administrators whether the badge is to be issued by the entire library, a specific department, or perhaps a dedicated committee. Badge issuers may also want to consider partnering with larger departments or schools and branding their badges accordingly (see chapter 10 of this volume). Institution-wide badging programs such as those implemented by Penn State University provide additional affirmation by associating the credential with the reputation of the university.

By awarding a badge, the issuer stands behind the badge's claim. The claim should therefore be carefully mapped to measurable learning outcomes. Higashi et al. state that "a valid assessment makes a claim that an individual knows something, backs that claim with evidence, and leads to a conclusion that is usable for a decision" (2017, 54). Badge designers should be explicit in the competency or ability that a badge represents and may want to consider issuing an expiration date for claims that will lose their value over time (e.g., technology expertise), which enables the earner to periodically reapply for renewal.

## Evidence

Evidence serves as the gauge for determining the degree to which a learner has achieved the desired results and as the primary validation of a badge's claim. By promoting authentic, performance-based assessment, badges can help shift the focus from teaching, which does not guarantee learning (McTighe and Wiggins 2012), to a demonstration of what a student has actually learned. As opposed to measuring learning by seat time, an outdated practice that is still reflected in course credits, the disruptive power of badges as credentials lies in their ability to "show versus tell."

While optional, according to OBI, evidence is one of the most valuable and transformative pieces of badge metadata. In alignment with the desired learning outcomes established in stage 1, evidence should be performance-based and demonstrate the transferability of the competency. "What will count as evidence *on the field*, not merely in drills, that they really get it and are ready to *perform with understanding, knowledge, and skill* on their own?" (ibid., 19; emphasis original).

A badge's evidence can be included as a file or a link, enabling flexibility in its format. The badge system prototype provided by Higashi et al. (2017) offers examples of four different kinds of evidence that might be included in a badge's metadata: experience (e.g., training or workshops), learning artifacts, endorsement (e.g., a written recommendation from an expert), and exams. The prototype presents the inclusion of all types of evidence as the ideal, enabling the triangulation of multiple sources to make a stronger claim about the quality of the assessment, but the authors also acknowledge that this may not always be possible (56).

The inclusion of learning artifacts as evidence presents a unique opportunity to directly align experience with competency. Rather than requiring the reviewer to sift through a candidate's portfolio to align their experiences with the desired qualifications, a badge serves as its own miniature portfolio and connects the dots for a potential employer or admissions officer.

## Endorsements

Endorsements allow outside evaluators, in addition to the badge issuer, to submit their own judgment of the claimed competency, similar to a reference letter written for a job applicant. Though this feature is one of the more recent fields to be added to the Open Badges specification, initial reports from early practitioners suggest that badges are enhanced "when they can be endorsed by multiple stakeholders after they are issued, based on the evidence contained in the badge" (Hickey and Willis 2017, 38).

Higashi et al. (2017) contend that "the major strength of this evidence category is in capturing intangible, yet historically reliable, assessments of expertise by knowledgeable others within the learning space. This type of evidence is also uniquely positioned to reflect on certain types of skills that are impossible to evaluate through other means, such as collaboration quality, which is inherently social" (62). The endorsement of information literacy competencies, which tend to be easier to evaluate via observation rather than testing, could certainly help enhance and clarify the credential beyond the original badge issuer's claim. Librarians working in collaboration with disciplinary faculty to implement badges might consider having the faculty member submit a statement of endorsement or an annotated rubric that was used to assess a culminating badge assessment in order to enhance the validity of the claim.

The full realization of the endorsement feature will require buy-in from experts such as internship mentors or employers, many of whom may still be skeptical of badges. But as badges gain broader recognition, external organizations will likely be more receptive to partnerships, presenting increased opportunities for professional endorsements (Hickey and Willis 2017, 37).

## STAGE 3, PLANNING LEARNING PATHWAYS: HOW WILL LEARNERS GET THERE?

The final phase of badge design involves creating the learning activities that prospective badge earners will need to complete in order to provide the necessary evidence that demonstrates the claimed competency. While badges represent the desired learning goal, a badge system can illustrate the steps learners will take to reach that goal. Considerations at this stage revolve around scaffolding and feedback mechanisms, such as, "How will we support learners as they come to understand important ideas and processes? How will we prepare them to autonomously transfer their learning?" (McTighe and Wiggins 2012, 6).

It is important at this stage in the design process to keep the purpose of the learning at the forefront of decision-making. Technology (or lack thereof) should not compromise the original intent or integrity of the learning experience, and in fact badge systems need not be overly complicated; using freely available tools, anyone can create and issue a badge in a matter of minutes. A basic badge system grounded in solid curriculum design is far more valuable than a complex system boasting bells and whistles that does not represent authentic learning. Furthermore, pilot programs that make use of existing resources can serve as prototypes that may help secure funding for future enhancements.

By depicting incremental goals and learning pathways, badge systems offer the opportunity to build scaffolding and feedback into the learning experience. Badging mechanisms can be leveraged during the curriculum design process to guide the learner's journey to the culminating badge.

## Badge Systems as Curriculum Maps

In essence, badge systems are illustrative curriculum maps that depict the pathways learners will take in order to achieve the desired outcome. As with any well-designed curriculum, broader learning goals, represented by the badge, should be broken down into measurable learning objectives and activity sequences that prepare learners to succeed in meeting a competency. The learning sequence that leads to a culminating badge can be depicted as a series of sub-badges or tokens of achievement. While culminating badges represent summative assessments, sub-badges can be used to indicate formative assessments (Higashi et al. 2017). In this respect, badge pathways provide mile markers on the learning journey, signaling opportunities for reflection and feedback.

By mapping out curriculum objectives in relation to broader learning goals, badge systems illustrate learning schemas that help maintain the transparency of purpose. A badge system might take many forms, such as a ladder of lower-level badges ascending to "summit" badges (see chapter 4), a hierarchy of sub-badges that accumulate to culminating meta-badges (see chapter 11), or thematic groupings, such as the educator professional development badges offered by Digital Promise (http://microcredentials.digitalpromise.org/).

Badge system diagrams may also be depicted as more fluid constellations, which can be used to convey flexibility when the order of learning activities is not prescribed. Whatever the design style, mapped badging systems illuminate and acknowledge not only the outcomes but also the learning *process* that leads to the culminating achievement.

Leveled badge systems are particularly pertinent to mastery learning, which "allows a student to keep trying until they reach a certain competency" as opposed to "traditional classroom assessments that score a student and then progress to the next lesson" (Rimland and Raish 2018, 215). Mastery-oriented systems, commonly used in game design, leave room for failure and "treat errors and mistakes the players make as an opportunity to provide diagnostic feedback and encouragement" (Blair 2011, 3). Badge systems should ideally allow learners multiple attempts to complete each learning activity and provide reinforcement for learners as they strive toward more complex goals at their own pace.

Several worksheets and guides are available for mapping out badge systems. Along with Wiggin and McTighe's curriculum planning resources, such as the 1-Page Template with Design Questions for Teachers (figure 1.2 in Wiggins and McTighe 2005, 22), readers may refer to DigitalMe's badge academy and Badge Design Canvas (https://www.openbadgeacademy.com/Getstartedwithbadges), the Sprout Fund's resources, including a badge design tools page (https://medium.com/sprout-digital-badges), Peer 2 Peer University's Badge Maker Course (https://badges.p2pu.org/en/about), and Little Bird Games's badge design guidelines and worksheets on designing a badge-based curriculum (http://dev.modcourse.com/students/classes/badge-based-curriculum-1). In accordance with the backward design model, the aforementioned resources begin with considerations about the broader purpose and learning goals before considering related instruction and activities.

## Signaling Progress with Achievements

While culminating badges communicate validated competencies to external audiences, incremental sub-badges can serve as internal achievement markers within a badge system. Lower-level achievements may not be considered worthy of credentialing status (i.e., displaying on a portfolio), and in fact the awarding of "lightweight" badges tends to raise concerns about diluting the badging ecosystem and undermining the legitimacy of badges as a serious form of credentialing. "It is to a learner's advantage," note Rimland and Raish (2018), "to earn higher-level badges to display a select few badges that convey more learning, rather than many low-level badges" (218). As achievement markers issued within a learning system, however, sub-badges indicate progress and provide positive reinforcement that can motivate the learner as they "level up" or work toward a culminating badge.

Achievements are a mechanism often used in gaming environments to engage players and encourage them to improve upon their performance. Providing achievement opportunities that range in difficulty encourages learners of all abilities to be more confident in attempting tasks that seem more attainable (Blair 2011, 2). Hickey and Willis (2017) advocate for the motivating effect of lower-level achievements, stating that badge systems are most successful "when initial badges are easy to earn and provide access to more advanced badges" (58). Lower-level achievements can provide an engaging entry point into a badging system by providing opportunities for early successes and positive feedback. While there is potential for collections of lightweight badges to communicate the bigger story of collective learning experiences, badge designers may want to reserve credentialing status for more robust culminating badges that clearly communicate demonstrated competencies while utilizing lower-level achievements as internal stepping stones contained within the learning system.

On the other end of the spectrum, challenging achievements, particularly those that offer social distinction for the earner, can engage learners by stimulating competition. Examples of successful badge programs suggest that "offering badges that are scarce and hard to earn" can be motivating for learners, especially if they unlock special opportunities or privileges (ibid., 51). Even if learners do not earn the achievement, they may be encouraged to put forth more effort in striving toward a meaningful goal. Vicarious experience or "seeing people around you succeed" also influences learners' self-efficacy, suggesting the potential benefits of social components such as leaderboards (Blair 2011, 2) and badges awarded for meaningful engagement and contributions within a learning community (see supplementary badges in chapter 9).

Until badges become more ubiquitous to the typical observer, the most immediate applications for lightweight badges are as guideposts and feedback mechanisms for learners. Carla Casilli (2014), who has directed badge design practices at Mozilla, Badge Alliance, and IMS Global, has advocated for lightweight badges largely due to their signaling power for the learner, for "in their accumulation they tell different stories to both the earner as well as the public" and serve as "markers and data points in the larger, more complex concept of self." To avoid learner confusion, badge designers should clearly distinguish between badges that may be earned and displayed and achievement markers that are internal to the learning system (e.g., with different badge shapes, sizes, or terms) while being mindful not to overwhelm learners with unfamiliar terminology.

**Flexible Learning Pathways**

By emphasizing achievements over seat time, badge systems offer opportunities for flexible and customized learning. While the culminating badge is anchored in the learning outcome and its associated criteria, the methods by which the learner reaches that achievement and the evidence provided can vary. Badge designers can build this flexibility into the badge system by offering multiple pathway options, choices in the evidence submitted, and personalization of the learning experience.

A choose-your-own-adventure-style badge system that allows learners to pursue different pathways depending on their preferences or aptitude might be considered the ideal design in terms of the flexibility and autonomy offered to the learner. This model might build on the gamified associations with badges by presenting branched pathways or triggering shortcuts upon demonstration of prior learning (e.g., earning 100 percent on a quiz). The design for this system would be complex, however, due to the additional content for each possibility and the triggering mechanisms required. As a simpler alternative, badge designers might allow learners to choose from groupings of activities (e.g., completing three out of five), based on their personal preferences, that all meet the same objective.

A badge system design can also differentiate the methods by which learners demonstrate their knowledge. Constructivist pedagogy asserts that "there are many ways to construct meaning, and there is not one universal way of processing that information" (Rimland and Raish 2018, 213). Allowing learners to meet criteria using their choice of format (e.g., written response, oral presentation, multimedia slideshow, etc.) or even a more open-ended choice of method encourages them to leverage personal strengths and take ownership of their learning. To earn a badge issued by Digital Promise, for example, educators must submit an application form describing how they have met the learning objectives and provide supporting evidence. Through this process, the learner gains practice in articulating competencies and is more connected to the purpose of the learning. An application system can also help with workflow by shifting responsibility to the badge earner to signal when an assignment is ready for review.

Finally, badge systems can offer flexibility through personalization. Rimland and Raish (2018) stress that the learning experience depends on the learner. "What is important to remember," they write, "is that it is impossible to design student learning. The instruction that should theoretically lead to desired learning outcomes for students can be designed, but it is impossible to state that we are able to design the student's learning experience" (211). Badge system designers should therefore provide opportunities for learners to make their own connections and meaning. Hickey and Willis (2017) encourage the incorporation of learner reflections and self-assessment models in badge systems, noting that "what seems particularly promising is asking learners to reflect on their *engagement* in learning rather than reflect on the *outcomes* of that learning (because focusing on the outcomes is likely to emphasize performance goals rather than learning goals)" (62; emphasis original). Along with reflecting throughout the learning process, learners might also submit culminating reflections or annotated learning artifacts to be included as evidence in the awarded badge's metadata.

## Technical Infrastructure and Logistics

Considerations regarding the technical infrastructure of badging systems are reserved for the final stage of design; while it may be tempting to start the design process based on the latest tool or trend, badge designers should avoid letting the technology dictate the curriculum. As badging system technologies will continue to evolve following the publication of this volume, the scope of this chapter remains focused on design principles. For more technical guidance, readers are referred to "Badging Platforms: A Scenario-Based Comparison of Features and Uses" (Dimitrijević et al. 2016), which provides a thorough overview and practical analysis of several badging platforms and their features.

## Badging Platforms and Learning Management Systems

When considering technology solutions, options typically include ready-made, modular, or custom-designed systems (see Bryan M. Mathers's visual representation of these options at https://bryanmmathers.com/choosing-a-badging-system/). While creating and issuing a standalone badge is fairly straightforward, out-of-the-box solutions for creating badging *systems* are scarce to non-existent at the time of writing.

One of the simpler options is to incorporate badging functionality into an existing learning management system (LMS). Third party badging applications—increasingly prominent in LMS environments, such as Canvas and Moodle—allow for the integration of badging features into a course using compatibility specifications such as Learning Tools Interoperability (LTI). The LMS facilitates the delivery and assessment of learning content associated with requirements for earning a badge and provides built-in technical support. Mechanisms such as triggers that unlock content upon successful completion of an activity are conducive to the awarding of incremental achievements. A learning management system can also be limiting, however, if its structure does not accommodate the desired badge system scheme. A hierarchical design, for example, may not be feasible using a linear, module-based LMS.

For more flexibility, badge designers might consider creating their own custom systems, which can be assisted by open source tools such as Badgr (https://info.badgr.io/). Alternatively, separate platforms may be used for content delivery and the issuing of badges (see the Badge Alliance's list at http://www.badgealliance.org/badge-issuing-platforms/). For example, online course content may be used in conjunction with tools such as Credly that can be used to manually issue badges for learning experiences completed online or in person, via emails sent to qualifying learners or activity codes that are revealed upon successful completion of a task. This method may be more labor-intensive but also requires less technological groundwork.

**Assessment Tools**

Authentic assessments—particularly for more fluid competencies, such as those related to information literacy—most often cannot be automated. Scaled assessment of badge assignments may be challenging, however, for librarians who are not teaching their own courses or who have a wide range of responsibilities beyond teaching.

Some of the more successful and sustainable badge designs use a combination of computer-based and human assessment (Hickey and Willis 2017, 43). Higashi et al. (2017) present a combination of assessment techniques for different types of evidence, including self-assessment, automated assessment (e.g., quizzes, workshop participation, etc.), and manual assessment by experts. Rimland and Raish (2018) likewise suggest consolidating and prioritizing instructor feedback for high-stakes activities, such as a "comprehensive reflection that has students consider their previous learning and connect it to what they feel they learned from the badge. . . . This allows for personalized responses to that particular step but lighter or automated assessment of previous tasks within that badge" (215).

Building on collaborative or co-teaching partnerships, librarians may also enlist faculty members to review the work of their own students—or perhaps graduate students, who may be able to assist with verifying submitted evidence. Rubrics can be used to facilitate scaled assessment and to ensure consistency in evidence evaluation (ibid., 218). Authentic assessment practices are essential to the validity of the badge claim and should not be compromised for the sake of expediency.

**Badge Design Team**

As a final point of consideration, badge program designs will benefit from diverse input and expertise. Assembling a model design and implementation team can be especially helpful when applying for grant funding. When embarking on a badge project, librarians may want to consider enlisting some (or all) of the following professionals:

- instructional designers
- game designers
- information technology professionals
- marketing or publicity specialists
- graphic designers
- Web developers
- badge design consultants
- graduate assistants (e.g., for help reviewing work, troubleshooting, or promoting the badging program)

## CONCLUSION

As an emerging educational technology, digital badging is still being defined by leading practitioners. In order for the badge ecosystem to thrive and for badges to be widely accepted as meaningful credentials, badge designers will need to ensure that badges represent relevant, transferable, and verifiable claims supported by detailed metadata and evidence. As flexible educational tools, badge systems can be used to orient and enhance authentic learning experiences around defined curricular goals.

Unlike degrees, courses, and job qualifications, which might be exaggerated or elaborated, badges cannot pretend to be something they are not. The best way to refute critics who doubt the validity of badges is to prove their value by example, in the design of carefully described, verifiable badges that represent demonstrated competencies.

Rooted in their originating values of transparency and recognition, badges are beacons of purposeful learning. They allow educators to promote and acknowledge significant learning experiences and to signal valuable competencies to employers. When thoughtfully developed and pedagogically grounded, badges can be used to enhance, communicate, and showcase quality teaching and learning.

Table 6.1. Badge Applications Aligned with Backward Design Stages

| Backward Design Stage | Role of the Badge | Design Considerations | Steps |
|---|---|---|---|
| Establish desired results. For example, the badge earner will demonstrate an understanding of their role in the scholarly conversation. | Showcase a learning competency. | What is the purpose of the badge? How is it relevant for the learner and potential reviewers? | 1. Evaluate institutional, local, and national needs. 2. Establish learning outcomes. 3. Create a tentative badge title and image. |
| Determine acceptable evidence. For example, the badge earner will demonstrate mastery of this competency by submitting a culminating project in the form of a reflective essay or media presentation. | Document and validate the learning experience. | Is the competency transferable? How will learners demonstrate competency? What criteria will be used to assess the submitted evidence? | 1. Identify suitable evidence (learning artifacts, test scores, endorsements, etc.). 2. Create assessments. 3. Create metadata according to OBI standards. |
| Plan learning experiences and instruction. For example, in preparation for meeting the learning outcome, the badge earner will be able to distinguish between popular and scholarly resources. | Illustrate learning pathways. | What scaffolding is required to help learners reach the learning goal? How might the larger learning goal be broken down into smaller learning objectives and formative assessments? What infrastructure is needed to support and sustain content delivery and assessment? | 1. Map the curriculum. 2. Determine and/or build supporting infrastructure (e.g., LMS, website, badge issuer integration, etc.). |

## REFERENCES

Bartoletti, Robin, Joyce Seitzinger, and Whitney Kilgore. 2015. "A Badges-First Approach to Learning Pathway Design in Higher Education." Presentation at the 8th Annual Emerging Technologies for Online Learning International Symposium 2015, Dallas, Texas, April 22. Presentation viewable online from http://olc.onlinelearningconsortium.org/conference/2015/et4online/badges-first-approach-learning-pathway-design-higher-education.

Blair, Lucas. 2011. "The Cake Is Not a Lie: How to Design Effective Achievements." *Gamasutra* (blog), April 27. https://www.gamasutra.com/view/feature/134729/the_cake_is_not_a_lie_how_to_.php.

Casilli, Carla. 2014. "The Myth of the Lightweight Badge," *Persona* (blog), February 26. https://carlacasilli.wordpress.com/2014/02/26/the-myth-of-the-lightweight-badge/.

Dimitrijević, Sonja, Vladan Devedzić, Jelena Jovanović, and Nikola Milikić. 2016. "Badging Platforms: A Scenario-Based Comparison of Features and Uses." In *Foundation of Digital Badges and Micro-credentials*, edited by Dirk Ifenthaler, Nicole Bellin-Mularski, and Dana-Kristin Mah, 141–62. New York: Springer International Publishing.

Hickey, Daniel T., and James Willis III. 2017. *Where Badges Appear to Work Better: Findings from the Design Principles Documentation Project*. Bloomington, IN: Center for Research on Learning and Technology, Indiana University. Retrieved online from http://www.badgenumerique.com/wp-content/uploads/2017/08/DPD-Project-Final-Report-Dan-Hickey-Willis-May-2017.pdf.

Higashi, Ross, Christian Schunn, Vu Nguyen, and Scott J. Ososky. 2017. "Coordinating Evidence across Learning Modules Using Digital Badges." In *Design Recommendations for Intelligent Tutoring Systems*, Vol. 5, *Assessment Methods*, edited by Robert Sottilare, Arthur Grasser, Xiangen Hu, and Gregory Goodwin, 53–68. Orlando: US Army Research Laboratory. PDF e-book.

McTighe, Jay, and Grant Wiggins. 2012. *Understanding by Design Framework*. Alexandria, VA: ASCD. http://www.ascd.org/ASCD/pdf/siteASCD/publications/UbD_WhitePaper0312.pdf.

Pagowsky, Nicole. "Keeping Up With Digital Badges for Instruction." *ACRL*. September 13, 2013. http://www.ala.org/acrl/publications/keeping_up_with/digital_badges

Rimland, Emily, and Victoria Raish. 2018. "Design Principles for Digital Badges Used in Libraries." *Journal of Electronic Resources Librarianship* 29 (4): 211–20.

Wiggins, Grant, and Jay McTighe. 2005. *Understanding by Design*. Expanded 2nd ed. Alexandria, VA: ASCD.

# II

# BADGING AND INFORMATION LITERACY: CASE STUDIES

# 7

# Pollak Library Spark Tutorials

*Lindsay O'Neill*

The Spark Tutorials are an online tutorial suite and digital badge system at Pollak Library at California State University, Fullerton (CSUF). The project was initiated in response to growing pressures to scale library instruction to a campus of 40,000 students, to support campus requirements for instructional assessment, and to accommodate CSUF's accrediting body's requirements for information literacy.

The Spark Tutorials program, which takes about an hour to complete, consists of four interactive e-learning tutorials that comprise an orientation to Pollak Library and the basics of library research:

- Services and Collections
- Finding Books
- Finding Articles and Databases
- Help and Support

The tutorials are housed in their own course in CSUF's learning management system (LMS), Moodle. The course is completely automated, and students self-enroll by following a link provided by their instructors. Successfully completing a tutorial with a score of 100 percent on the final quiz triggers issuance of a tutorial-specific digital badge. Completion of all four tutorials in the Pollak Library module triggers issuance of an additional meta-badge to recognize completion of the entire module.

This is the first of four planned modules that, together, will lay a foundation in information literacy for students at California State University, Fullerton. This module and the remaining three are based on a set of learning objectives intended to put students on the path toward mastering ACRL's *Framework for Information Literacy for Higher Education.*

This chapter outlines the inspiration for Pollak Library's Spark Tutorials badges program, its structure, its initial and continuing development, lessons learned, and next steps.

## SETTING

California State University, Fullerton, is a large regional commuter university that offers 109 degree programs with courses taught by more than 2,000 faculty members. In fall 2017, the student body at the campus reached 40,439 enrolled students, a record high for the university (Strategic Communications and Brand Management 2018).

Pollak Library, the sole library on campus, has fifteen instruction librarians who collectively teach more than six hundred one-shot library instruction sessions per year by request from campus faculty. Due to the large and growing student body and limited librarian and library classroom availability (the library has three heavily used computer classrooms), instruction librarians are only able to reach a small percentage of students. Additionally, the instruction program does not have set outcomes or a plan for strategically integrating information literacy instruction across campus curriculum.

Like many other institutions of higher learning, CSUF has been experiencing several challenges over the last few years, including an increased focus on formal assessment of both performance and learning and a growing number of online classes and programs. CSUF is also about to undergo a periodic reaccreditation. CSUF's accrediting body, Western Association of Schools and Colleges Senior College and University Commission (WASC-SCUC), refers to ACRL for its information literacy requirement, which is now one of the required five core competencies for reaccreditation (http://www.ala.org/acrl/issues/infolit/standards/wasc-scuc). However, academic librarians across the United States have been engaged in deep and prolonged discussions about information literacy instruction. When the ACRL *Framework for Information Literacy for Higher Education* was officially adopted in January 2016 by the ACRL board, the old standards were rescinded.

I was hired in mid-2014 as the library's first-ever instructional design librarian. In this new role, I was charged with exploring solutions to expand library instructional offerings both in-person and online, as the library's online offerings were extremely limited (for example, the newest video on the library's YouTube channel was four years old). In the first year of employment, I developed several new videos and also worked on developing an interactive tutorial with my new colleagues. One resulting tutorial, developed in 2015 in collaboration with the librarian serving as the coordinator for CSUF's first year experience program, was the Fluent Information Research tutorial, or FIRe for short. The FIRe tutorial was tested in a very small pilot in fall 2015 as a potential activity for students to complete individually before meeting in person for library instruction, allowing more information literacy instruction to be incorporated into the First Year Experience program. Three instructors in the first year program agreed to have their students complete the tutorial. No formal assessment was performed of the tutorial's efficacy, but it did receive some positive feedback from instructors and students. The FIRe tutorial showed potential for scaling up instruction, or at least facilitating "flipped" instruction, but it was relatively long at thirty minutes and was not tied well enough to ACRL's information literacy standards.

The FIRe tutorial's minor success coupled with the accrediting body's designation of information literacy as a core competency led to a directive from the provost that reached me via the university librarian: *Develop a ten-minute library tutorial that all freshmen will be required to complete.* The university librarian also asked me to chair a new task force to write learning objectives for the library's instruction program based on the new ACRL framework.

The goal for this objective-writing project was to officially ground the library's instruction in formal standards, specifically the ACRL framework because of its use by the accrediting body as its information literacy standards. Ideally this project would give more structure to the library instruction program, allow librarians to better assess students' grasp of information literacy, show progress toward satisfying the accrediting body's information literacy requirement, and facilitate development of new instructional objects and methods to scale up instruction. Overall, a complete set of learning objectives would allow instruction librarians to be more strategic about delivering information literacy instruction and embedding it into curriculum.

More immediately, this project's short-term outcome was a set of information literacy tutorials, which came to include digital badges.

## ANALYSIS

I expected that this project would ultimately take years to complete. It would take a lot of time and concerted, collaborative effort for librarians to write learning objectives tied to the ACRL framework and aligned to campus curriculum. While the university librarian asked for a ten-minute tutorial, it was clear that such a short length would only be able to give a brief overview of the library. It would make more sense to develop a suite of tutorials, which would allow the library to scale basic information literacy instruction and facilitate a foundation in information literacy for all students. Designing and developing tutorials would consume many hours: anywhere from ten hours of design work for a simple, hour-long PowerPoint–based tutorial to eighty hours per hour of seat time for a complex, branching, more simulative tutorial (Blunt 2015). However, the significant time investment in tutorial development would result in expanded learning options that would allow the library to teach more students than ever before.

## A "Required" Tutorial

When the university librarian gave the directive to develop a library tutorial that all freshmen would be required to complete, the word *required* stood out as something especially difficult to accomplish. Clearly it would be critical to be able to track student completion so that the library instruction program could perform more scaffolded information literacy instruction. That is, if *all* freshmen got the basics of library research, librarians who taught sophomores, juniors, and seniors would be freed to teach higher-level skills.

Yet librarians are generally unable to "require" anything of students. Sometimes librarians collaborate with faculty members to require students to complete a library-related assignment, but the faculty member has to do the "requiring," usually by awarding points for the assignment. For a tutorial to be "required," it was clear that there would have to be careful marketing and consensus building with campus partners, particularly programs and classes that targeted freshmen, so that the tutorial would be incorporated as a mandatory part of those classes and programs. This project would also require a method of tracking student completion.

One way to mark student completion is to issue certificates to students who complete the tutorials, but this decentralizes student progress: librarians would not know which students did the work, as only students would have the certificates. Another solution we identified was to issue digital badges for completing the tutorials.

Digital badges originated in video games as motivation and rewards for players to accomplish tasks or to level up. Game characteristics that are reused to gamify another context most often include points, leaderboards, and badges (Hamari, Koivisto, and Sarsa 2014, 3027).

However, it is important to use digital badges with a specific goal in mind, not just because they are a trendy technology. "Popular positive belief in the effectiveness of gamification," says Hamari (2017), "has often been based on the anecdotal conception that, because most games are 'fun' and intrinsically motivating, then any service that uses the same mechanics should also prove to be 'fun' and effective in invoking positive further behavioral outcomes" (469). When used as part of information literacy instruction programs in academic libraries, digital badges do not seem to be "fun" enough to drive student motivation on their own. For example, the library at University of Maryland developed a program that issued badges for workshop attendance and assignment completion on a variety of topics (Baeza and Ippoliti 2017). This co-curricular program aimed to attract participants by offering digital badges for specific accomplishments and also sweetened the deal in its initial format by offering an entry in a drawing to win an iPad upon program completion. Yet only two students completed the work that was required to qualify for the drawing.

A group of librarians at Nova Southeastern University constructed a competency-based digital badges program for information literacy that focused on lower-level skills (Tunon et al. 2015). The authors "envisioned library modules (e.g., find a book in the catalog, find scholarly articles in a database, cite a journal article according to APA, etc.) as well as special customized modules that could be used to meet the different library skills needed for specific academic programs" (159). Students who completed each module would receive a badge. The authors' goal for this program was a "systematic method for documenting information literacy learning outcomes across academic programs instead of the piecemeal system of documentation being used at the time" (159). The badges were intended as a tracking tool, "not an internal motivation tool" (167). The authors experienced some technical issues through the course of the project. Ultimately they were disappointed by their inability to use badges to systematically track student learning due to technical issues, but they plan to troubleshoot and try again.

Ford et al. (2015) at Portland State University designed an information literacy program aligned to campus outcomes that included badges. The authors stated that "too often innovation is championed for innovation's sake rather than to improve pedagogical aims" (35). The authors sought to align learning objectives, assessments, and syllabi to create an effective instructional program that would succeed independent of badges and badge technology (37). Ultimately, they found that program design was an incredible amount of work, and at the time their article was published they had yet to launch their badge-equipped instructional program.

At this relatively early stage in structuring and scaffolding library and information literacy instruction at CSUF, integrating digital badges into this project is mainly a means to an end. "A common mistake among organizations that utilize a gamified application is thinking about the type of technology platform to use first instead of thinking about exactly how they want to design their program" (Ting 2014). An educational program should be design-focused, not technology-focused. Starting with gamified elements rather than effective instructional design will not result in a successful program.

Research on the motivational effect of digital badges in educational contexts is complex. The motivational effect of badges varies based on several factors, including learners' prior knowledge and how the badges are used, particularly whether to reward participation or recognize learning (Abramovich, Schunn, and Higashi, 2013). Digital badges were not found to have much of a motivating effect in other library's experiences (Tunon 2015, 166; Baeza and Ippoliti 2017). Thus digital badges in the Spark Tutorials program would not be intended to serve as a motivational tool, but instead as a useful signifier of accomplishment and as a tracking system so that individual instructors and librarians alike could judge students' progress toward information literacy. The project focused on building an automated online instructional program, and the digital badges were included as an add-on that would allow students to prove to their faculty that they had completed library and information literacy instruction.

### Information Literacy Learning Objectives

The new task force for writing information literacy learning objectives would be key to this project. Aligning library instruction to objectives based on the ACRL framework would allow the library to build a library instruction program that was strategic in deploying information literacy instruction; it would allow individual librarians and the program coordinator to perform more thoughtful assessment, and it would support CSUF's need to show the accrediting body that graduating seniors are information literate.

Many library instruction programs have set learning outcomes, though many are also rewriting their outcomes to match the new framework. Rather than starting with overarching programmatic outcomes, the curriculum team started with the basics to facilitate tutorial development: a set of foundational learning objectives that, if mastered, would provide freshmen with a solid foundation in information literacy. These objectives would put students on a scaffolded path toward mastering the framework. They will also feed into overarching learning outcomes for the library instruction program that are yet to be written but will be based on the framework at a higher level.

## DESIGN

### An Information Literacy Curriculum

Members of the information literacy task force were drawn from the library's instruction and reference unit. Final task force composition included six librarians (including myself) who all had experience teaching information literacy and library research skills to freshmen. To tie into the "FIRe" theme of the Fluent Information Researcher tutorial, the group named their new task force CINDEr: The Committee for INformation literacy DEsign.

The task force approached their work with an eye toward building a competency-based framework for information literacy. Just as the rescinded ACRL standards provided measurable learning objectives, CINDEr's goal was to write learning objectives that, when mastered by students, would prove them competent and ready to move on to higher-level tasks and knowledge. The designers of the ACRL framework intended for the knowledge practices and dispositions to be non-prescriptive so that it is up to local institutions to write their own learning outcomes as needed. Thus the CINDEr task force used the framework to inspire a local information literacy curriculum.

CINDEr performed its task by brainstorming common research assignments that freshmen receive and thinking about the skills and knowledge freshmen would need to be successful with their assignments. Team members also carefully studied the framework and pulled out themes and dispositions for inclusion. Committee members gathered research assignments and lesson plans and extracted common lessons from one-shot library instruction sessions. The ideas were organized into categories and hierarchies. For example, students would need to know what a database *is* before being able to explain *why* it is a useful search tool. Most of the ideas were basic concepts and skills that all students should know to be successful in their college courses that have an information literacy component.

The team focused on writing learning and performance objectives using verbs at the bottom two levels of Bloom's revised taxonomy: *remembering* and *understanding* (see a visual representation of the taxonomy at https://cft.vanderbilt.edu/guides-sub-pages/blooms-taxonomy/). The benefit of focusing on the bottom rungs of Bloom's revised taxonomy is that the resulting learning objectives are translatable into automated tutorials. Learning activity verbs at the remembering level (the lowest level) include *defining*, *identifying*, *indicating*, *matching*, *memorizing*, *recalling*, and *recognizing*. At the understanding level, verbs include *classifying*, *differentiating*, *predicting*, and *summarizing*. Both of these groups of verbs may be fairly easily converted into automated activities such as multiple-choice quizzes, matching exercises, or drag-and-drop exercises.

I hold a second masters in instructional design and so served as the team's instructional designer, organizing and structuring the team's work into specific and measurable learning objectives, which the team then reviewed and critiqued. This was a recursive process, continuing until the team had created a structured, foundational set of learning objectives organized into four modules: Pollak Library (an overview of the library and basic library skills), Evaluation, Searching, and Citations. Each section is divided into subsections that include overarching learning goals and specific learning objectives (http://libraryguides.fullerton.edu/cinder).

Work was considered provisionally complete when the team felt that the curriculum would facilitate freshman students' success in their first-year courses. Additionally, students who mastered these objectives would be set on the path toward working on higher-level information literacy skills. The resulting document is a work-in-progress: it will continue to be revised and built upon as librarians on the CINDEr task force write higher-level, scaffolded learning objectives that integrate into campus curriculum. Further work on the CINDEr curriculum will likely hinge on subject librarians analyzing their departments' curriculum and identifying courses and assignments that align well with a hierarchical information literacy curriculum, as individual subjects and programs will have unique information literacy needs.

### Naming and Storyboarding the Tutorials

Members of CINDEr agreed to offer design input and feedback on the tutorials, which began with naming the project. As the CINDEr team set out to create a suite of tutorials, they decided to continue using the "FIRe" theme to name the new tutorials the "Spark" Tutorials. The word *spark* also connotes "sparking" information literacy in students and has served as a useful branding tool.

Name decided, it was time to begin designing the tutorials. First, the team created a text-based storyboard in Microsoft Word to begin designing assessment, practice, and content for each learning objective. Second, we translated the draft text storyboard into a visual storyboard using PowerPoint. We created a slide in PowerPoint for each slide that would appear in the tutorial. Incorporating feedback from CINDEr team members was crucial to ensuring the inclusion of all essential information and to spotting problematic phrasings in the tutorial voiceover.

### Badges and Competency-Based Learning

This project aimed to align each badge with specific learning objectives. Digital badges are often associated with a competency-based model of instruction and "serve as a way . . . to certify that a learner has gained competence or expert knowledge in a certain skill, concept, or phenomena" (Raish and Rimland 2016).

As tutorial design began, we wrote the assessment, practice, and content to match the learning objectives for each tutorial, using a process commonly referred to as "backward design" (Wiggins and McTighe cited in Bowen 2017). In this model, instruction and assessment are aligned to specific and measurable learning objectives, and the assessment is designed first. Competency-based assessments are simply "authentic measures of mastery in a given domain" (Lammers 2015), so each tutorial was designed to simulate library research activities to facilitate transfer to the real world.

After CINDEr wrote the learning objectives (http://libraryguides.fullerton.edu/CINDEr), the next step was to design aligned learning experiences. For the Services and Collections tutorial, for example, one of the learning objectives is to "differentiate between librarians, Circulation, and Interlibrary Loan." The aligned content for this part of the tutorial consists of three short videos that explain the difference between these services (as well as how to locate them). The practice activity for this learning objective is a game in which students earn points for identifying the service where they would accomplish specific tasks. Then, the final assessment remixes the game along with several multiple-choice questions to verify that the learners are now able to differentiate between librarians, circulation, and interlibrary loan. Students who complete the tutorial with 100 percent accuracy (they can try more than once) prove that they have mastered the aligned learning objective.

Using the competency-based model is not only important because it keeps a tutorial focused and creates a more effective learning experience. It is also important that when students complete the tutorial and earn a badge for their efforts the badge is meaningful due to their mastery of the learning objectives. Rather than sitting through a video or another passive activity, students are active and engaged.

## Choosing a Delivery Platform

It is easy to decide that badges should be incorporated into an online learning program. It is another challenge altogether to figure out how to deploy tutorials and digital badges. The task force evaluated several badge platforms, including Purdue's Passport (https://www.openpassport.org/), which would be incredibly expensive for CSUF, due to the pricing model that is calculated based on the size of the student body (CSUF has forty thousand students). We also considered the WordPress–based website option, in which the Badge OS and LearnDash WordPress plug-ins can be combined to issue badges for online learning. In addition, there were a variety of other plug-ins and add-ons available to integrate into learning management systems (O'Neill 2017). After thorough research, I concluded that adding a freely available badges module to the campus learning management system, Moodle, would be the best choice for CSUF.

Deploying library e-learning and digital badges in the campus learning management system was ideal, because students were already using the platform for most of their classes. Even if all of their classes are in-person, many CSUF instructors use Moodle to store syllabi and collect assignments. So I started lobbying CSUF's Moodle administrators to add the badges module. After about a year of identifying stakeholders and engaging in persuasive conversations, the Moodle administrators added the badges module, and I was the first to hold the badge coordinator role in Moodle.

While it is very simple to set up a course in Moodle to offer library tutorials (the Moodle administrators were more than happy to help), each course is private, and faculty could only check student completion of the tutorials if they were each individually granted an "instructor" role in the course. Adding instructors was time-consuming because it had to be done manually, and it also opened up concerns about student privacy and other issues. Faculty would be able to see *all* students' progress, not just those enrolled in their home courses, and they would be able to edit course content, which could lead to problems.

However, by enabling digital badges, instructors would be able to verify student completion of the modules without requiring instructor access to the course. The badges would appear in students' Moodle profiles, and because badges have metadata, instructors could see what the students had to do to earn the badge, confirming that the students reached a minimum grade. For this project, the badges were only issued for scores of 100 percent.

**Development Phase**

Once fully storyboarded, I used Articulate Storyline 2 to develop the tutorials. Storyline is an effective choice of software because it may be used to develop tutorials that are as interactive as desired, up to and including simulations (e.g., of database searches). Furthermore, tutorials produced with Storyline may be technically packaged in such a way that, when embedded into a learning management system like Moodle, they will communicate student behavior and performance to the grade book.

This technical packaging is known as SCORM, which is simply an industry-standardized format for e-learning products. According to their website, "SCORM tells programmers how to write their code so that it can 'play well' with other e-learning software" (http://scorm.com/scorm-explained/). Major tutorial authoring software like Storyline, Adobe Captivate, and TechSmith's

Camtasia have the capability to publish tutorials as SCORM, as well as HTML5 and Flash.

Developers have two options for making tutorials usable for learners: Published tutorials can either be hosted on a server for public access as HTML5 or Flash (as if they were Web pages), though they would not collect any learner information, or tutorials may be packaged as SCORM and embedded into an LMS. In this case, the tutorials are still published as HTML5 or Flash as well, but they are zipped into a folder that contains SCORM files that facilitates reporting back to the LMS. These zipped files are uploaded into the LMS.

The very first tutorial, which is about fifteen minutes long, took about twenty-two hours to develop, but subsequent development of each of the remaining ten- to fifteen-minute tutorials took eight to ten hours, since the first could be reused as a template and formatting took much less time. Overall it took about seventy-five hours to design and develop all four tutorials and to successfully integrate them into Moodle. Once complete, the tutorials underwent thorough user testing to eliminate bugs and ensure an effective learning experience.

Simple badge art was designed using a free online badge builder from Credly (http://credly.com). The library course was created in Moodle, and I embedded the tutorials and configured the course to issue digital badges for 100 percent scores on the tutorials. A meta-badge is also issued for completing all tutorials in a module.

Faculty can check their students' Moodle profiles to verify that they have earned the badges. Meanwhile, the library gets hard data on students who complete online library instruction, including the number of badges issued for successful tutorial completion and data on student behavior within the tutorials.

## Buy-In from First Year Experience Program

At the same time that tutorial development was underway, CSUF's First Year Experience program was undergoing a dramatic transformation. From 2002 to 2016, Freshman Programs at Cal State Fullerton was a first-year seminar program for a limited number of freshmen (about six hundred) who had to apply and be accepted. Students in the program enrolled in a three-unit section of a course called UNIV 100 in their first semester. Officially titled Foundations for College Success and Lifelong Learning, the course offered an introduction and semester-long orientation to what Cal State Fullerton had to offer.

The Pollak Library is a long-time partner in this program, appointing a librarian each year as the Freshman Programs liaison. Each section (usually about twenty-five students) was assigned a liaison librarian, and the librarian collaborated with the faculty member to teach an instruction session to help the students complete a research assignment.

The program was very successful in retention rates of enrolled freshmen. For example, in 2013, 97 percent of freshmen enrolled in Freshman Programs moved on to become sophomores, in contrast to only 84 percent of all other freshmen (California State University, Fullerton, 2013).

In 2016 the program director retired, and the program was rebranded as First Year Experience (FYE). The new interim director performed a major redesign of the UNIV 100 course. The redesigned course was submitted to and approved by the campus curriculum committee as counting toward general education requirements.

After the new interim director was announced, I, as instruction coordinator, reached out to the new director along with the newly retitled FYE liaison librarian. Development of the Spark Tutorials was well under way, so the two coordinators pitched the tutorials as a new option for library instruction instead of or in addition to the traditional one-shot session. UNIV 100 instructors could choose a one-shot session, have students complete the tutorials, or both. Regardless of the content of the one-shot session, if they completed the Spark Tutorials, students would all have the same foundation in library research/information literacy skills. The director of the First Year Experience program loved the tutorials idea because of the standardized learning experience and tracking ability and wrote them in as a required assignment in the syllabus.

## IMPLEMENTATION

The first four Spark Tutorials were completed in August 2016. They went live in Moodle at the beginning of the fall semester after thorough testing and debugging. The FYE instructors were provided with the permalink to the course with the direction to have their students self-enroll in the course to complete the tutorials. As soon as each tutorial was completed with a 100 percent score, students were notified that they had earned the corresponding badge. Once students completed all four tutorials, they received an additional meta-badge signifying completion of the first module.

The implementation went very smoothly. A feedback form and contact information were included in the course's information so that any student who experienced a problem could reach out for help. There were only a couple of issues reported that were swiftly and easily resolved.

Just under seven hundred students completed the Spark Tutorials in fall 2016. Most of these were likely students enrolled in the FYE program (which is about six hundred students), as the tutorial suite was not actively marketed to faculty other than as a bullet point in a library newsletter e-mail and as a link on the library's instruction Web page.

## EVALUATION

At the end of the 2016–2017 academic year, 882 participants were enrolled in the Spark Tutorials course. Over 2,400 digital badges were issued to students who completed one or more of the four tutorials, and an additional 556 meta-badges were earned by those completing the entire module (table 7.1).

At the time of writing, the existing Spark Tutorials are almost two years old. While almost complete, the next module is not yet ready, because designing and developing it is such a time-consuming process. It took seventy-five hours to design and develop the first module, which has to be completely revamped due to the library's adoption of the discovery tool PRIMO as well as a complete library website redesign. There are three multi-part modules still to be developed, which will probably take several years, because I am the

Table 7.1. Badges Issued for Spark Tutorial Completion, 2016–2017

| Spark Tutorial | Badges Issued 2016/17 |
|---|---|
| Pollak Library Finding Articles and Databases | 611 |
| Pollak Library Finding Books | 586 |
| Pollak Library Help Support | 561 |
| Pollak Library Orientation | 556 |
| Pollak Library Services and Collections | 658 |

sole driver behind this project, doing all the design and development, and I have many other demands on my time as a reference and instruction librarian.

This project has yet to be formally assessed, so feedback is piecemeal and anecdotal. While several FYE faculty gave positive feedback on the tutorials, *all* of the instructors still elected to have the librarian teach a one-shot session. The faculty liked that the tutorials extended library instruction beyond just the one-shot session. Assigning the tutorials in advance also allowed the one-shots to include more hands-on time for students to work on research skills rather than being overly informational and allows librarians to address higher-level ACRL framework concepts. One or two FYE instructors complained that the process to check student completion of the tutorials was too onerous: the digital badges are only visible in students' profiles, so faculty have to check each students' profile for the badge.

The LMS collects information on how students answer each question and interact with each activity within the tutorials, but the data is massive and difficult to parse. It will be a future project to examine student behavior within the tutorials themselves.

Marketing of the Spark Tutorials was minimal, partly because I have limited time to do the legwork, and partly because the first year served as a pilot that would facilitate identification of shortcomings with the platform or opportunities for improvement. The project became more time-consuming to further develop over its first year as increasing pressure came from library leadership to market and assess this project on top of designing, developing, maintaining, and troubleshooting it, with no additional assistance offered.

Because students self-enroll in the Moodle course, it is unknown what prompted them to log in, in the first place, or even whether they were completing the tutorials because they were assigned or voluntarily for their own knowledge (as several graduate students reported to me that they did). It is possible that news of the library tutorials spread by word-of-mouth, as FYE faculty only teach for the program part-time and work in other departments as well.

Through the handful of responses sent through the in-course feedback form, and a few comments sent directly to me, students said that they liked the gamified style of the tutorials and were gratified to get the positive reinforcement of the digital badge. Moodle sends a message to students about an earned badge as soon as they complete a tutorial successfully. In the future, a survey will be sent to students enrolled in the course to gather their feedback.

While much work remains, the module that is complete has served as an important and successful demonstration of the possibilities of expanding library instruction online. This project attracted interest from CSUF's campus assessment office as crucial evidence of meeting the accrediting body's information literacy requirement as the campus ramps up its reaccreditation efforts.

As each tutorial was developed, the newly created embedded videos were also uploaded to the library's YouTube channel so that they could be used by librarians and faculty. While each video has less than one hundred views, they are a satisfying step toward expanding the library's online instruction.

These tutorials also allow librarians to continue to offer instruction to classes that are not able to either come into the library or have a librarian come to them. Online classes are especially well served by the availability of online tutorials. While automated tutorials are best suited for lower-level learning, fleshing out an ACRL framework–based badges system opens up opportunities for higher-level project-based activities that would allow even online students to master more sophisticated framework content with a librarian's guidance, by reviewing student work and offering meaningful feedback.

Aligning the tutorials with learning objectives based on the framework was a significant accomplishment that grants the project more cachet. Librarians are able to pitch faculty on the pedagogical underpinnings of the tutorials and relate them to campus curricular goals. This is a crucial feature that faculty and CSUF administrators understand and appreciate.

In fact, the support of faculty and administrators, particularly the interim director of Online Education and Training, helped the library gain better representation in Moodle beyond the Spark Tutorials course. A new library widget was added to the current version of Moodle that automatically appears in every course. The widget includes a search box for library resources, a link to the Spark Tutorials, and a link for students to get help from librarians.

## LESSONS LEARNED AND NEXT STEPS

### Challenges

Being the first adopter of digital badges at CSUF has certainly come with a learning curve. It was very challenging to lobby for the badge technology, to learn how to use it, and to communicate its value to others across campus. While it was gratifying to be approached by other CSUF departments as a "badge expert" who could advise on this topic, it was aggravating to navigate the challenges of being first and having no on-campus resources to call upon for help. However, as badges catch on at CSUF, it is likely that several of these challenges will be worked out.

Each year, the campus creates a brand-new Moodle system rather than updating the current system. Existing courses must be transferred to the new

Moodle. Unfortunately, course enrollments cannot transfer along with the Spark Tutorials course to the new system. Furthermore, most distressingly, the digital badges earned by students will not transfer either. That means that the digital badges earned by students will only remain in the Moodle version in which they were earned. Thus students would have to complete the tutorials again anew each year to earn back the badges and prove to their faculty that the tutorials were completed.

It should not be this way. Moodle employs the Open Badge standard created by Mozilla, which is commonly used by most badge platforms. According to CSUF's Moodle administrators, there is supposed to be an additional server component, Mozilla Backpack, which should store badge information and make it transferrable to any other system that supports the Open Badge standard, which would include the new version of Moodle. Unfortunately, for an unknown reason (LMS administrators are mute on this), it does not work, and it is not a priority project for CSUF's Moodle administrators, so the badges will remain locked in whatever Moodle version they were earned.

However, there is another version of Moodle on campus, called Communities, that is used as an online space for campus groups and committees to chat and store files. It lives side-by-side with the main instance that contains students' courses. It is simply updated each year, not re-launched as a completely new instance. I will likely re-create the Spark Tutorials course and badges in this parallel Moodle so that students can make progress and keep their earned badges in one place for however long they are students on campus. I really liked having the Spark Tutorials in the same place as students' regular courses, but the stability of the Communities Moodle is very important.

An additional challenge is that the Pollak Library's website has been completely redesigned and a new discovery search tool implemented. The website looks dramatically different than it did, and the library now uses PRIMO as a discovery layer instead of the previous homegrown solution. While much needed, these aesthetic and mechanical changes mean that each Spark Tutorial has to be overhauled both with new screenshots and video captures of the website, and the website simulations will have to be completely redeveloped to match the new mechanics of PRIMO.

## Successes

The fact that 882 learners self-enrolled in the Spark Tutorials in its very first year with extremely minimal marketing and only one formal program partnership, with FYE, is fairly impressive. The library is still far from requiring all freshmen to complete the Spark Tutorials, but the provost has directed that the FYE program expand to encompass all freshmen and transfer students by fall 2018. Unfortunately the program now has yet another new interim director for the 2017–2018 academic year who is, again, redesigning the course. But the FYE coordinator librarian and I have participated in initial redesign efforts and feel confident that integrating the Spark Tutorials into the course syllabus will result in many more students completing the tutorials than ever before. This will put the library a major step closer toward implementing a CSUF–wide information literacy co-curriculum.

Future plans for writing more learning objectives will involve greater partnerships with faculty across campus, as upper-division courses have subject-specific needs that blanket objectives will not meet. Ideally subject librarians will develop their educational technology skills so that they can adapt or develop tutorials that are discipline-specific. This might mean multiple versions of a tutorial or custom tutorials created from scratch, all of which will be part of a larger, cohesive system.

Overall, these tutorials are part of a culture change occurring at CSUF that focuses on greater student success and better services and support to all students, including those that are enrolled in hybrid or online courses. Integrating digital badges into this project has helped its structure become visible to students and faculty and is a step in the right direction toward tracking student learning and also facilitating a full information literacy instructional program.

From the start it was obvious that this was going to be a multi-year project because of the incredible time involved in designing learning objectives and designing, developing, and testing the tutorials and technology. However, it seemed like it would be possible to have designed and developed more than one module in a full year. The pressure from library leadership to manage, market, and assess every aspect of the Spark Tutorials on my own was unexpected and led to much greater time investment than initially expected. In the future, it will be essential to train and include more librarians and staff in this project so that it can grow. Maybe they will even get a badge for their efforts!

## REFERENCES

Abramovich, Samuel, Christian Schunn, and Ross Higashi. 2013. "Are Badges Useful in Education? It Depends upon the Type of Badge and Expertise of Learner." *Educational Technology Research and Development* 61 (2): 217–32.

Baeza, Victor, and Cinthya Ippoliti. 2017. "Digital Badges: A Tool for More than Micro-credentialing." Presented at Electronic Resources and Libraries, Austin, Texas, April 3.

Blunt, Rick. 2015. "Innovations in Interactivity and Interactions." Presented at DevLearn, Las Vegas, Nevada, October 2.

Bowen, Ryan S. 2017. "Understanding by Design." Center for Teaching, Vanderbilt University. https://cft.vanderbilt.edu/understanding-by-design/.

Burnette, Diane. 2016. "The Renewal of Competency-Based Education: A Review of the Literature." *The Journal of Continuing Higher Education* 64 (2): 84–93.

California State University, Fullerton. 2013. "Freshman Programs: Welcome!" http://www.fullerton.edu/admissions/welcomeday/freshmanprograms_2013.pdf.

Ford, Emily, Betty Izumi, Jost Lottes, and Dawn Richardson. 2015. "Badge It! A Collaborative Learning Outcomes Based Approach to Integrating Information Literacy Badges within Disciplinary Curriculum." *Reference Services Review* 43 (1): 31–44.

Hamari, Juho. 2017. "Do Badges Increase User Activity? A Field Experiment on the Effects of Gamification." *Computers in Human Behavior* 71 (June): 469–78.

Hamari, Juho, Jonna Koivisto, and Harri Sarsa. 2014. "Does Gamification Work? A Literature Review of Empirical Studies on Gamification." Presented 2014 47th Hawaii International Conference, Waikoloa, Hawaii, January 6–9. Published by IEE, pp. 3025–34. http://ieeexplore.ieee.org/stamp/stamp.jsp?tp=&arnumber=6758978.

Lammers, Darci. 2015. "Assessment Strategies for Competency-Based Learning." Presented at DevLearn, Las Vegas, Nevada, October 1.

O'Neill, J. Lindsay. 2017. "Digital Badges Exposed: Technology behind a Library Badges Program." Presented at Association of College and Research Libraries Virtual Conference, March 23.

Raish, Victoria, and Emily Rimland. 2016. "Employer Perceptions of Critical Information Literacy Skills and Digital Badges." *College and Research Libraries* 77 (1): 87–113.

Strategic Communications and Brand Management. 2018. "[2017] Fact Sheet." California State University, Fullerton (website), June 1. http://news.fullerton.edu/_resources/multimedia/factsheet.pdf.

Ting, Deanna. 2014. "Rules of the Game." *Incentive* 188 (6): 12–18.

Tunon, Johanna, Laura Lucio Ramirez, Brian Ryckman, Loy Campbell, and Courtney Mlinar. 2015. "Creating an Information Literacy Badges Program in Blackboard: A Formative Program Evaluation." *Journal of Library and Information Services in Distance Learning* 9 (1–2): 157–69.

# 8

## Competency-Based Education, Badging, and the Library

*Michael Fosmire and Amy S. Van Epps*

Competency-based education (CBE) has experienced a resurgence in popularity in recent years as the spiraling costs of higher education have led thought leaders to seek ways to decrease time to degree completion and to deliver instruction more affordably. By focusing on mastery rather than on course-based success metrics, CBE can award credit for students' prior experiences and expertise. With advances in learning and information technologies, students also have many more options for navigating their learning path, including utilizing freely available online learning objects. As long as students can demonstrate their mastery of subject matter, through badges or other performance assessments, they can work toward their degree at their own pace, potentially saving time and money for themselves and their institution.

We came to the intersection of competency-based education and badging through our involvement with an initiative at the Purdue Polytechnic Institute (PPI). After being at the university for a year, our new university president issued a challenge to the campus to develop a competency-based degree program, with the first successful department or program receiving $500,000 in funding (Hamon Kuns 2014). PPI submitted the winning proposal for the competency-based program to create what would become the transdisciplinary studies in technology (TST) degree (ibid.). The libraries have had a longstanding relationship with the PPI, working with them to integrate information literacy into their first-year Introduction to Design Thinking course, which is required of all their majors. The TST degree provided an opportunity to expand our involvement, as it was founded on an inquiry-based approach to learning that incorporated authentic, hands-on problem solving. In order to switch from a course-based model to an outcome-based model of measuring student achievement, the TST program developers realized they needed to create different structures for capturing and monitoring progress toward mastery of the outcomes required to earn the degree.

In tracing our path through CBE and badges, we need to start with a discussion of what CBE is, where it came from, and why it is currently experiencing a resurgence of interest in higher education. We will then discuss how the relatively new technology of digital badging can enable the scalability of CBE experiences. Finally, we will demonstrate an implementation of the CBE/digital badging nexus through the case study of Purdue University's TST degree program.

## COMPETENCY-BASED EDUCATION

Over the years, competency-based education and, indeed, the concept of competence have held different meanings depending on context. Fundamentally, a competency-based approach to education focuses on determining what a student needs to be able to do in a particular situation and then developing an assessment tool or method that enables the student to demonstrate their competence to meet that need. Grant (1979) describes CBE as deriving "a curriculum from an analysis of a prospective or actual role in modern society and that attempts to certify student progress on the basis of demonstrated performance in some or all aspects of that role" (6). A more formal, and detailed, definition describes CBE as "a data-based, adaptive, performance-oriented set of integrated processes that facilitate, measure, record, and certify within the context of flexible time parameters the demonstration of known, explicitly stated, and agreed upon learning outcomes that reflect successful functioning in life roles" (Spady 1977, 10). The Competency-Based Education Network (2017)—or C-BEN, as it is known—takes a process-based approach, where "competency-based education combines an intentional and transparent approach to curricular design with an academic model in which the time it takes to demonstrate competencies varies and the expectations about learning are held constant. Students acquire and demonstrate their knowledge and skills by engaging in learning exercises, activities, and experiences that align with clearly defined programmatic outcomes. Students receive proactive guidance and support from faculty and staff. Learners earn credentials by demonstrating mastery through multiple forms of assessment, often at a personalized pace."

At its core, CBE focuses on performance rather than time spent on a task, so that a student can chart a self-paced course through a curriculum and competencies may be acquired through a variety of activities. A performance (e.g., writing a paper, solving a problem, building or operating an artifact, giving a speech) demonstrates the student's underlying competence, which is used to certify the student's achievement. The traditional educational model provides course-level certification of mastery, typically with a grade indicating degree of achievement. This model leads to certain questions: What does a C grade in calculus actually mean? Can the student differentiate a function but not integrate or integrate some functions but not others? At the course level, a C might signify excellence in one content area and incompetence in another or, alternatively, a mediocre skill level across all topics. CBE attempts to provide more specific and timely indicators of achievement. If a student masters differentiation in the first week of study, that competency can be certified, and the student can move on. If the student never manages to integrate in polar coordinates, that too is reflected in the record. Compared to a C in calculus, a CBE record can be much more informative. The processes by which competencies are identified, assessed, and scaffolded are manifold and provide a breadth of CBE case studies.

## History

Competency-based education achieved a level of popularity in the 1960s and 1970s as a response to pressures to decrease cost and duration of academic programs, a desire for individualized paths to learning, and a desire to better align educational content with skills needed in the workforce. Many of these pressures still exist today and, in combination with innovative, educational technologies such as digital badge platforms, are fueling the current resurgence of competency-based programs. In the 1960s, the federal government, through Fund for the Improvement of Postsecondary Education (FIPSE) Grants, supported the development of several pilot competency-based educational programs. By the end of the seventies, however, CBE had mostly disappeared from higher education, except in a few smaller institutions, such as Alverno College.

Gallagher (2014) identifies several challenges of the initial CBE movement that led to its lack of success. While sidestepping the question of whether higher education is responsible for credentialing workers or educating citizens, we note Gallagher's assertions that early CBE programs suffered from high attrition in the program, lack of buy-in from students and faculty, the "unbundling" of the teaching process (with different entities responsible for instruction, certification, and content creation) leading to fractionalization and lack of coherence, a proliferation of increasingly specialized competencies, the lack of readiness of students—particularly those most in need—for self-directed and intentional learning, and the isolating nature of self-paced or individualized learning. While Torshen (1977) extols the potential for CBE to focus on "the goals most relevant and important for students to attain, to design and implement instruction that maximizes likelihood that students will attain those goals" (24), he acknowledges that a true CBE program would require a complete transformation of the educational system and training of instructors, as well as requiring many more resources to address the specific, individual learning needs of students. Any discussion of current CBE innovations needs to consider these challenges.

A new door of opportunity opened for CBE development around the turn of the twenty-first century, with the reauthorization of the Higher Education Act in 2005, which allowed for direct assessment of learning outcomes and the proliferation of online instructional materials and programs. Some of the key concepts of CBE, such as personalized learning and persisting until mastery, have been recognized by national organizations. The National Academy of Engineering (2008), for example, named advancing personalized learning as a Grand Challenge (http://engineeringchallenges.org/challenges/learning.aspx), and the New Media Consortium (Adams et al. 2017) identified "processes for assessing nuanced skills at a personal level" (2) as one of their "key trends" in technology and education and identified "integrating formal and informal learning" as a key challenge (22). The Lumina Foundation (2014) sponsored the development of the Degree Qualifications Profile, which can form the backbone of a CBE program. The C-BEN network, with thirty-three current member institutions, provides a community of development for CBE programs. While most institutions are still experimenting, introducing a program here or there to test the waters, some of the more robust, notable examples are the University of Wisconsin's Flexible Option and Southern New Hampshire University's College for America (see Klein-Collins 2012 for a review of CBE programs).

CBE programs tend to fall into one of two categories: course-based programs and direct assessment programs. Course-based programs, such as Alverno's, involve students learning in a formal classroom environment. The courses address a variety of competencies, but the students must be certified independently for those competencies—that is, passing the course does not by itself fulfill a competency. Direct assessment programs, such as Western Governors University, have no required courses; rather, students can demonstrate competencies at their own pace, acquired through coursework or work or life experiences.

## Digital Badges and CBE

Digital badges (Olneck 2012) and CBE (Johnstone and Soares 2014) both have advocates who proclaim them disruptive technologies, with Olneck asserting that digital badges are "insurgent credentials" that can subvert educational institutions' monopoly on credentialing achievement. Lipscomb University's Customized, Outcome-based Relevant Evaluation (CORE) badges (http://www.lipscomb.edu/professionalstudies/core-badges) provide an example of a badging system for competencies that complement content-based student outcomes, based on the OSI Polaris® Competency Model (Organization Systems International 2015), popular in industry. Lipscomb's badges are organized into seven domains: Communication, Conceptual, Contextual, Interpersonal, Leadership, Management, and Personal. Within those domains, the badges signify and certify the domain, specific competency earned, and level of competency.

The characteristics of digital badges have been explained elsewhere in this volume, so we will focus on the application of digital badges in a CBE environment. A digital badging framework can serve a number of purposes in support of CBE, among them tracking, transparency, organization of and access to learning materials, and motivation.

Digital badges, particularly ones compliant with the Open Badges Specification (IMS Global Learning Consortium 2017), are portable and transparent. They contain metadata about the acquisition of the competency and may provide evidence of the performance that earned the competency. Such a digital badge framework adds significant value to the competency process since the student can display their competency in an information-rich way—for example, linking from a CV to the curated portfolio from a digital badging system. The digital badging platform can also provide a clearinghouse for instructional content related to the competency being worked on. One of the challenges of a personalized learning approach advocated in CBE is the requirement for a wide variety of resources to meet the specific needs of each individual user. With education and information technologies, access to customized sources, including adaptive learning environments, can be organized and deployed more efficiently and easily than previously.

**Student Motivation**

Creating and sustaining student motivation is perhaps the most important, and challenging, aspect of creating an effective learning environment. Many of the challenges of CBE mentioned above can be classified as motivational considerations, for the students or the instructors. Pintrich (2003) lists five factors that impact student motivation: self-efficacy, self-determination and personal control, personal and situational interest, value calculations, and goal-orientation. Fosmire (2014) describes how these factors are frequently expressed in the context of information literacy instruction—for example, that overconfidence leads to a lack of motivation to improve searching and evaluation skills.

Self-efficacy relates to students' belief that they are capable of learning. If they believe they can learn something, they are more likely to try. If students believe they have control over their own learning and behavior, they will also be more successful. If they feel they are being led through a series of tasks, on the other hand, they might be successful in the short-term, but the long-term effect is a decrease of interest in the topic. Personal and situational interest relate to students' innate interest in a topic, while value calculations refer to students' internal cost-benefit analysis of the competing factors of interest, utility, importance, and cost associated with a task. Finally, goal orientation refers to the specific, intrinsic goals students have for being in the classroom, which may or may not be the same as the instructor's goals (Pintrich 2003).

Within CBE, digital badge platforms can address some of the challenges of motivation, if properly constructed. Badges can improve self-efficacy by providing specific, targeted feedback on the status of a student's competency and expertise. Utilizing adaptive learning techniques, the digital badging environment can provide real-time feedback for students to address challenges and provide scaffolded content of appropriate difficulty for the student's current level. By focusing on outcomes rather than tasks, badges can provide a variety of paths through the competencies. These paths can potentially link to a variety of underlying resources that students can choose from to create their personalized, self-paced journeys through the content.

Within the outcomes-based approach, CBE allows students to follow their own personal interests as long as the artifacts they produce or performances they demonstrate meet those outcomes. By disaggregating courses from outcomes, a CBE program may allow students to choose the content area they work in to achieve those outcomes. Value calculations can be complicated, since a variety of factors need to be weighed. However, one could argue in favor of a few factors of the value calculation. Decreased cost for students, in time and money, can be a valuable advantage. When a competency is mastered, a student can move on to another one, rather than waiting around while the rest of the community masters a topic. Finally, in the area of goal orientation, CBE and badges make the learning outcomes explicit at the outset of the program. Regarding goal orientation, Pintrich (2003) remarks that learning for mastery rather than comparative performance is an important design principle for promoting goal-orientation motivation. Since CBE is a mastery-based approach to learning and badges directly signify mastery, this approach aligns well with this factor.

While CBE in a digital badging environment can be an effective pedagogy, we do not mean to imply it is the only way to achieve an effective learning environment. Indeed, a CBE approach improperly implemented can be as ineffective as any other environment. For example, in a self-paced, student-directed environment, a significant challenge may be students' lack of preparation for personal management and self-direction. Many students do not have the self-regulation skills to work on complex tasks and skills independently, so providing guideposts, feedback on progress, and encouragement to persist in their efforts is vital for student success. Badges, while providing timely and specific feedback, may also be viewed as extrinsic motivators, decreasing students' self-direction and leading to a perspective of "checking the boxes." Abramovich, Schunn, and Higashi (2013) note that in an educational setting, different kinds of badges can motivate, or demotivate, students differently based on their prior preparation. As with any technique, implementation of a CBE badging program needs to be mindful of the potential pitfalls for students, to encourage "deep learning" and persistence in the program.

## CBE AND BADGES IN THE PURDUE TST PROGRAM

To track student progress toward their degree, the transdisciplinary studies in technology (TST) degree program chose to use Passport (http://www.openpassport.org), a home-grown digital badging platform developed by Purdue University's Teaching and Learning with Technology group, compliant with the Mozilla Open Badges Infrastructure (OBI) (Mozilla Foundation 2016).

The initial collection of badges was designed specifically to reflect the content in the two signature courses offered in the TST program, a hands-on design course centered around a major "build" project and a seminar course focused on synthesizing and communicating ideas related to a contemporary transdisciplinary issue in technology. Each badge was created to be equivalent to one credit hour of work, to help make achievements commensurate, and transferrable, to more traditional degree programs. In this model, granular certifications for each learning outcome were instantiated in the challenges that make up each badge. Most of the badges contained between three and five challenges.

As information literacy is a required component of the university's core curriculum, librarians have been part of the TST degree development from the beginning, and there was widespread support for incorporating information literacy into the competency and badge frameworks. In the first semester of implementation, fall 2014, the two signature TST courses were the Design Lab, roughly equivalent to the Introduction to Design Thinking class required for all PPI majors, and Digital Narratives, which combined the content of standard intro English composition and speech communications courses.

Since the original Introductory English Composition and Introduction to Design Thinking courses meet the university's core curriculum requirements for information literacy, there was a good fit to include an information literacy badge in the context of both Digital Narratives and Design Lab.

In the Digital Narratives class, which was co-taught by a librarian and several disciplinary faculty, the librarian facilitated much of the content for the information literacy badge. Instruction on the use of information in support of design decisions was also included in the Design Lab class, introducing students to the value of information literacy in the technical realm. Artifacts generated in either Digital Narratives or Design Lab, or any other course the students were taking, could be used to demonstrate competency for the information literacy badge.

The original information literacy badge contained five challenges, which paralleled the structure of the other badges in use in the 2014–2015 academic year. The challenges were written collaboratively by the TST faculty fellows, including two librarians, to map directly to the ACRL Information Literacy Competency Standards (ACRL 2000). Achieving the badge was straightforward for students who completed the activities designed for the class sessions dedicated to information literacy. The work of identifying keywords, crafting a research question, identifying databases, comparing results from databases, and evaluating the quality of the results were all tracked on worksheets that could be completed and submitted to meet the initial challenges. The final two challenges included (1) the use of information, which required the submission of a paper that used information appropriately and contained proper citations and references, and (2) an understanding of intellectual property, which was demonstrated through completing a quiz after reading online content.

This model for competence development worked relatively well, and the badging platform functioned as something like a learning management system, where assignments were submitted, assessed by the faculty, and returned to the students. The faculty learned two important lessons during the initial implementation: First, we had overestimated students' readiness to embrace this freedom and pursue the badges on an independent schedule. We were not adequately prepared to work with first year students who are the product of the current K–12 system, which tends to promote test taking and meeting specific deadlines and does not allow for a lot of individual exploration or autonomy in assignments. Second, we found that students were unprepared for the process of multiple revisions on an item to strengthen and hone the work until they demonstrated mastery. Instead, they wanted to submit once and move on to the next item, accepting whatever grade they had earned from that work. This mind-set is antithetical to the process of competency-based education, which requires demonstration of mastery of each competency, however long it takes to achieve.

When looking at the entire degree, there were some drawbacks to the model of having each badge equivalent to one credit hour of course material. To embrace true transdisciplinarity, the program does not have course restrictions or rigid plans of study beyond two signature classes offered by TST each semester. Instead, it is up to each student to build their educational path, according to the future they envision for themselves, while ensuring that the university's core requirements are fulfilled, course prerequisites are met, and they achieve significant depth in at least one field and strength in a second field not normally paired with the first. However, to implement a completely competency-based degree program with the credit-hour equivalent badges, we would need to develop badges to capture all coursework students take. The TST faculty fellows realized they would not be able, nor was it appropriate, to write badges and challenges for the content of all of the other courses that the TST students might possibly take.

## First Revision

After realizing the misalignment of our first model with creating and sustaining a full degree, the TST fellows shifted to a new model, in which the badges represented the competencies expected of the graduates of this program, independent of specific course content. Many of these skills and abilities fall into what are often referred to as *professional skills* or *soft skills*—those that, for example, address working independently and in groups, meeting deadlines, communicating effectively, and engaging aesthetically.

Our first revision of the program resulted in the development of forty-two competencies grouped into eight families, with each competency badge available to be earned at the Developing, Emerging, and Proficient levels (figure 8.1). Each of the new badges contained a single challenge requiring the student to identify an artifact they created demonstrating facility with the competency. Students submitted the artifact along with a reflection explaining how the artifact exemplified the expected skills and abilities. The combination of artifacts and reflections allowed students not only to demonstrate their skills but to articulate those skills as well.

With the shift away from assignment-based badges to the forty-two new, more conceptual competencies, information literacy remained. As with all the badges, however, it was reduced to the single requirement to submit one or more artifacts and a reflection that discussed how those artifacts demonstrated the competency. In the case where the new competencies included

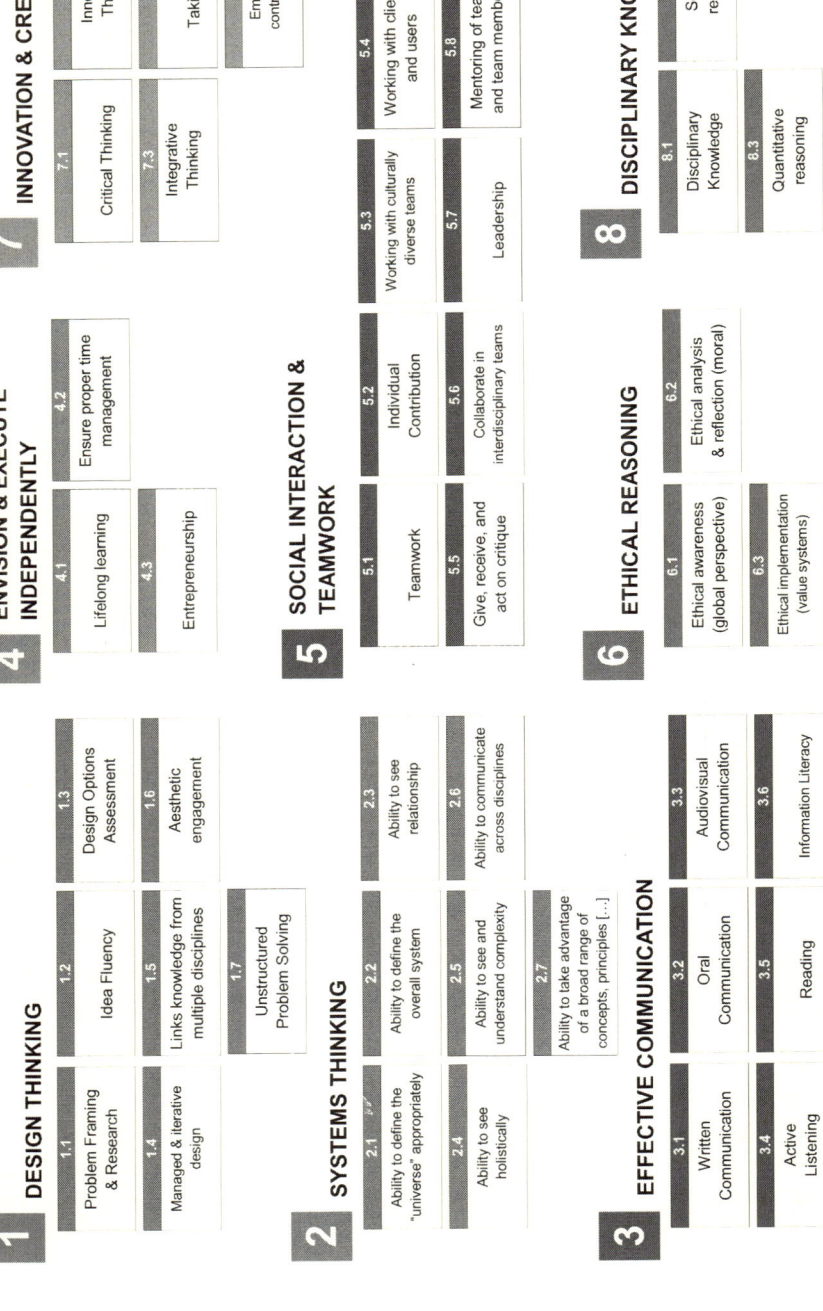

Figure 8.1. TST Degree Competencies, Grouped into Families

several learning outcomes, it was expected that the artifacts and reflections would address all the relevant outcomes, unless otherwise stated.

For the information literacy badge at the Developing level, the learning outcomes were listed in a way that roughly parallels the ACRL information literacy standards, and all five outcomes were expected to be demonstrated at a novice level. This expectation meant that, in most cases, multiple artifacts were needed to fulfill all of the outcomes. At the Emerging level, the information literacy badge focused on scientific and technical literature. It included the ACRL Information Literacy Standards for Science and Technology (ALA, ACRL, and STS, n.d.), related to being "knowledgeable of sources that are specific to the field—e.g., manual, handbooks" (found under "Standard Three: Performance Indicators"). In addition to using technical literature, the Emerging level outcomes expected the student to assess the quality of discovered information and appropriately synthesize and use that information while maintaining the fidelity of the source. The Proficient level learning outcomes expected sophisticated information organization, determination of what is enough information for a task, analysis of information through different lenses, and managing one's own intellectual property.

Students had a difficult time making the transition to the forty-two competencies, where the challenges were not directly tied to particular class assignments. They had problems determining what materials could be used for particular badges when something beyond a specific assignment was required (Van Epps et al. 2016). The process of writing a reflection and referring to multiple artifacts in a coherent way challenged the students, so they tended to avoid badges requiring such synthesis.

To complete the competency requirements for their degree, students were expected to achieve all forty-two competencies at the Developing level, a subset of twenty-nine of those at the Emerging level, and then an even smaller subset of sixteen at the Proficient level. With the ability to select which competencies to pursue at a higher level of development, the students tended to just select the ones that appeared most approachable rather than those that aligned with a passion or professional goal. As a result, many of the badges with multiple learning outcomes, information literacy in particular, were not attempted at higher levels. The TST signature courses continued to include work that would easily translate to many of the badges, including information literacy, but the students did not easily see the connections or pursue those badges.

After a year utilizing this set of forty-two competencies, difficulties became clear. Students struggled to understand how to connect their existing work with the competencies, how to demonstrate behavioral competencies through an artifact or document, and how to navigate the extreme level of

142                                Chapter 8

granularity and occasional duplications embedded in the competencies. This led the fellows to reduce the number of badges that needed to be earned from the original forty-two to the expectations for the current cohort of students that they earn twenty-eight Developing level badges, seventeen at the Emerging level, and twelve at the Proficient level. As before, students determine which of the competencies they wish to pursue at the higher levels.

**Second Revision**

The fellows once again revised the competencies for new students entering the program in the fall of 2017. In this new version, they created a new, smaller set of overall competency families that is easier to understand, especially by those outside the program, and includes fewer competencies overall. The new competencies contain five competency families, with each family containing between three and five competencies (figure 8.2).

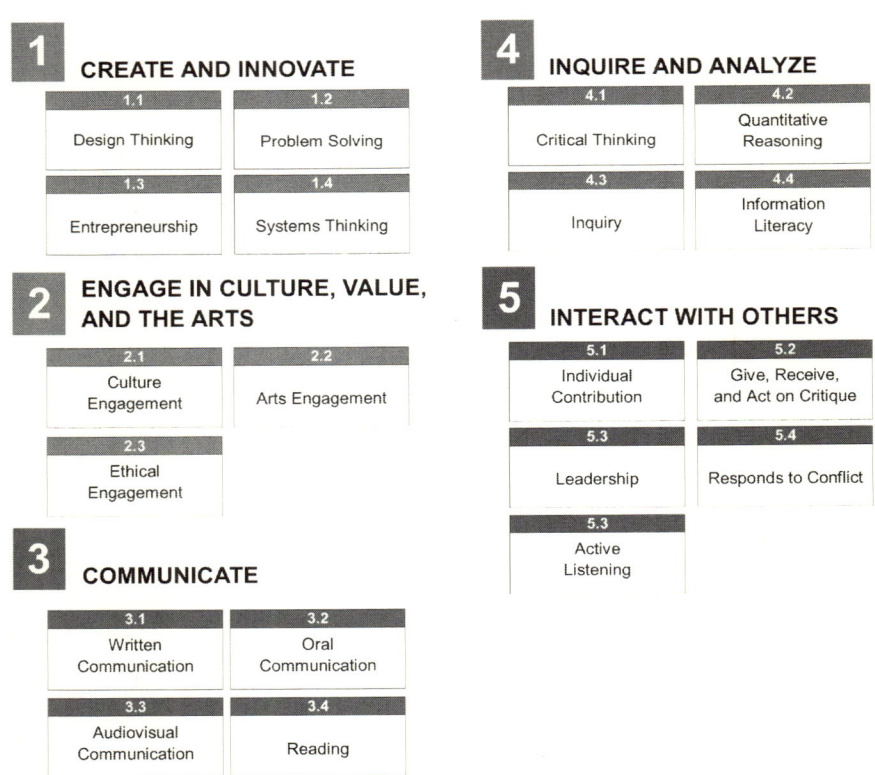

Figure 8.2.  TST Degree Competencies for Incoming Students in Fall 2017

The new set of competencies removes areas where different competencies overlapped or complemented each other. This is particularly evident with the information literacy competency. Information literacy now is part of the inquire and analyze family of competencies. The other competencies in this family include critical thinking, quantitative reasoning, and inquiry. Within this group, inquiry includes identifying a question or problem, finding information to address that question, and synthesizing that information; critical thinking includes interpreting and analyzing information from multiple sources. Given the definitions of these two other competencies, information literacy is represented within this family as encompassing the ability to use information gathering tools and sources, to organize that information, and to properly document that information with citations and references. This representation is not an attempt to simplify information literacy or make it easier to achieve. Rather, is it an acknowledgment that there is overlap between the skills that make up information literacy and other inquiry and analysis tasks and that there is not a need to evaluate those skills within multiple badges.

## LESSONS LEARNED

One of the biggest challenges the TST faculty faced as the students worked to achieve the competencies through the badge framework was the need to have some sort of example or artifact of the work attached to the badge. For competencies like written communication, it is straightforward to select a piece of writing that highlights the skills of the writer in organizing and presenting a coherent argument. Similarly, oral communication can be documented through a video of a presentation. Competencies such as "Give, receive, and act on a critique" become more challenging without, for example, a third party writing a letter describing characteristics observed that could be included in a badge submission.

We did stumble into some of the pitfalls of CBE and badging described earlier. Gallagher (2014) noted a tendency for the proliferation of specialized competencies in CBE programs, as stakeholders continually want to add "just one more" competency and the program ends up with an overwhelming number of requirements specified at a very granular level. We experienced this firsthand in our initial program, and, as illustrated by the progression of competencies, the TST faculty allowed the competencies to balloon before taking a step back to clarify and simplify them to make the program easier for the students to understand and navigate. The other major consideration was the students' preparedness to be self-directed and intentional about their learning from day one, considering their exposure to lecture and test-focused K–12 educational systems. The students in our cohort who were most enthusiastic and capable of thriving in this environment came from non-traditional educational systems.

Using Pintrich's (2003) six facets of student motivation, the CBE program was successful in addressing self-determination and personal control and fostered personal and situational interest through the student-led, inquiry-based learning environment of the studio course. However, the self-efficacy factor was a challenge for students, operating in an entirely new learning environment. The instructors did not realize how much scaffolding students needed in order to work successfully. The students' value calculations related to the program also varied over time, as it was easy for them to question what the program was leading toward without seeing examples of the career paths a transdisciplinary degree leads to after graduation.

While there were challenges—which is to say, learning opportunities—with the implementation of the competencies, the librarians were welcomed wholeheartedly into the TST program as equal contributors, valued not only for their information skills but also for their instruction background and other life experiences. One of the authors was asked to teach each of the two signature courses in different semesters and to develop and organize the mentoring program for students, which is the main venue for helping students become reflective learners and chart their path through their degree program. As partners from the beginning, we were able to deeply embed "information literacy thinking" throughout the curriculum in a way that would be more difficult in an established program. Overall, the project provided an engaging opportunity to completely embed information literacy into a new program. We learned valuable lessons on the impact of the structure of the competencies and the achievement mechanisms on student motivation and completion of competencies. As such, we understand much better how to structure digital badges and how to reduce overlap of competencies. It will be interesting to see how the revised information literacy competency is pursued by the incoming cohort of TST students. Once the revised competencies have been tested by the cohort, the next step will be to incorporate concepts from the ACRL's *Framework for Information Literacy for Higher Education* into the TST curriculum.

## REFERENCES

Abramovich, Samuel, Christian Schunn, and Ross Mitsuo Higashi. 2013. "Are Badges Useful in Education? It Depends upon the Type of Badge and Expertise of

Learner." *Educational Technology Research and Development* 61 (2): 217–32. doi: 10.1007/s11423-013-9289-2.

ACRL (Association of College and Research Libraries). 2000. "Information Literacy Competency Standards for Higher Education." Chicago: ACRL and American Library Association. https://alair.ala.org/bitstream/handle/11213/7668/ACRL%20 Information%20Literacy%20Competency%20Standards%20for%20Higher%20 Education.pdf?sequence=1&isAllowed=y.

Adams Becker, S., M. Cummins, A. Davis, A. Freeman, C. Hall Geisinger, and V. Ananthanarayanan. 2017. *NMC Horizon Report: 2017 Higher Education Edition*. Austin: New Media Consortium. http://cdn.nmc.org/media/2017-nmc-horizon-report-he-EN.pdf.

ALA, ACRL, and STS (ALA/ACRL/STS Task Force on Information Literacy for Science and Technology). n.d. "Information Literacy Standards for Science and Engineering/Technology." American Library Association (website). http://www.ala.org/acrl/standards/infolitscitech.

Competency-Based Education Network. 2017. "What Is Competency-Based Education?" http://www.cbenetwork.org/competency-based-education.

Fosmire, Michael. 2014. "But Do They Care? Pintrich on Motivation in Learning." What I've Been Reading. *Issues in Science and Technology Librarianship* 75 (Winter). doi: 10.5062/F4RJ4GD4. http://www.istl.org/14-winter/reading.html.

Gallagher, Chris W. 2014. "Disrupting the Game Changer: Remembering the History of Competency-Based Education." *Change: The Magazine of Higher Learning* 46 (6): 16–23.

Grant, Gerald, ed. 1979. *On Competence: A Critical Analysis of Competence-Based Reforms in Higher Education*. San Francisco: Jossey-Bass.

Hamon Kunz, Amanda. 2014. "Daniels Awards Prize for Competency-Based Degree to Purdue Polytechnic Institute." Purdue University (website), September 4. https://www.purdue.edu/newsroom/releases/2014/Q3/daniels-awards-prize-for-competency-based-degree-to-purdue-polytechnic-institute.html.

IMS Global Learning Consortium. 2017. "Open Badges v2.0: IMS Candidate Final/ Public Draft." IMSGlobal.org (website), March 8. https://www.imsglobal.org/sites/ default/files/Badges/OBv2p0/.

Johnstone, Sally M., and Louis Soares. 2014. Principles for Developing Competency-Based Education Programs. *Change: The Magazine of Higher Learning* 46 (2): 12–19. doi: 10.1080/00091383.2014.896705.

Klein-Collins, Rebecca. 2012. *Competency-Based Degree Programs in the U.S.: Postsecondary Credentials for Measurable Student Learning and Performance*. Greenwood Village, CO, and Chicago: CAEL Publications. http://www.cael.org/ pdfs/2012_competencybasedprograms.

Lumina Foundation. 2014. *The Degree Qualifications Profile: A Learning-Centered Framework for What Colleges Should Know and Be Able to Do to Earn the Associate, Bachelor's, or Master's Degree*. Indianapolis: Lumina Foundation. https:// www.luminafoundation.org/files/resources/dqp.pdf.

Mozilla Foundation. 2016. "What's an Open Badge?" Open Badges (website). https:// openbadges.org/get-started/.

National Academy of Engineering. 2008. *NAE Grand Challenges for Engineering*. Washington, DC: National Academy of Sciences, on behalf of the National Academy of Engineering. Updated 2017. http://www.engineeringchallenges.org/File.aspx?id=11574&v=ba24e2ed.

Olneck, Michael R. 2012. "Insurgent Credentials: A Challenge to Established Institutions of Higher Education?" Presented at Education in a New Society: The Growing Interpenetration of Education in Modern Life, at Radcliffe Institute for Advanced Study, Harvard University, Cambridge, MA, April 26–27. Draft retrieved from https://www.hastac.org/documents/insurgent-credentials-challenge-established-institutions-higher-education.

Organization Systems International. 2015. "Polaris® Competency Model Development Guide (version 4.0)." Purchasing information. OSI (website). http://orgsysint.com/products/polaris-competency-model-development-guide/.

Pintrich, Paul R. 2003. "A Motivational Science Perspective on the Role of Student Motivation in Learning and Teaching Contexts." *Journal of Educational Psychology* 95 (4): 667–86. doi: 10.1037/0022-0663.95.4.667.

Spady, William G. 1977. "Competency Based Education: A Bandwagon in Search of a Definition." *Educational Researcher* 6 (1): 9–14. doi: 10.3102/0013189X006001009.

Torshen, Kay Pomerance. 1977. *The Mastery Approach to Competency-Based Education*. New York: Academic Press.

Van Epps, Amy S., Iryna Ashby, Colin M. Gray, and Marisa Exter. 2016. "Supporting Student Attainment and Management of Competencies in a Transdisciplinary Degree Program." Paper presented at ASEE's 123rd Annual Conference and Exposition, New Orleans, Louisiana, June 26–29. ASEE. doi: 10.18260/p.25977. Paper downloadable from https://www.asee.org/public/conferences/64/papers/15132/view.

# 9

## Hot Neoliberal Commodities or Tools for Empowerment? A Badges Case Study and Conversation

*Emily Ford, Jost Lottes, Betty Izumi, and Dawn Richardson*

In the United States' political and economic climate, higher education has become less of a public good and more a means to an economic end. In other words, instead of college being where students go to learn to participate in democratic society, students attend college to get a degree and then a job that will allow them some personal economic success. Accrediting agencies in many disciplines are focused on competencies and skills, further solidifying and codifying competency-based approaches to education. This tension between neoliberalism—the commodification of education—and the historical purpose of education for the public good is felt by many educators. It affects how we approach students, how we develop curricula, and how we deliver those curricula.

Digital badges represent this same tension. They can be viewed as a kind of currency that perpetuates the marketization or commodification of students' skills. But they might also be used as a tool to empower students to dismantle systems that reinforce stark political and economic disparities. This chapter presents a case study and reflective conversation about planning for and implementing badges, while questioning neoliberal approaches to higher education today. First, we outline the background of our project, providing details about collaborative efforts in curriculum mapping and design. Next, we discuss the project implementation and its challenges. We end our chapter with the transcript of a discussion regarding the project itself, which highlights our collaborative work, our frustrations, our wins, and our thoughts on the role and power of badges in higher education today.

# DIGITAL BADGES FOR
# CREATIVITY AND CRITICAL THINKING

The student population at Portland State University (PSU)—an urban public access university in downtown Portland, Oregon—consists of a high percentage of first generation, non-white, nontraditional, and part-time or commuter students. Exemplary of this environment is the fact that in fall of 2016, 62 percent of PSU's new undergraduate students transferred in from other colleges. Many PSU students work full-time and support families. Additionally, the university's outreach efforts to Middle Eastern and Southeast Asian countries have resulted in a visible Muslim student population. This diverse student population presents challenges to the university and in the classroom to reach students from a variety of backgrounds, ages, experiences, and knowledge. Teaching in such a diverse environment is quite rewarding yet poses many challenges. For one, it is hard to know students' individual skill and ability levels. In any one class, students' information literacy, digital literacy, and critical thinking skills can range from very basic to advanced. Digital badges are one way that teaching to this disparity could be addressed.

In 2012, the new PSU provost announced reTHINK PSU, a new internal grant-funded initiative, which aimed to support discovery and experimentation in learning by improving the affordability and flexibility of education, with a focus on projects utilizing innovative technological approaches and tools. It was around this same time that the librarian for the university's College of Urban and Public Affairs, one of the authors, had been trying to better integrate information literacy instruction in public health courses. The Health Studies major was one of the university's largest (and growing) undergraduate programs, and it was evident that students were lacking a clear understanding of information evaluation skills and concepts. The Association for Schools and Programs of Public Health (ASPPH)—the accrediting body for undergraduate public health education—valued information literacy, and positive relationships between the librarian and the School of Community Health suggested potential for a collaboration to improve information literacy instruction in public health courses. Badges presented a potential mechanism to deliver, reinforce, and acknowledge information literacy skills, and this funding opportunity would provide the support and resources to develop a collaborative project with Community Health faculty. After garnering support from key stakeholders, the reTHINK PSU proposal was funded in full at $20,000. The provost viewed the project as a "proof-of-concept" that could inform the university regarding badging in higher education. Digital Badges for Creativity and Critical Thinking was born.

## PLANNING FOR BADGES

The Urban and Public Affairs librarian formed a project team with three Community Health faculty members and one instructional designer, all of whom were dedicated to discovering and experimenting with badges. While the project was largely driven by interest in the technology, the project was in essence a curriculum mapping and instructional design project. Experimenting with badges and micro-certification was the icing on the proverbial cake. We were curious to see if badges would allow students to acknowledge and communicate their skills, and we were motivated by the ability to engage in curriculum mapping curriculum development and to improve existing courses.

In order to create a badge curriculum, we collaboratively reviewed learning outcomes in the three participating courses to identify commonalities and themes. This work built on an existing curricular mapping exercise of Community Health courses mapped to ASPPH Undergraduate Learning Outcomes (http://www.aspph.org/educate/models/undergraduate-learning-outcomes/). From there, the team mapped participating course outcomes to the Portland State University Library's learning outcomes and developed badges that aligned with each outcome. Next, for each course we outlined how students would achieve the outcomes, be assessed, and earn their badges. Although badges and their associated learning outcomes were the same for each course, each class used unique course assignments and activities via which students achieved these outcomes and earned badges. As an example, table 9.1 outlines the core badge curriculum as delivered in the Social Gerontology course.

The curriculum included two in-class library instruction sessions to support student success with research and writing assignments. In addition to core badges, which affiliated specified learning outcomes to course assignments, we used supplemental "fun" badges to acknowledge student achievements and dispositions (table 9.2). The supplemental badges were not included on a course syllabus but were a surprise to students receiving them.

The end result of our curricular design efforts and badge creation was a rich collaboration among members of the project team. During the fall quarter of 2013, the librarian and teaching faculty members worked to deliver the curriculum and award badges in each course, which are listed below:

- *Our Community Our Health (PHE 250):* The required breadth course for Health Studies majors. This was a large lecture course of 120 students. Taught by Dawn Richardson.
- *Social Gerontology (PHE 354U):* An elective course for general education and for Health Studies majors. A requirement for the aging specialization. This course had thirty-five students. Taught by Jost Lottes.

Table 9.1. Core Badge Matrix: Social Gerontology

| Badge | What does the badge certify? | What did students need to do? |
|---|---|---|
| CREDLY CROWN | Credly Crown: Earners of this badge have successfully created a Credly profile and are ready to accept badges they'll be earning throughout the term in their Community Health course. | • Create an account in Credly<br>• Complete and submit the Credly Account Creation form |
| WEB NINJA | Web Ninja: Earners have learned how to evaluate websites for currency, relevance, authority, accuracy, and purpose. | • Passing grade on Website Evaluation assignment |
| SOURCE SLEUTH | Source Sleuth: Earners can distinguish the characteristics of information sources produced for different audiences (scholarly, popular, professional, etc.) in order to select appropriate sources. | • Find three articles (professional/popular/in-between)<br>• Passing grade on Policy Paper |
| HACKER | Keyword Hacker: Earners can execute keyword searches and use basic Boolean search commands to retrieve results appropriate to the searcher's information needs. | • Complete a D2L quiz on search techniques<br>• Successfully find a research article for Article Review assignment |

Table 9.2. Supplemental Badges

| Badge | What does the badge certify? |
|---|---|
| PROBLEM SOLVER | Problem Solver: The earner of this badge took initiative to creatively solve a problem for the class, specifically related to issues with course mechanics (D2L, submissions of quizzes & papers, keeping on track, etc.). |
| REFLECTIVE READ | Reflective Reader: Earners of this badge showed thoughtful reflection on assigned course readings. |
| ENERGIZER | Energizer: The earner of this badge thoughtfully contributed to a fantastic class discussion with a comment about the assigned reading. Their contribution helped to energize the class and stimulate engagement. |
| ELOQUENT EMCEE | Eloquent Emcee: Earners of this badge offered, without being asked, to stand up in front of classmates and share their knowledge. |

**Table 9.2.**   *(Continued)*

| | |
|---|---|
|  | Group Guru: Earners of this badge showed the ability to communicate effectively, remain organized, and contribute to a team's work. |
|  | Research Moxie: Earners of this badge showed moxie—energetic drive and engagement in their research. |

- *Community Nutrition (PHE 327U):* An elective course for general education and for Health Studies majors. This course had thirty-four students. Taught by Betty Izumi.

## IMPLEMENTATION AND CHALLENGES

In each course, information about badging and badges was presented in course syllabi as well as in Desire2Learn (D2L), the university's course management system. Each course included its own badge matrix (table 9.1, above) and an FAQ, and we outlined directions and instructional activities for badges in D2L.

The librarian, teaching faculty, and paid teaching assistants collaboratively managed the badges for each course. Because D2L did not support badges integration, the project utilized a paid Credly account to create and distribute badges. Teaching faculty and teaching assistants tracked student progress and achievements using shared spreadsheets as well as grade books in D2L. Teaching assistants used this information to award badges in Credly. The librarian served in a supportive badge management role, fielding student, faculty, and teaching assistant questions regarding the platform, workflows, and other issues. While this seemed straightforward, we quickly learned that it was not.

Our paid Credly account included the ability to upload spreadsheets to award batches of badges; however, this buggy feature often only processed partial data. As a result, some students who earned badges did not receive them. When this came to our attention, teaching assistants had to again cross-reference student progress with badges successfully and unsuccessfully awarded in Credly. For students who should have received badges but did not, teaching assistants manually awarded them. Because using Credly was so unwieldy, both students and faculty considered it a large impediment to the project's success.

In addition to Credly's technological failures, using the platform introduced several other layers of complexity. Because we chose an external platform, students needed to set up personal accounts and profiles on Credly. Credly did not automatically send badges to the profiles of users who had earned them. Instead, students received a system-generated email notification of their award and needed to log in to Credly and accept them. For Portland State students, additional logistics such as remembering and maintaining usernames and passwords, receiving extra emails, and accepting badges added more to their already full school, work, and home lives. A minority of students also struggled with digital literacy skills. In addition to using basic computer skills, such as using a mouse and keyboard, the badges project required these students to use D2L, Credly, and the Internet, which exponentially amplified their confusion and frustration. In these cases, the librarian answered numerous email, phone, and in-person questions as well as providing consultative support to students who needed it. Finally, some students did not see the value in displaying their badges or did not fully understand how to use their badges once they had earned them. Although the librarian and teaching faculty introduced badges and continued the conversation about badges throughout the term, many students did not accept badges as valid or did not fully understand their value.

Despite the project's challenges, we were able to discover and experiment with the idea and actuality of badges. Despite badges being the most attractive portion of the project to funders, the success of the project has little to do with awarding 622 badges to students. We regard our greatest success as the deep collaboration among ourselves and the high-quality curriculum we developed. In fact, the curriculum, without badges, is still used in some courses, and some components of it have been adopted and re-used in criminology and criminal justice, public administration, and other disciplinary courses.

PSU has not yet moved forward with badging at an institutional level, but there continues to be some interest in badging as the university moves more and more classes online. To date there is no PSU–wide badge curriculum, and neither is there a library-wide badge curriculum. Instead of moving toward badges wholesale, the university has put its resources behind the acquisition and support of an e-portfolio system, PebblePad. This system was selected, in part, because it does allow for badging. However, it is up to individual faculty members to create and use badges as they see fit. Additionally, the ongoing funding from the reTHINK PSU initiative funds the development of flexible, online degree programs. As such, faculty are re-structuring courses for online delivery. While this work requires and includes deep collaborations with the library and librarians, much of this work is done on a course-by-course, instructor-by-instructor scale rather than from a programmatic or general education scope. Finally, the nature of the PSU community and PSU's general education curriculum poses challenges to implementing badges. The large disparity in knowledge and skills of students, coupled with institutional policies dissuading prerequisite courses, means that providing appropriate curricular scaffolding is difficult.

## THE CONVERSATION

Four years after completing the Digital Badges for Creativity and Critical Thinking project, the project team gathered to record a discussion of our experience. Our discussion, reflected in the following transcript, surfaced many of our wins and challenges. We discussed positive and negative experiences with technological implementation, layout and presentation of badges, course content and course level, student feedback, and institutional buy-in. Additionally, we discussed issues in higher education such as defunding, neoliberalism, contingent faculty, and other institutional issues. Readers will notice our camaraderie and signs of our deep collaboration, which stemmed from working so closely together on this project. Our hope is that the discussion of our experience contributes to the body of qualitative knowledge about badging for information literacy and badging in higher education in general.

EMILY: *Why did you participate in the badges project?*

BETTY: Students are really lacking in library skills and information literacy skills. This seemed like a really fun way for them to practice and learn their skills. I felt like it could be easily integrated into my class, which emphasizes research.

DAWN: When you [Emily] had first talked to me about the project concept [five years ago], you said something about science literacy, and that's the part I latched on to. Then, as we went forward, I realized, "Oh—these are library skills." When you really looked at it, it was science literacy. Just noticing trends in my classes—this general anti-intellectualism, anti-science feeling among students—I thought a lot of it seemed to stem from students not having the soft or hard skills to even engage with that material. It seemed perfect to integrate into a basic class like Our Community, Our Health. It seemed ideal, and it seemed fun.

JOST: Very similar reasons for me, actually. I had spent many, many terms wondering about the lack of information literacy skills, and it shocked me how all those students now have all this data at their fingertips and don't seem to be able to use it, more than prior generations. They are intimidated by it and don't know what to do with it. It was a great opportunity.

EMILY: For me it germinated from my past experiences. I knew that the community health discipline was pre-disposed to understand information literacy and noticed from working with students in Community Health that their skills were lacking. I felt like there was room for us to make improvements.

DAWN: Had it been a librarian I didn't know, or someone I had no interest in working with—

BETTY: Or not a librarian.

DAWN: —I don't know that I would have been as interested. Then, as you fleshed out the team in our department, I could really see how this could work in 200-, 300-, 400-level classes. There is something to be said for the collaboration aspect of it, in terms of our personalities and expertise.

EMILY: *In your experience, what worked, and what didn't?*

DAWN: I was a big fan of it. The hardest part was the application because of the platform [Credly]. It wasn't Credly per se that was the issue. Had it been more streamlined, had it been in D2L, or had there been some other way of doing it that was more intuitive for the students . . . Not to say Credly wasn't intuitive. It was just too bulky. Too much of a hard sell.

BETTY: I think that it needs to be more seamless if there are going to be electronic badges that are distributed, and I think that students would have prioritized it more or would have been more excited about it at all levels if it was institutionalized at PSU.

JOST: There was a little bit of resistance from students, because they said it's extra work. That's always something they don't like, of course. That's definitely one of the downsides, and I agree that the execution of Credly was just very cumbersome. But I think it was a great project. I really enjoyed it. I enjoyed working with you guys; I enjoyed redesigning the syllabus. That was one of the reasons I participated in this, because I had to do that anyway. Going through that process, and thinking about learning goals and how they can be meshed with information literacy goals, was a really good part of the experience. I still use a lot of these assignments in my classes to this day.

BETTY: What was successful is that the videos were developed and the assignments were developed. I think that it's most appropriate for freshmen. When you're a senior and you're just learning how to give credit where credit is due, that's a problem. For my Freshman Inquiry class, we use the badges activities, but we don't distribute the badges. And I've shared—especially the professional/popular/in-between activity [part of the Source Sleuth badge]—with colleagues across the country, because not being able to recognize a professional source is such a serious issue.

JOST: That video ["Information Cycle"—part of the curriculum for the Source Sleuth badge] has something like 7,000 views, so others must be using it. It's a sign that students all over the country don't really know that skill and that faculty all over the country are struggling with these issues.

DAWN: All the tools were great, and I'd second what Jost said about the opportunity to revamp the class. That's also something that didn't work for me in the end, because that was the last time I taught the class. Depending on who you are and what classes you teach, you may not have ownership of the curriculum. Whoever is teaching it now is definitely not using any of those materials. It's unfortunate, because there is a lot of good stuff there that could have been built upon, but it didn't go anywhere. I don't teach another class that the badges material will fit for. I teach graduate and senior or 400-level classes.

EMILY: On the other hand, that points to issues in higher education in general. The division of labor—especially for lower-level courses, which are frequently relegated to contingent labor—introduces problems with consistency. The technology made it very, very challenging. Credly was our best option, because we didn't have a lot of money. If only we had a programmer, a server, et cetera.

BETTY: We still would have needed D2L to accept it.

EMILY: Exactly. Working with proprietary systems is not tenable. When our TA was trying to upload Excel spreadsheets to get them to award badges, it was missing rows of students, and then we'd have to go back in and double-check the spreadsheets against each other . . . There was just a lot of work.

BETTY: That was never going to be sustainable—having a TA award badges. It really needs to be, as soon as you finish a badge activity, a badge automatically appears, and it's on your e-portfolio.

JOST: In some cases, it was a week or two between turning in the assignment and receiving the badge. That doesn't work in terms of motivating them. It just feels like busywork at some point for them if they don't see the connection.

BETTY: A challenge at PSU—especially in the School of Community Health—is that our classes don't have prerequisites. When it comes to these badges, in my 300-level class, I had students who were freshmen all the way to seniors. The freshmen and sophomores, maybe juniors, could have benefitted from badges being required assignments. But that would mean that, for seniors and other students who already had these skills, it would be busywork. Several students who were really strong students academically—the type of students who did everything assigned—did the badge activities even though they already knew the information. To them it was, "Why am I doing this? I don't care about badges. I just want to do well and graduate."

DAWN: I had the opposite experience. I remember hearing some of the negative feedback from some of the others [Betty, Jost, and Emily], but I didn't get a lot of that. I heard a lot of positives. Students were upset about the Credly stuff, but, regarding the badges, feedback was generally positive. People were saying, "I never knew this was the skill until you told me. I knew I could do this, but it helps me articulate." That's partly a function of me having more students—nearly a hundred—which provides more opportunity for more people to say more things.

BETTY: What you just said about "I never knew this skill"—that's really important. Students can now see it as a skill that they can put on their résumé.

EMILY: That's really heartening for me to hear—who, over the years, has been not so happy with badges on a theoretical level. That was the point: Students could surface and acknowledge for themselves what they already knew or what they were learning. It provided a way for them to do that.

DAWN: The other negative thing I heard was that people felt like they were learning great stuff but nobody would care because it wasn't an established thing. That isn't that people think this is baby work or this is stupid; they saw value in it. Their frustration was that they couldn't use that value; it didn't have currency beyond the class. It tells me they actually saw the value but just weren't able to spend it anywhere. And they were right; that's an accurate, valid concern.

BETTY: I wonder if that could have been addressed in another badge, where they would have to translate their badges into employable skills.

EMILY: There's only so much you can do in one class. This is co-curricular stuff.

BETTY: These types of skills are critical to learn as an undergraduate, so, in an ideal world, by the time students graduate, they would have all of these skills and they would be able to articulate them as skills on their résumé, whether or not they have badges. Doing everything in one class is a lot because we have content to cover.

JOST: In an ideal world, we would have classes that build on each other, so students would earn different levels—like gold, silver, platinum versions of those badges.

BETTY: And in an ideal world, students would come with some base level of skill around information literacy. Freshmen are high school–plus three months, and in high school they're learning rote memorization. They're not learning how to articulate their opinions, and they're not learning referencing and in-text citation. I probably didn't learn it, either. It's a big leap.

EMILY: For librarians, what we see is a result of the state of libraries in public schools in Oregon, where budgets have been slashed and there are hardly any school librarians any more. We are seeing the first waves of Common Core educated students come to public universities. These are perceptions that I have, but I don't have evidence to show that that's part of the problem. I would like to think that it used to be better, but I'm not sure.

BETTY: Even ten years ago, students didn't have as much access to this much information at their fingertips. The problem of fake news wasn't as rampant in the US. Now we're just talking about something so different.

DAWN: In sociology, too, it's pretty well documented that there's a very hard and fast anti-intellectual movement in the US. It's not just passive; it's very active, and it pushes back against these efforts. It pervades all levels of education, and it's bipartisan in some ways, too. That's a real structural factor that makes this hard—teaching people how to engage with information, how to engage with science, how to figure out what is a fact or not, and how to connect your thinking to a larger body of thought. "Alternative facts." We joke about that, but there are people for whom that is very real and acceptable. I'm not talking about fringe groups, either.

EMILY: When you were talking about some students, Betty, opting not to do it, that was a little different in your class than in both Dawn's class and Jost's class, where badges were required and part of the grade or the assignment, so it was all seamlessly mapped.

JOST: We surveyed students before and after the course and gathered a lot of data showing that a lot of them thought they had certain skills but then they didn't actually have them. In my class, they had to do badges. If I had given them the chance to opt out, I don't know what they would have done. A lot of them probably would have said, "This is so easy. I can do it anyways. It's a waste of my time," and we did get those sentiments from some people. They said "Oh, this is so high school" and "It's demeaning that you're making me do this."

BETTY: I wonder what it would have been like if I had assigned points to badges. They were part of the class, they were required, but there were no points assigned to it, and I think when there are no points assigned to it, it's not really a requirement.

DAWN: In my class, the badges weren't presented as something distinct from the grade. It was so integrated that maybe that's why I didn't get the busywork comments. It might be because of the way it was presented in the syllabus and how we talked about it in class. It wasn't badges and grade; they were the same thing. I had students emailing me at the end of class that they'd already gotten grades and they wanted their badges.

BETTY: That's how I've done it in my freshman class this year. The activities are all online and facilitated by the student mentor. It's funny, though—they will do the badge activities, and then I notice a lot of errors in class on what they say is a professional source. They'll say the *New York Times* is a professional source, or CNN, and so we go over this again. Then I get comments from students: "Boy, it sure would have been nice if we learned about this before we had to turn in our draft." And I thought, "But you *did* learn it." I don't know where the breakdown was this year. But the way it was structured [for the badges project] was easy: you just click on the badge activities, there's the video, the quiz, and everything, and it's all there, and you get feedback. That didn't happen in the same way this year, because that kind of execution requires resources: you [Emily].

EMILY: That's what's interesting. I was present in each class at least twice when we did this. There were in-person instruction sessions. Plus, I was on the back end, providing feedback via D2L and tweaking quizzes. In Public Health–speak, the in-person instruction and online instruction were an intervention. We're looking at this as an intervention with outcomes.

DAWN: A senior in a 200-level class might have been more willing to engage in that kind of thing, whereas somebody in a 300-level class might not. They might have already had diminished expectations. So those factors could have impacted people's willingness and attitudes.

BETTY: It's their expectations about a class and about the class material. If I'm teaching a 300-level class, I tell my freshmen, "Look, you can take this class, but my expectations and the material are at a 300-level."

EMILY: *I hoped we could capture if there were any funny stories or anecdotes that we had. I think, Dawn, you got an unexpected badge from a student?*

DAWN: I got two. They went into Credly, and they created a badge. [One of them was the Crystal Clear badge: "This badge recognizes and applauds your repeat efforts to help students understand the purpose of badging."] It's interesting that they wanted to create their own badges and award them. I think it happened because you [Emily] came to class, and you were talking about the one that Jost had made for you. [Tonsillectomy Readiness badge: "Awarded for calmly facing impending tonsillectomy."] And I was like, "What?? *I* don't get badges!" And after that, the two students did it.

JOST: You came to my class and talked about that badge [Tonsillectomy], and I had two students complaining. In the survey they said, "Oh, this is just silly, this tonsillectomy badge thing. What a waste of our time."

EMILY: It could be a different kind of motivation, too. Although the research about badges is minimal, if we look at extrinsic and intrinsic motivation, some students might be motivated by fun, whereas others might be approaching education as a very serious endeavor. How do you even balance that in a classroom?

You have to balance motivation styles but also someone's personal circumstances that lead them into education, taking it very seriously. "I'm paying all this money. Why are you talking about badges for tonsillectomies?"

BETTY: On the one hand, the Girl Scout badge idea is really awesome; everybody can identify it. But I wonder if people also feel that it's not as serious, because it has that same look and feel in the doling-out of the badges. I think that you gave a new badge to one of my students, too: the Eloquent Emcee. In somebody's class students were giving each other badges, right?

EMILY: Dawn approached me and said, "Hey, I want to have a fun badge for group work," so that's how we thought about these other ones.

DAWN: They did end up in some groups, giving each other badges.

BETTY: That could help to build more social cohesion in the class.

DAWN: So much of it could be the content of the class. In my class, people don't come to it to leave with some hardcore content knowledge, and so the expectations they had of the class and of themselves, they felt freer to just do the fun stuff, because they knew that's kind of what the class was about. The way I describe that class is, "This is the sampler platter of public and community health. You're not going to leave here with depth, but you're going to leave here with a broad understanding, some connections in the field, and some idea of where to go next." Lower stakes, maybe. More fun.

BETTY: My class is an elective, so students who take it are more serious about the topic. Of course, there are students who take it for other reasons, but most students who take it are really interested in the depth.

EMILY: And Jost's class is in the middle, because it meets general education requirements, although it is required of a certain concentration of students in a major.

DAWN: We [Jost and Dawn] had a shared student. I remember her saying that she liked the badges because she got to see them slightly differently or how they built on each other. She was very positive about badges in class. In fact, it's like they were getting double rewards for the same work, which is how we pitched it.

EMILY: *If we could make badges work, in an ideal world, in an ideal Portland State, what would that look like?*

JOST: The first thing is that the technology needs to be in place. It needs to be simple for the students, and it needs to be simple for us. It also needs to have very quick turnarounds—not the way we collected, graded, and then matched badges to achievements; it has to be instantaneous. I think the most successful ones were those ad hoc, fun badges, and I think for motivation those can work really well. But, until the infrastructure is in place and integrated with D2L, it's an uphill battle to try to use badges in classes.

DAWN: It needs to be student-driven, community-driven, from the ground up.

For example, what is the platform? What should the badges look like? Should they be called *badges*? Then the process should be replicated on a somewhat consistent, timely basis so that students know that this comes from their ranks and it doesn't feel like it's this imposed or applied thing.

BETTY: It has to be institutionalized. It has to be seen as valuable by the PSU community. There also has to be currency; it has to mean something to people outside of the institution or these classes so students are developing badges and potential employers are participating in that process so that they can say, "Yes, that's a really valuable skill." We did have one for group work. That's a critical skill, right? Working together to figure out what makes sense for students and then what is desired by the employer.

JOST: What we need is the ability for students to take those badges with them and to show them and to have meaning. That is also connected to the fact that you need to do the work in order to get it. We were very generous. If we had been stricter, I would say no more than half of the students would have gotten that final badge [Master Information Analyzer]. That was the culminating badge; you had to do all the work in order to get it. We did end up giving it to probably 85 to 90 percent of students, so badges might have been less meaningful for that reason.

EMILY: *I have previously shared with you some of my concerns about having students become a commodity on a marketplace level. It's very disheartening to see—as public education has been defunded on a legislative level and in our current economic marketplace—that institutions are viewing student credit hours as money. A student is money for an institution. Generally, a student's aim is to get a job. Everything that they're doing in higher education is to participate in a capitalist economy, and thereby those students become products in and of themselves. In essence, this is neoliberalism, morphing higher education away from being a public good and instead becoming a financial and social commodity enabling people to participate in a capitalist economy. I am very conflicted; while surfacing learning outcomes and skills is very helpful, badges are also playing into this economy of selling one's skills in order to participate in capitalism. I would like to hear what you think about that kind of tension: Do badges amplify this capitalist paradigm? Do they further neoliberalism?*

BETTY: Is the concern that students who don't participate in badges or can't go to college don't have the badge?

EMILY: My concern is that it's no longer a public good to have an education; it's just a commodity—something that's going to be sold. As a result, we're taking away the value of an education as a public good and contributing to an economy full of worker bees.

DAWN: The commodification of not just higher education but of the people within higher education—the faculty—is a huge issue. Clearly this is a terrifying trend, particularly with MOOCs [massive open online courses] and online courses. That said, the way badges can be done, going back to the ideal world, can be hugely empowering for students. And if done in the right way, whatever that would be deemed to be, could be a tool for students to counteract those systems. It doesn't necessarily have to be about getting the job and being in the system and participating as a capitalist cog. It can also be about critical thinking skills, and pushing back on the system, and engaging in ways that allow you to dismantle.

BETTY: You could get a badge for participating in policy making or engaging as a citizen.

DAWN: Or even using these badges in ways that then counteract the prevailing system. I don't think it's about the badges; I think it's about the application, because the arguments that are being made about badges can be made about grades; they can be made about résumés, CVs—any markers of achievement could have those same views attached to them. I think it's about the systems.

BETTY: I don't see badges as a problem, except for right now when I was saying that students who don't have access [to higher education] then don't have the skill as marked by a badge. It's more a problem in higher education. With or without badges, higher education is no longer a place to learn about yourself or to learn how to participate as a responsible person in our society. It's really about needing a degree because you need to get a job. And without this degree, studies have shown that your salary will be X dollars lower. And we live in a capitalist society.

DAWN: That doesn't mean we can't change it. People say, "Oh, we live in a capitalist society," but we don't have to. I personally believe that some of the skills that we're giving them are important skills that can dismantle systems—and not just economic systems but political systems. Obviously, there's been a ton written in the past six months about how we got to the current place we are politically and economically, and that's because people lack these very skills that were on our syllabi. Badging them could be a force for a lot of good.

EMILY: In my thinking about badges and this neoliberal problem, they could be used to dismantle systems in that way, but how? How would we map that out? When I have said, "I would never do this again *unless* . . ." my caveat is that I will not use badges again unless we can use badges themselves to help students think critically about a badging system, it's neoliberal implications, and higher education in general. I want badges to help students gain that disposition, but I don't know how to do that.

DAWN: That's a laudable goal for me, but I would do this again even without that. If all a student learns how to do is tell the difference between popular media and professional media, isn't that a win? Isn't part of the problem that people don't know how to interrogate information so that leads them down these paths that are not good? I agree it would be great to do that, but I don't know how we would do that in my class. For an education class or a social justice class—or they're teaching a great class on campus now, Social Justice Pedagogy, that would be an ideal place to do that.

EMILY: It's separating out the digital object of a badge from the curriculum. You can teach those skills, such as information sources and formats, without having to have a digital object on top of it.

BETTY: I don't see how that badge activity would really drive change in terms of changing our capitalist system. I feel like that's our whole society. If it's about education and changing our society, that needs to happen way early on. By the time students are in college, they have been participating in this capitalist economy for twenty years. It's easy to be complaisant and just say, "Well, forget it; there's nothing I can do about it," but it's not just the Trump Administration. I mean, previous administrations, they were all capitalist; they all functioned in a capitalist economy. So what is the alternative?

JOST: I think it's more about whether badges contribute to turning our students into mindless worker bees. I do see that concern—by making them more marketable—because there is that push throughout the entire university. We've been talking about some of these things. What do employers want? Well, if you think of universities, the way they should be, or were at some point in time, students would go in, and they would learn how to be better people, make the world a better place. It's not something that we do anymore necessarily.

DAWN: It's like the difference between our education [at public universities] and a liberal arts education. But there are some small vestiges of liberal arts—private universities that are hanging on.

BETTY: I just don't see badges in and of themselves as being able to shift us more in that direction. Because we live in a capitalist society. And because of the way that our institution is funded.

DAWN: Emily is saying that the badges could shift us more toward capitalism; that's her concern. I'm not taking the counter; I'm saying that I don't think it's a done deal, that by badging we're moving further toward marketizing students. I think there are ways to do it that can help countervail that.

EMILY: To use the badge as critical inquiry.

BETTY: But to really counter those forces, it's more than badges.

# 10

## Badging and Workplace Information Literacy
Helping Students Prepare for the Professional World

*Megan Blauvelt Heuer*

In fall 2016, as subject librarian to the Advertising Division and recently appointed head of Information Literacy, I had been discussing with faculty the possibility of mapping information literacy learning outcomes to the curriculum but had not seen the progress I had wished for. When, as an alternative to this approach, one professor suggested implementing a more focused information literacy certificate program that could be delivered within the scope of her courses, I was happy to oblige. The professor had learned from area employers that recent graduates in the field of advertising were lacking in necessary research skills for the available entry-level jobs. At the time, advertising students at Southern Methodist University received one-shot information literacy instruction by instructor request, a piecemeal approach familiar to many librarians. What we have developed since then is a rigorous program with two levels of digital badges representing research competencies needed in the advertising field. This chapter describes the considerations for developing a badging program for workplace information competencies, the specific curriculum and assessment for our badges, and the initial responses from students to the badging.

### WORKPLACE INFORMATION LITERACY

Workplace information literacy can look very different from the information literacy skills needed for the academic environment. A traditional approach to information literacy as a set process with associated universal competencies does not necessarily produce graduates with sufficient lifelong information skills; indeed, much work in the area of workplace information literacy emphasizes that practices of information use should be seen through a sociocultural lens and that the practices and understandings of information literacy are shaped within the context of a community of practitioners (Lloyd 2010). Individual workplaces each represent a community of practitioners for whom the "rules" of how information is sought and used varies greatly from the structured world of academic work. According to Lloyd, "Workplaces and workplace interests are incredibly diverse, complex, and messy. Learning about the requirements and practices of work occurs at both the formal and informal levels and requires access to both explicit and tacit sources of information. Information literacy may not follow the systematic research-based process that is advocated by the higher education setting" (71). Indeed, because learning itself is highly influenced by the context of where the learning is occurring, the transfer of understanding from education to work is particularly difficult because the context and the culture are so different (Eraut 2009). For example, the information environment in the workplace is much more fluid and is developed socially with both informal and formal sources of information used. Additionally, information problems tend to be ill defined and have very different time parameters than academic work.

The *Framework for Information Literacy for Higher Education* (ACRL 2015) recognizes that information literacy is influenced strongly by context; therefore, it can be used in developing educational experiences that speak to workplace information literacy if we are able to develop an understanding of those workplace information practices. In reviewing the literature on workplace information literacy, consistent patterns emerge around students' inabilities to use information critically and to communicate effectively, to recognize formal and informal sources of information, and to integrate information practices with other aspects of professional work. Bruce (1999) characterizes the use of information at work as requiring the ability to collaborate with a team rather than work individually, the intellectual abilities to use information rather than technological skills, and the ability to connect information skills with broad professional requirements. As such, she recommends that information literacy education emphasize learning as new ways of understanding and recognizing information practices rather than training specific skills that may be short-lived. Cyphert and Lyle (2016) find that, although employers expect a broad range of critical thinking and communication skills, recent graduates lack the abilities to recognize what information is needed and to seek out alternative methods of problem solving when typical strategies fail. In Head's study (2012), employers reported that recent graduates lacked persistence in solving information problems, did not work with other team members to gain information, and had difficulty finding patterns and meaning.

Grounded in workplace information literacy research and the ACRL framework, the following principles are the foundation of Southern Methodist University's Information Literacy certificate program:

- Performance on information tasks should mimic a context that is as similar as possible to the workplace and should address multiple literacies.
- Students should be given the opportunity to practice solving ill-structured information problems.
- Learning and problem solving should emphasize social interaction and communication.
- While students need to learn specific information tools in order to perform tasks, the emphasis should be on developing both persistence and deeper understanding of information.
- Students should explicitly understand the need to adapt to new information environments.

This means that the program needs to help students focus on the process of using information and bring attention to how decisions are made when finding and using information. Rather than adhering to an authoritative model of finding and using information, students need to be encouraged to develop their own heuristics through critical reflection and through conversations with others so that they can acclimate to future workplace environments.

## BADGING AND CAREER COMPETENCIES

Due to the Advertising Department's requirement that students acquire multiple professional certifications and their interest in developing and representing soft skills for the students' résumés, an information literacy badging program for the department was a natural fit. While formal degrees do not capture soft skills like information literacy, badges represent more granular competencies in a documented way that is transparent to employers (Knight 2012). Nevertheless, while employers are open to the idea of using badges to assess applicant skills and a majority find grades to be insufficient measures, badging is still new enough that employers may need to be educated more about them (Raish and Rimland 2016). This education may happen organically as employers tend to research applicants online as social media and the "reputation economy" evolves, and badges offer a way for students to establish a positive online presence. Because it is still unclear how much time an employer would spend verifying the claims of badges, particularly if applicants possess many of them (Berge and Muilenburg 2016), summative badges are a better approach than progressive ones for career competencies. The burden of determining how learning experiences quantify into significant achievement should not be placed on the employer. For that reason, we created two summative badges for the Temerlin Information Literacy Program that represent milestone stages in learning, and there are no badges for the individual modules.

Employer trust in the value of a badge is essential. The badging program at SMU is endorsed by the Advertising Department and bears its name—the Temerlin Information Literacy Certificate Program. This title serves to align the program with the expectation of quality education associated with the Temerlin Advertising Institute. Having the brand of the school itself speak to the quality of the badge means that employers may not feel the need to investigate further; however, we still provide as much transparency as possible should they wish to do so. This method for ensuring the quality of a badge by relying on the same system of authority as traditional college credit was purposeful. The power of branding and the expediency of relying on a known authority likely outweighs the tendency of the employer to research and verify badges, particularly in a time when open digital badges are still a relatively new concept to employers.

A badge can become a talking point in an interview for either an employer or a recent graduate. Employers value information competencies but may not be explicitly aware of them (Cyphert and Lyle 2016), and an information literacy badge starts the conversation. It is important that students be able to articulate the value and the rigor of what they have learned. An employer may learn more about what a job candidate has achieved in an interview than in independent verification of the badge curriculum and assessment. In the long run, however, the proof is in the pudding: if students with a Temerlin information literacy badge lack demonstrable research skill in their internships or in their first jobs, the result is a diminished reputation for the school that should be avoided at all costs. It is, therefore, important that the program be of the highest quality and that we ensure all students receiving badges are able to perform. Indeed, there is no reason that badges cannot be a method of ensuring rigorous authentic assessment, despite the roots in gamification that lead some to believe digital badges are trivial (West and Randall 2016).

Motivation is a recurrent theme in the badging literature, despite mixed results as to the efficacy of motivating learners and the debate over the merits of extrinsic rewards (Pagowsky 2013; Grant 2016). In fact, research has shown that extrinsic motivators like digital badges can actually erode students' intrinsic motivation (Deci, Koestner, and Ryan 2001; Hanus and Fox 2015). However, for workplace information literacy badges, the main purpose of the badge is not for motivation, so the question as to whether a student finds receiving a digital badge motivating or not is not particularly pertinent. A career competency badge has value in a wider environment, and this changes how the badge affects the motivation of the student as compared to a badge that only has value within the context of the classroom. Social capital, rather than the badge itself, is the reward for a career competency badge (West and Randall 2016). Ultimately, students are highly aware of the need to find employment after graduation. Indeed, 92 percent of twenty- to twenty-three-year-olds attend college in order to improve their employment opportunities (Fishman 2015). The earner of a workplace information literacy badge needs to believe in the value of what is being learned as a career competency, and therein lies the intrinsic motivation. This further supports the idea that formative badges are not as essential as summative badges, since they are not being used as a motivational factor.

The literature raises concerns about badging and competency-based education, and this chapter aims to address some of those arguments in relation to career competency badging programs like the Temerlin Information Literacy Program. First, according to Ford (2017), badging can be seen as supporting a neoliberal view that the purpose of education is to supply a new generation of workers for the marketplace and that this destabilizes a balance between the societal good of education and career preparation. It is not within the scope of this chapter to consider whether badging or competency-based education should completely replace traditional education, which is a different proposition than a badging program that acts as a supplement to traditional learning, as is the case with the Temerlin Information Literacy Program. General education, which serves that societal good, is still a part of the curriculum, and, given the soaring costs of college and the demands placed on recent graduates for employability, it is an imperative that the university also help prepare them for the workplace. Whether we consider the badge to emphasize education as a commodity seems to be beside the point: students already see their education as supporting their career development. In that way, grades are no less a commodity than badges. The only difference is that badges represent more specific skills and learning. "For educators," says Ford, "there must be a balance between learning outcomes, assessment, and the point at which they cause harm. How can we use and reinforce learning outcomes with this in mind? How could we use and interrogate badges in the classroom so that students viewed them with a critical eye rather than steps to neoliberal 'success'?" (ibid., 21). The answer lies in how well designed the educational experience is that the badging program affords. Does the badge set a single "right" path toward being information literate for career success, or does it teach critical thinking about research? Just because students receive a badge that recognizes their efforts does not necessarily mean that the instruction or educational experience is unsound.

Another argument against badging programs is that badging is a system of individual achievements that can be stacked up to earn a micro-credential and that, as such, learning is compartmentalized (Lodge 2016). According to Lodge, badging neither encourages nor represents the development of the whole self; therefore, badges should be reserved for lower level, vocational competencies. However, a badge can be used to represent summative learning. Teaching and measuring critical thinking and deep learning as well as motivating students in order to develop the whole self is difficult, whether for a grade or for a badge; and both systems have the potential to create a learning situation in which students are expected only to meet strict outcomes rather than being allowed to explore and learn beyond those outcomes. As the following section illustrates, a badge's main functions are (1) to highlight a competency—such as information literacy—to students, faculty, and potential employers and (2) to promote learning until mastery. The effectiveness of how the student is taught, what they learn, and how they are assessed is influenced by many factors, foremost the quality of the education, but not by the badge.

## TEMERLIN INFORMATION LITERACY CERTIFICATE PROGRAM

In the current version of our program are two levels of badges, each representing multiple lessons and activities, delivered through online tutorials in LibWizard, as well as through live instruction and group work in class. Delivering some content online helps scale the program and facilitates a flipped classroom model, but it is important to also include in-person learning that provides students with opportunities to engage in more complex learning and communication that is impossible within a static tutorial. Tutorials are reserved for the delivery of content and for introducing some of the library's research databases. The badging program is embedded within a few courses, but any advertising students not taking those courses have the option to participate in the program if they so wish. A course was created in the university's learning management system to facilitate delivering materials to enrolled students and keeping track of their progress.

Developing programming that focuses on workplace information literacy requires much collaboration with disciplinary faculty, particularly in the case of an embedded program like Temerlin's. At the outset of creating the program, I developed a document listing the various components to be created and areas of responsibility in delivering the program. This allowed me and the disciplinary faculty to discuss and agree upon the intended audience and scope of the program—who would track the participants' work, who would develop the educational components and how they would be delivered, who would grade the tests, and who would develop the badge design, marketing, and Web presence. The components created for this program include

- documentation of the scope of the program
- student learning outcomes for each level of badge
- documentation of the series of modules for each badge
- a website that describes the program
- Credly badges
- online tutorials
- lesson plans for live sessions
- and tests, practice tests, and rubrics for assessment.

## STUDENT LEARNING OUTCOMES

Developing the learning outcomes from the program involved considering how concepts from the ACRL framework (ACRL 2015) might be translated into learning outcomes that make sense for advertising. Preliminary discussions with several professors about the assignments that their students complete, common struggles students experience with research, and the kinds of research tasks that are required in entry level positions also helped influence the program planning. Although there is not much in the literature of advertising education on this topic—possibly because there is a mismatch in understanding and in language about information literacy between librarians and advertising professors and professionals—one article by Spiller and Marold (2015) on needed competencies for an advertising competition proved insightful as to what advertising professionals and faculty want from student research.

The resulting badging program has five overarching objectives that can be mapped to ACRL framework concepts, as shown in table 10.1. Elements of the entire framework can be seen in these learning objectives, though they are not an exact match, because the needs of the Temerlin program relate to the workplace rather than to traditional academic inquiry. It was critical that the Temerlin Information Literacy Program communicate what is being learned in a way that resonates with students, faculty, and potential employers; therefore, the objectives highlight areas of need specific to advertising in the language of the profession rather than in library terminology. For example, the third objective, "Demonstrate both strategic, critical thinking and persistence in solving information problems," was crucial to this project, given issues raised in the literature and by the faculty. Persistence is presented as one of the dispositions of "Research as inquiry" in the ACRL framework, and while the idea of strategy is presented in the frame "Searching as strategic exploration," the term *critical thinking* does not actually appear in the document, though it is certainly implied. Critical thinking and persistence are considered very important by stakeholders, and, in fact, employers do not actually associate information skills with the more highly desirable critical thinking and problem solving abilities, though educators and librarians do (Cyphert and Lyle 2016). Because of this, critical thinking and persistence were elevated as a main objective of the Temerlin program. These learning objectives break out into specific student learning outcomes that can be seen in table 10.1.

For a badging program that has multiple modules, this system allows for learning outcomes that are specific to the individual modules and that relate to broader objectives representing the total learning for the program.

## ASSESSMENT OF LEARNING

In order to have a rigorous program, a test of authentic skill in research is required for a student to receive either of the badges. In creating the tests and the rubric, we considered the skills we wanted students to demonstrate, as well as the tendencies and attitudes that would support them in transferring their learning successfully to work situations. We also considered how the Temerlin program objectives would be manifested in the students' work, as shown in table 10.1.

The tests require the students to complete real-world information tasks and record their answers, their search methods, and an annotated list of resources used. This helps us see not just their results but also the thought process behind their searches and evaluations. Although it is difficult to get the students to record their searches, and it is an artificial aspect of delivering a test, it is important to be able to ascertain how the students are thinking in order to judge their behaviors and their grasp of concepts rather than only seeing the end product. The students are allowed to work on the tests over several days. The test for the Level 2 Badge is an extended project that allows them to dig in deeper with their research and communicate with the professor and librarian.

Because the Temerlin Information Literacy Program is delivered for the most part within the scope of advertising courses, the students do receive a

Table 10.1. Temerlin Information Literacy Program Objectives Aligned with ACRL Framework Concepts

| Temerlin Information Literacy Program Objectives | Evidence of Application of Objectives in Student Work | Corresponding ACRL Framework Concepts |
| --- | --- | --- |
| Recognize established and emerging sources of information in the field of advertising. | <ul><li>Identifies information by type rather than by container</li><li>Uses all relevant source types</li></ul> | Information creation as process |
| Understand how information systems are organized in order to access relevant information. | <ul><li>Successfully retrieves specifically relevant sources</li></ul> | Information creation as a process/Searching as strategic exploration |
| Demonstrate both strategic, critical thinking and persistence in solving information problems. | <ul><li>Able to break down problems</li><li>Uses multiple sources and perspectives for complex questions</li><li>Demonstrates connection of information need to source type</li></ul> | Research as inquiry/Searching as strategic exploration |
| Choose appropriate sources of information with an understanding of application context. | <ul><li>Tolerates ambiguity</li><li>Recognizes weaknesses of information used</li><li>Uses specifically relevant sources</li></ul> | Authority is constructed and contextual/ Scholarship as conversation |
| Apply ethical practices using information in advertising. | <ul><li>Distinguishes between plagiarism and copyright</li><li>Makes ethical choices for real-world scenarios</li></ul> | Information has value |

grade on the test for their course. Grading the tests is a collaborative effort between the librarian and the course instructor, partly because there is a good deal of legwork needed in order to accurately assess student performance. Grading research by only looking at a reference list and the drawn conclusions does not give a real picture of that student's level of research skill. All sources cited in the test need to be found and assessed, and a grader also needs to have an idea of what information is available that may help answer any test question a student may have missed. Certainly the fact that all students taking the test are researching the same questions makes this process easier, as opposed to grading diverse research topics, but it is still a lengthy process. As the librarian, I perform the first pass of grading—hunting down students' sources, giving comments on strengths and

---

### SAMPLE TEST QUESTIONS FOR THE LEVEL 1 BADGE

Your agency has been hired by Prosper Pure Life to increase sales for their product, Advanced Probiotic Life, to an American market. They generally promote natural solutions to wellness and are proud that their products are free of preservatives and artificial ingredients.

What are the opportunities and challenges that would be pertinent to advertising the product?

Who is (are) their target market(s)? What preferences or attitudes are important to be aware of?

1. Document your search process. What search terms, tools, or strategies did you use to find this information? What type(s) of information might answer this question and why?
2. What are your answers? Be sure to provide evidence to support these answers.
3. Provide references to your selected information. These should be selected because you think they are the best sources. Say why you used the source and how the source was limited or possibly biased, if applicable.

You are working on some communications copy, and you happen to see that another company's official communications copy really speaks to what you are trying to say. You decide to use most of the copy for your purposes, because there is no copyright notification on the original material. Can you use this content ethically? If so, how? If not, why not?

weaknesses in their research and analysis, and suggesting a rubric score in each area. The instructor then reviews the tests with my comments and suggested rubric scores and assigns a final rubric score and numerical grade for the course. This process allows me to understand what the students learned or did not learn and has helped me to learn more in general about students' thought processes in finding and using information.

In order to receive the badge, students must perform at the proficient level in all areas of the rubric, as shown in table 10.2. Students who do not perform at proficiency may retake a similar test until they are able to pass and receive the badge, extending their learning until mastery. This is one of the advantages of embedding a badge within a course: students may receive a B or C grade on the test, and that may be sufficient to their grade for the course, but the badge requires that students master the information literacy competencies. Indeed, in our initial offering, the challenge of earning a badge inspired students. Every student who did not achieve proficiency in all areas retook the test until they were able to receive the badge.

In putting together the learning activities for the program, iterative practice with feedback on information tasks and extended learning with informal networks through group work serves as the basis for learning. In past instruction sessions, students repeatedly asked, "What does good research or source evaluation look like?" This provided a helpful starting point. The question might have stemmed from students' natural desire to discover what is expected in order to receive a good grade, but it also enabled us to discuss how they had performed research in the past and how they might start to develop strategies for research based on the context of their environment. Though challenging, it is important that an instructor not impose an artificial concept of good research that is academic- or library-centric. Rather, it is helpful to work with examples of good and bad research, allowing the students to assess various examples using the rubric, and to discuss the many paths that research might take. The program also includes practice tests with what are termed *possible* answers rather than *definitive* ones, which students use to study for the final test.

Thinking must shift in order for a student to consider the act of research itself rather than focus solely on the product of research as they normally would for class projects. The culminating learning activities for both badges are problem-based inquiries, and in both cases the tasks match the types of tasks the students perform on the tests, which adds to the iterative practice the students receive. A breakdown of the modules with associated learning outcomes appears in table 10.3. Descriptions of some of the lesson plans used in this program appear in *Disciplinary Applications of Information Literacy Threshold Concepts* (Heuer 2017).

Table 10.2. Rubric for Level 1 Badge

| Criteria | Performance Indicator | Proficient | Emerging | Little or No Evidence |
|---|---|---|---|---|
| Understanding of Information Ethics | Recognizes ethical choices in the academic and professional use of information | Demonstrates good judgment and reasoning when making ethical choices | Sometimes demonstrates good judgment when making ethical choices; may lack reasoning about ethical choices | Does not demonstrate understanding of ethical choices |
| Search Strategies | Able to match research needs to information sources; refines search strategies and terminologies as needed | Identifies all relevant source types and understanding of the uses, advantages, etc., of source types; identifies effective search strategies | Identifies and understands uses, advantages, etc., of some relevant source types; may perform limited search strategies, which may not be refined as needed | Does not identify relevant source types, and shows little understanding of their uses, advantages, etc.; ineffectively performs search strategies |
| Use of Information Tools | Effectively uses databases, search engines, and demographic and psychographic tools | Locates all needed information; effectively uses information tools | Locates some needed information; sometimes effectively uses information tools | Frequently does not locate information; does not effectively use information tools |
| Application of Information | Chooses authoritative and relevant information; seeks and synthesizes multiple perspectives | Locates all appropriate, current, and credible sources; uses specifically relevant information; acknowledges and analyses possible limitations or bias of sources; finds multiple sources and synthesizes them to establish perspective | Locates mostly appropriate, current, and credible sources; uses somewhat relevant information; sometimes acknowledges possible limitations or bias; sometimes finds but may not synthesize multiple sources | Chooses poor sources; provides limited, superficial, unreliable, and/or irrelevant information; does not recognize possible limitations or bias |

Table 10.3. **Learning Modules and Associated Student Learning Outcomes**

| | Level 1 Badge | |
|---|---|---|
| Module | Student Learning Outcomes | Mode of Delivery |
| Introduction to Advertising Research | • Locate library advertising resources.<br>• Perform searches in typical information tools for company, industry, and consumer research, using subjects, limiters, and Boolean operators. | Online LibWizard tutorial |
| Source Comparison Chart | • Identify uses, advantages, disadvantages, and means of access for various business, market, and advertising information sources.<br>• Match research needs to potential information sources and search tools. | Live session |
| Simmons OneView Tutorial | • Build a cross-tabulation chart in order to determine consumer demographics, psychographics, media consumption, and brand/category indexes. | Online tutorial |
| Information Ethics in Advertising | • Identify concepts related to plagiarism.<br>• Identify examples of plagiarism outside of academia.<br>• Distinguish between plagiarism and copyright violation. | Online Tutorial and live session |
| Evaluating and Synthesizing Information | • Develop criteria for evaluating advertising sources.<br>• Evaluate survey information.<br>• Recognize and synthesize competing pieces of information. | Live session with practice activity |
| Advanced Internet Skills | • Identify how Internet search engines function and how that impacts search.<br>• Create Internet search strategies using various techniques.<br>• Find statistical information online. | Live session with practice activity |

*(continued)*

Table 10.3. (Continued)

| | Level 1 Badge | |
|---|---|---|
| Module | Student Learning Outcomes | Mode of Delivery |
| Information Types in Advertising | • Identify how and why various types of information for advertising research are produced.<br>• Refine skill in using typical information tools for company, industry, and consumer research. | Online tutorial |
| Problem-Based Case Studies | • Determine how limitations of various types of information impact research.<br>• Develop alternative research methods given limitations of information sources.<br>• Compare proprietary and free sources of information, and determine appropriateness. | Live workshop delivered in two sessions |
| Research Skills Test | • Research specific information tasks; provide answers, search methods, and annotated list of resources used. | Take-home test |

| | Level 2 Badge | |
|---|---|---|
| Modules | IL SLOs | Mode of Delivery |
| Research Deconstruction | • Recognize perceived industry value of specific information sources.<br>• Match research needs to potential information sources and search tools. | Live session |
| Concept Mapping | • Break complex information problems down into solvable questions.<br>• Develop alternative methods of research given limitations of information sources. | Live session |
| Client Project | • Determine all avenues of research needed; create a client presentation synthesizing what was learned, providing annotated list of resources used. | Long-term individual project with consultations from faculty and librarian |

## CONCLUSION

Since first starting, the Temerlin Information Literacy Program has been recognized by the chair of the department and the dean of the school as an innovative idea that should be supported and possibly replicated in other departments. Sharing stories about the gains the students made, even with a small starting sample, helped faculty see the benefits of this kind of instruction. One semester, the students took a pre- and post-test, and the before and after comparisons make for very compelling evidence.

The Temerlin program has raised the importance of information literacy among the advertising faculty as a whole. Relying on a single faculty champion to help deliver an intensive program like this makes sustainability a concern, so it was an important step for us to gain the support of the department and the school. This journey started out with an attempt to develop curriculum mapping of information literacy, but with the development of the Temerlin Information Literacy Program there is not the same need for curriculum mapping. In fact, there are benefits to delivering intensive instruction within a few weeks as we do with this program rather than spacing it out over the course of several semesters. With too much time between information literacy instruction sessions, students oftentimes forget what has previously been learned. In the Temerlin program, concepts and skills are reinforced immediately. Also, students work through all parts of the research process rather than in an intermittent fashion, allowing for greater understanding of how all those parts fit together. Because of this, students develop enough proficiency that they are able to use and refine a full suite of skills.

Another benefit of packaging learning within a badging program is that it highlights information literacy as an important skill to the students. The badge helps communicate the value of information literacy as a career competency to the students and provides them with a focus for working on these skills. Even though students performed research and received information literacy instruction prior to the establishment of the Temerlin Information Literacy Program, there was little explicit recognition on the students' part of the development of those skills—much less enough awareness that they would add it to their résumé or discuss it with an employer. However, students gave less credence to the badge itself than we thought they would. In a survey given to the participants at the end of the semester, they were asked, "What aspect of the Temerlin Information Literacy Certificate Program do you value the most?" Not a single student identified the badge or the ability to add a line to their résumé or a skill to their LinkedIn profile, though the résumé credential had been of interest for the students at the outset of the program. The survey responses overwhelmingly mentioned learning how to use new sources, learning how to ask questions and evaluate sources, and learning about how to apply the information found. In other words, they valued what was learned, which makes a strong point. No matter whether educators are giving grades or badges, we hope that the purpose is learning and an appreciation of what was learned by the student. A badging program can be rigorous, can address deeper learning, and can encourage students to continue learning until mastery, and it is essential that a badging program for career competencies include these criteria. For a badge to avoid being a checklist of tasks completed or a series of hoops navigated, the learning achieved should be both relevant and transformative for the student.

## REFERENCES

ACRL (Association of College and Research Libraries). 2015. Framework for Information Literacy for Higher Education. Chicago: ACRL. http://www.ala.org/acrl/standards/ilframework.

Berge, Zane L. and Lin Y. Muilenburg. 2016. "In the Eye of the Beholder: Value of Digital Badges." In *Digital Badges in Education: Trends, Issues, and Cases*, edited by Lin Y. Muilenburg and Zane L. Berge. New York: Routledge.

Bruce, Christine Susan. 1999. "Workplace Experiences of Information Literacy." *International Journal of Information Management* 19 (1): 33–47.

Cyphert, Dale, and Stanley P. Lyle. 2016. "Employer Expectations of Information Literacy: Identifying the Skills Gap." In *Information Literacy: Research and Collaboration Across Disciplines*, edited by Barbara J. D'Angelo, Sandra Jamieson, Barry Maid and Janice R. Walker, 53–79. Fort Collins, Colorado: The WAC Clearinghouse and University Press of Colorado. Available at https://wac.colostate.edu/books/perspectives/infolit/: University Press of Colorado.

Deci, Edward L., Richard Koestner, and Richard M. Ryan. 2001. "Extrinsic Rewards and Intrinsic Motivation in Education: Reconsidered Once Again." *Review of Educational Research* 71 (1): 1–27.

Eraut, Michael. 2009. "Transfer of Knowledge between Education and Workplace Settings." In *Knowledge, Values and Educational Policy: A Critical Perspective*, vol. 10, edited by Jill Porter, Hugh Lauder, and Harry Daniels. 65–84. London: Routledge.

Fishman, Rachel. 2015. *2015 College Decisions Survey: Part 1, Deciding to Go to College*. Washington, DC: New America ED. https://dev-edcentral.pantheon.io/wp-content/uploads/2015/05/FINAL-College-Decisions-Survey-528.pdf.

Ford, Emily. 2017. "To Badge or Not to Badge? From 'Yes' to 'Never Again.'" *C&RL News* 78 (1) (January): 20–21. Retrieved from http://crln.acrl.org/index.php/crlnews/article/view/9602/10991.

Grant, Sheryl. 2016. "Building Collective Belief in Badges: Designing Trust Networks." In *Foundation of Digital Badges and Micro-credentials*, edited by Dirk Ifenthaler, Nicole Bellin-Mularski, and Dana-Kristin Mah, 97–114. New York: Springer.

Hanus, Michael D., and Jesse1 Fox. 2015. "Assessing the Effects of Gamification in the Classroom: A Longitudinal Study on Intrinsic Motivation, Social Comparison, Satisfaction, Effort, and Academic Performance." *Computers & Education* 80: 152–61.

Head, Alison. 2012. *Learning Curve: How College Graduates Solve Information Problems Once They Join the Workplace*. Project Information Literacy, October 16, 2012, http://www.projectinfolit.org/uploads/2/7/5/4/27541717/pil_fall2012_workplacestudy_fullreport_revised.pdf.

Heuer, Megan. 2017. "Using the Frame Information Creation as a Process to Teach Career Competencies to Advertising Students." In *Disciplinary Applications of Information Literacy Threshold Concepts*, edited by S. Godbey, S. Wainscott, and X. Goodman, 79–91. Chicago: Association of College and Research Libraries.

Knight, Erin. 2012. *An Open, Distributed System for Badge Validation* (Working Paper). Mozilla Foundation, December 18, 2012, https://docs.google.com/file/d/0BwJ_PQhV0lJTSnYtQzV5Q0FxNDA/edit Lloyd, Annemaree. 2010. *Information Literacy Landscapes: Information Literacy in Education, Workplace and Everyday Contexts*. Cambridge: Woodhead Publishing.

Lodge, Jason. 2016. "Keep Calm and Credential On: Linking Learning, Life and Work Practices in a Complex World." In *Foundation of Digital Badges and Microcredentials: Demonstrating and Recognizing Knowledge and Competencies*, edited by Dirk Ifenthaler, Nicole Bellin-Mularski, and Dana-Kristin Mah, 41–54. New York: Springer International Publishing.

Muilenburg, Lin Y., and Zane L. Berge. 2016. *Digital Badges in Education: Trends, Issues, and Cases*. Florence, Italy: Taylor and Francis.

New America. 2015. "Reasons for U.S. Adults to Go to College in 2015, by Age." *Statista*. https://www.statista.com/statistics/554328/reasons-for-us-adults-to-go-to-college/.

Pagowsky, Nicole. 2013. "Keeping Up with . . . Digital Badges for Instruction | Association of College & Research Libraries (ACRL)." American Library Association (website). http://www.ala.org/acrl/publications/keeping_up_with/digital_badges.

Raish, Victoria, and Emily Rimland. 2016. "Employer Perceptions of Critical Information Literacy Skills and Digital Badges." *College & Research Libraries* 77 (1): 87–113. doi:10.5860/crl.77.1.87. http://crl.acrl.org/content/77/1/87.

Spiller, Lisa, and Dave Marold. 2015. "Enhancing Student Performance in Collegiate Marketing Competitions: The ECHO Judges' Perspectives." *Journal of Advertising Education* 19 (2): 30–46.

West, Richard, and Daniel Randall. 2016. "The Case for Rigor in Open Badges." In *Digital Badges in Education: Trends, Issues, and Cases*, edited by Lin Y. Muilenburg and Zane L. Berge. New York: Routledge.

# 11

## Failing Better

### Scaffolding Learning with the Metaliteracy Badging System

*Kelsey L. O'Brien*

Since its inception in 2012, the Metaliteracy Badging System, collaboratively produced by educators from across the State University of New York (SUNY), has undergone several trials and transformations. Over the course of this iterative journey, the educators involved have learned a great deal about badges and, more broadly, about adaptability, creativity, and innovation.

With the metaliteracy framework as its foundation, our badging program evolved from the need to address students' increasingly participatory roles in social online environments. Congruous with the values of the Open Badging movement, metaliteracy promotes lifelong learning by cultivating self-improvement and empowering students to take ownership of their educational accomplishments.

The Metaliteracy Learning Collaborative leveraged the emerging badge system infrastructure to implement badges not just as learning capstones but also as progress markers and feedback mechanisms that support learners as they grapple with increasingly advanced concepts. The scaffolded design of the system leaves room for students to fail, reflect, and grow as learners; likewise, this project has encouraged the librarians and faculty involved to adapt and persist throughout the course of its development.

Over the last several years, the Metaliteracy Badging System has served in often-unexpected ways as a flexible educational tool that facilitates meaningful curriculum design and collaborative teaching. This chapter provides an overview of the design and implementation of the system, along with our challenges and goals moving forward. Just as we teach our students to fail better, we too have drawn on our setbacks as opportunities for growth and improvement.

# PREPARING TWENTY-FIRST-CENTURY LEARNERS TO BE GLOBAL CONTRIBUTORS

## Setting

Located in New York's capital, the University at Albany, State University of New York (SUNY), serves a diverse population of about seventeen thousand undergraduate and graduate students. As one of sixty-four campuses in the SUNY system, the University at Albany (UAlbany) leverages its consortial status with expansive opportunities and shared online programs and resources offered through Open SUNY (http://navigator.suny.edu). Minority students make up nearly half of the university's undergraduate population, and its robust international program has attracted students from more than ninety nations (Admissions, UAlbany, SUNY, n.d.). Branded in 2008 as "the world within reach," and led for the past several years by presidents proudly representing minority backgrounds, the university values diversity, inclusion, and global awareness (for more information, visit https://www.albany.edu/about-ualbany).

Information literacy, one of four required academic competencies in the university's General Education Program (see https://www.albany.edu/generaleducation/), plays a central role in preparing UAlbany students to engage critically and ethically in increasingly globalized information environments. The university has a two-tiered general education requirement that encompasses information literacy, writing, oral discourse, and critical thinking. The required Writing and Critical Inquiry course introduces students, generally in their first year, to all four competencies, while the upper level requirement is embedded within each major. The University Libraries' Information Literacy department, in conjunction with subject librarians, supports both levels of the information literacy competency. Through credit courses and instruction integrated throughout the curriculum, the department "empowers students to be confident users and creators of information in a dynamic and continually evolving information landscape" (University Libraries, UAlbany, SUNY 2015). Our instruction therefore focuses not just on developing skills, but fostering mindful engagement and practices across the spectrum of information communities, both within and beyond the classroom.

## Metaliteracy Framework

The metaliteracy framework, based on Mackey and Jacobson's seminal article, "Reframing Information Literacy as a Metaliteracy" (2011), informs the University at Albany's information literacy general education requirements, as well as ACRL's *Framework for Information Literacy for Higher Education*.

Metaliteracy expands on information literacy concepts to acknowledge and support learners' roles as active participants and contributors in dynamic and inherently social online environments, in which the lines between consumer and creator are often blurred (Mackey and Jacobson 2011). While students may not view themselves as authors or publishers, their ability to share information on global platforms with the click of a button positions them with a greater latitude and responsibility than had students of previous generations and calls on information specialists to help them do so critically, safely, and ethically. Metaliteracy therefore addresses not only students' skills but also their ways of thinking and interacting in the world.

The Metaliteracy Learning Collaborative, a diverse team of SUNY librarians, disciplinary faculty, instructional designers, and administrators, assembled in 2012 with the goal of updating information literacy standards for twenty-first-century learning environments (SUNY 2013). Envisioning a comprehensive literacy infused throughout students' academic careers that would transcend disciplinary boundaries, the collaborative developed the metaliteracy learning objectives (Mackey, Jacobson, and Metaliteracy Learning Collaborative 2018). The "meta" in *metaliteracy* might be considered twofold in meaning, indicating both the all-encompassing nature of the competencies applicable across educational settings and also its self-referential qualities, which encourage learners to reflect on their learning processes and essentially learn how to learn.

Flexible by design, the metaliteracy learning objectives are applicable across a range of disciplines and learning contexts, aiming to support learners in participatory roles as they collaboratively produce, share, and repurpose information. Metaliteracy addresses behavioral (i.e., skills and competencies) and cognitive (i.e., comprehension and understanding) components of learning and more notably incorporates two additional domains—metacognitive and affective—that take learners' dispositions, attitudes, and thought processes into account. As twenty-first-century learners engage in increasingly complex and fraught information environments, the metaliteracy principles provide pertinent guideposts, preparing our students to participate as informed consumers and responsible digital citizens.

The Metaliteracy Learning Collaborative's work coincided with higher education's first ventures into digital badging. As a promising new credentialing mechanism that offered more granular recognition of learning across formal and informal contexts, badging presented a venue in which to explore a more broadly scaled implementation and assessment of the learning goals established by the metaliteracy framework. Thus the collaborative began investigating the potential for a SUNY–wide metaliteracy badging program in 2012 and first piloted the system at the University at Albany in the fall of 2013.

Over the course of its development, the Metaliteracy Badging System has been supported by three SUNY–funded Innovative Instruction and Technology Grants, one small online teaching and learning grant, contributions from the university provost, and substantial funding from the University Libraries' dean for the most recent upgrades and enhancements on a customized platform. In many instances, we set out to accomplish goals for a particular grant only to discover further applications and possibilities for the system in the process, which required additional funding but also propelled us to strive toward a full realization of the potential held by this flexible educational tool.

## DESIGNING SCAFFOLDED LEARNING

The content of the Metaliteracy Badging System maps to the learning goals and objectives established by the metaliteracy framework. Scaffolded in design, the system facilitates mastery learning by enabling self-evaluation and feedback and by fostering a sense of learner agency.

Using WordPress, the BadgeOS plug-in, and the Credly API, we created leveled badge trees and achievement triggers that enable the issuing of Open Badges upon successful completion of prerequisite assignments. While the core functionality discussed in the following section has remained intact, the technical infrastructure of the system has evolved over the course of its development, as discussed in the final section of this chapter.

Metaliteracy places the emphasis on the learner by fostering learner agency, ownership, and identity. Likewise, the Metaliteracy Badging System is oriented around the metaliterate learner. Both in content and structure, the system guides students as they explore their roles as empowered learners and contributors, reflecting on their own thinking and learning processes and recognizing their achievements as the fruition of both their successes and failures.

### Badges as Identity Markers

The Metaliteracy Badging System consists of four core *master badges*: Master Evaluator, Digital Citizen, Producer and Collaborator, and Empowered Learner (figure 11.1). The Metaliterate Learner figure (figure 11.2), which situates the learner at the nexus of their learning and expands out as concentric circles representing a variety of active learner roles, inspired the design of the culminating Metaliterate Learner badge. The quadrants of the culminating badge represent the four comprising master badges, as well as the four interrelated learning domains that span across the metaliteracy learning objectives.

*Failing Better*

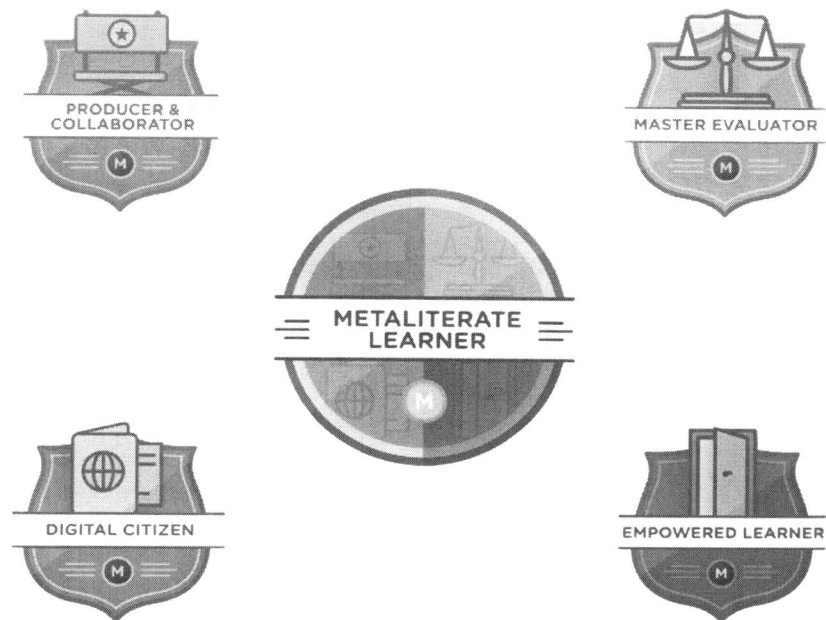

Figure 11.1.  The Metaliteracy Badges

The metaliteracy badges correspond to the goals outlined by the metaliteracy framework (Mackey, Jacobson, and Metaliteracy Learning Collaborative 2018), as illustrated in table 11.1 (Please note: badges were aligned with the 2014 learning goals and objectives, which have since been revised). The badges thus establish the desired roles and responsibilities that we cultivate in our students as they prepare to contribute knowledge in academic and professional contexts.

The naming convention for the metaliteracy badges intentionally indicates transformative titles claimed by the earner. A metaliteracy badge does not simply represent the final outcome of a learning experience but rather the translatable role assumed by the learner and the corresponding dispositions and ways of thinking that may be applied to future learning situations. As the information landscape and its affiliated technical demands constantly fluctuate, metaliteracy concepts foster adaptability and self-efficacy, rather than focusing on isolated skills or experiences.

The metaliteracy badges thus empower the earner to be a lifelong learner. In gaming environments, achievements earned for milestone accomplishments or exceptional performance become a part of the player's identity. Displayed on a social profile, earned achievements signal specialized skills and establish the

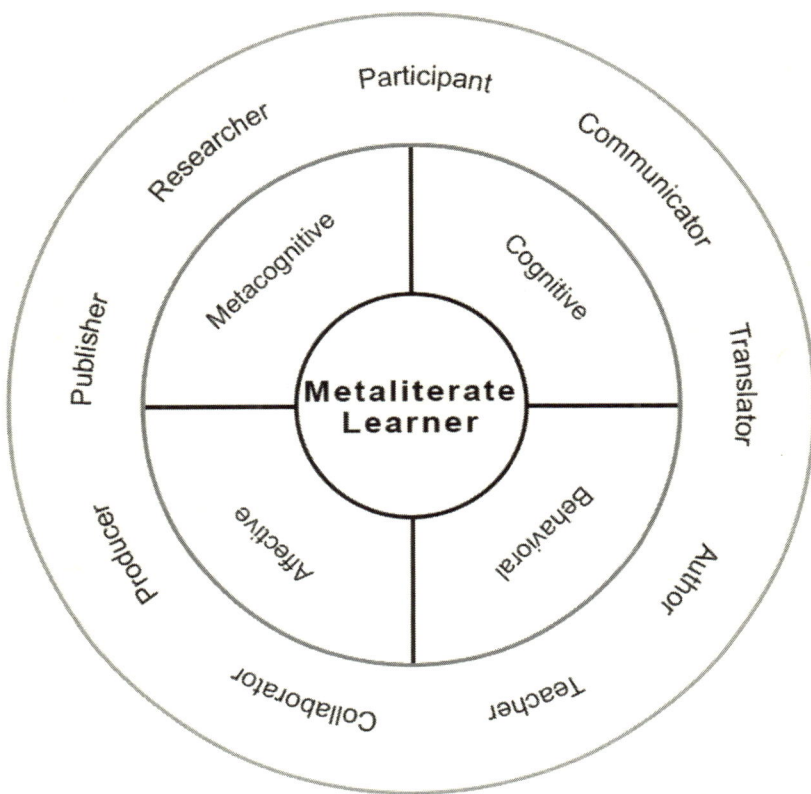

**Figure 11.2. The Metaliterate Learner**
[FC>Mackey and Jacobson 2014.

player's value within the wider gaming community (Blair 2016, 66). Likewise, metaliteracy badges showcase the earner's accomplishments and their value to wider academic and professional communities. Compared to a typical course assignment, which often consists of an isolated transaction between instructor and student, a metaliteracy badge represents a more fully realized role and responsibility placed on the earner.

While the culminating metaliteracy badges indicate transformative roles incorporated into the learner's identity, the component sub-badges in the system prepare learners to take on these roles by continually reflecting on their own learning processes.

### Sub-badges as Progress Indicators and Feedback Mechanisms

Using the metaliteracy framework as our guide, we employed a backward design approach to map out the badge system content. Considering what stu-

Table 11.1. Metaliteracy Badges Aligned with Learning Goals (2014)

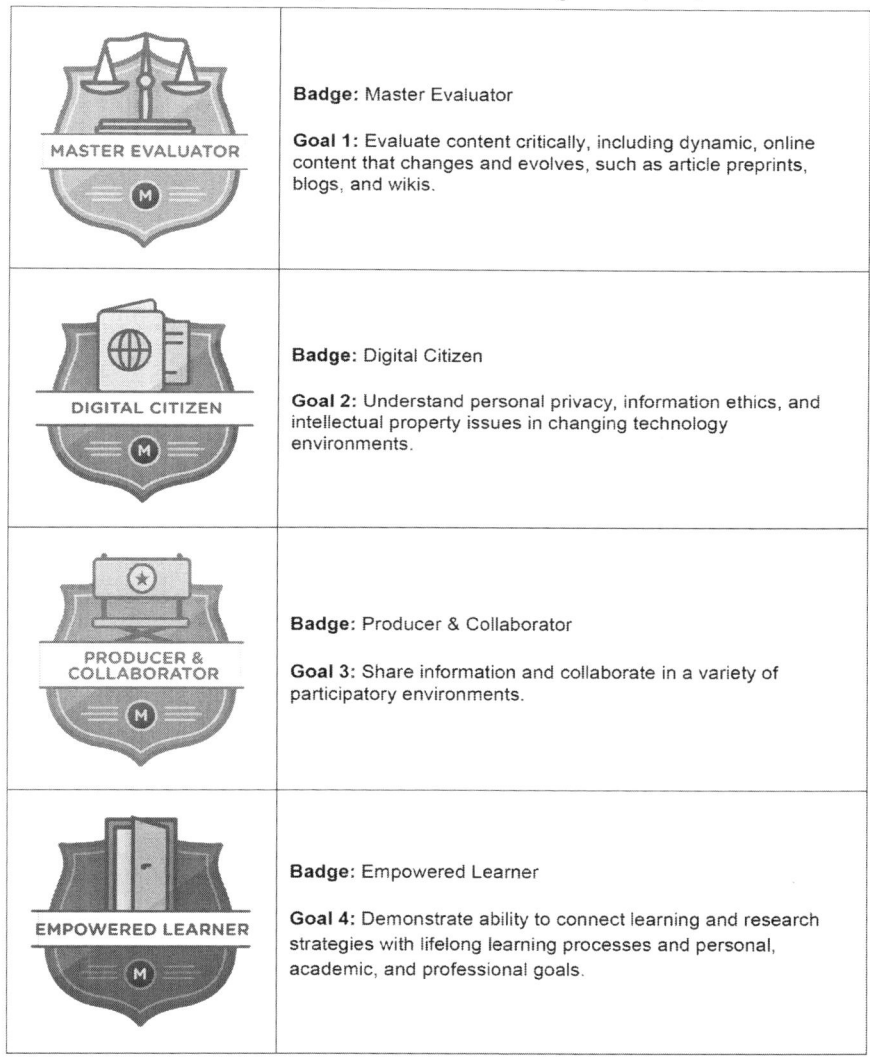

| | |
|---|---|
| MASTER EVALUATOR | **Badge:** Master Evaluator<br><br>**Goal 1:** Evaluate content critically, including dynamic, online content that changes and evolves, such as article preprints, blogs, and wikis. |
| DIGITAL CITIZEN | **Badge:** Digital Citizen<br><br>**Goal 2:** Understand personal privacy, information ethics, and intellectual property issues in changing technology environments. |
| PRODUCER & COLLABORATOR | **Badge:** Producer & Collaborator<br><br>**Goal 3:** Share information and collaborate in a variety of participatory environments. |
| EMPOWERED LEARNER | **Badge:** Empowered Learner<br><br>**Goal 4:** Demonstrate ability to connect learning and research strategies with lifelong learning processes and personal, academic, and professional goals. |

dents would need to be able to do and understand in order to accomplish the four broader outcomes, we delineated the metaliteracy learning objectives into measurable assessments and activities that would lead to the earning of each metaliteracy badge. In designing the curriculum we found that several of the objectives overlap and intersect across the four broader learning goals; so, while the badge system content does not directly align with each objective laid out by the metaliteracy framework, it does address every learning objective.

In what amounted to a visualized curriculum mapping exercise, we created a tiered constellation of prerequisite learning activities and assessments for each badge. Figure 11.3 presents the Master Evaluator constellation as an example.

Each badge constellation consists of four cumulative levels: quests, challenges, content badges, and master badges. Students advance from the lowest quest level to the master badge level, at which point they may earn and share an open, metadata-enhanced badge via Credly. The incremental badges that make up the three lower levels serve as progress markers in that they are only awarded within the system and are not programmed to be issued via Credly. A metaliteracy badge displayed on an earner's profile is therefore a meaningful and robust credential that represents authentic learning and in-depth engagement with the metaliteracy concepts.

The hierarchical structure of the badge constellations lends itself to a scaffolded curriculum design that allows students to make multiple attempts as they advance through increasingly complex concepts at their own pace. By mapping out the learning scheme for students, visualizing their progress, and providing consistent checkpoints, the badge system enhances learners' recognition and understanding of their own learning processes.

Blair (2016) notes the double value of achievements in games, in that they "act as a goal before they are earned and an artifact of the accomplishment

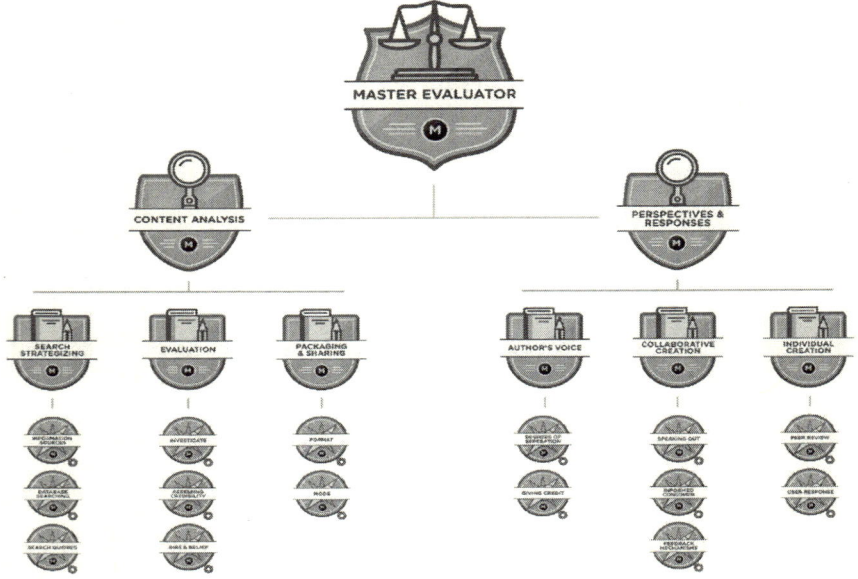

Figure 11.3. Master Evaluator badge constellation

afterwards" (63). Before students embark on the metaliteracy quests, the badge constellations provide visual roadmaps of the learning activities that they will progress through in order to earn a master badge, in effect heightening their awareness of broader curriculum goals and the relationships between introductory and advanced concepts. As students engage with the content and successfully complete each component, the constellations serve as illustrative progress maps, providing positive reinforcement in the form of earned achievements that fill in the corresponding icon on the learner's profile, marking their advancement as they strive toward the master badge.

While students may complete quests in any order, they must master the lowest levels in a series before they advance to the next level. The scaffolded structure of the badge system thus facilitates self-paced learning and provides opportunities for continual feedback. Upon successful completion of prerequisite quests, capstones unlock at the challenge and badge levels, prompting students to synthesize what they have learned thus far. The system allows students multiple attempts, enabling them to resubmit based on reviewer feedback and to build on their understanding rather than simply accepting that they have failed the assignment. An earned badge therefore indicates not only completion but also persistent engagement and mastery of the concepts.

The scaffolded design also encourages learners to slow down and reflect on their learning processes, counteracting habitual information-seeking practices that often prioritize instant gratification over quality. Quest level activities aim to meet students where they are by introducing foundational concepts within familiar contexts. Quests that fall under the Master Evaluator badge, for example, include discussions about Google and Wikipedia and teach students how to conduct a more effective Web search. As students advance through each level, activities become increasingly metacognitive, prompting students to synthesize and apply what they have learned. At the challenge level of the aforementioned badge, for instance, students begin to consider the varied perspectives and voices (including their own) of information creators, applying what they have learned in preceding quests to develop a search strategy for a research project. Upon reaching the master badge level, students submit a culminating assignment that demonstrates mastery and serves as a learning artifact of the badge's claimed competency.

The badging system content incorporates a variety of multimedia and interactive elements, including embedded YouTube videos and self-check quizzes. The activities include both original content written by the Metaliteracy Learning Collaborative and open online content, including Web articles, blogs, and Creative Commons–licensed videos and images. The activities thus promote openly shared resources while also simulating real-world scenarios, preparing students to navigate online resources and encouraging exploration beyond a contained learning environment.

## Teaching Students How to Fail

Many educators can attest to the common challenge of students' hesitation to contribute during class activities and discussions, which often seems to stem from a fear of failure; indeed, it seems that millennials are particularly risk-averse, often favoring image among their peers over genuine academic inquiry (for more on this discussion, see chapter 3). The metaliteracy content in the badging system aims to make students more comfortable with failure, helping them to recognize their initial struggles as a natural part of the learning process.

The Empowered Learner badge, for example, incorporates several exercises that encourage students to develop metacognitive practices for problem solving and self-directed learning. In the Failing Better challenge, students reflect on their past failures and learn about the benefits of adapting a growth mindset, as defined by social psychologist Carol Dweck (2006). The challenge concludes with a capstone for which students anonymously post on a "failure wall," a Padlet-generated page of student stories that has become a communal testimony to the ubiquitous experience of failure. Likewise, in the Adapt and Persist challenge students learn how to be strategic and flexible when attempting difficult tasks, even when things do not initially go according to plan, a mantra that can be especially useful when teaching students about the research process.

By scaffolding learning activities and acknowledging students' feelings as they grapple with the concepts, the Metaliteracy Badging System aims to support and empower students as they learn to navigate and contribute to complex information environments. The metaliteracy exercises thus cultivate an underlying mindset that helps students develop resilience as researchers and learners.

## IMPLEMENTING A COLLABORATIVE TEACHING MODEL

Librarians teaching information literacy courses and a lecturer in the Writing and Critical Inquiry (WCI) program first piloted the Metaliteracy Badging System in the fall of 2013. Since then, applications of the system have expanded exponentially across dozens of courses and a wide range of disciplines, including English, psychology, informatics, criminal justice, and education. Undergraduate students, particularly first-year students enrolled in WCI, are the primary users, but an ongoing grant-funded project with an instructor in the School of Education has demonstrated potential expansion of the content for graduate students (SUNY 2016).

Due to metaliteracy's focus on metacognitive proficiencies, the assignments in the Metaliteracy Badging System are reflective in nature, typically consisting of short essay-style responses that require manual grading. In order to scale and sustain this assessment process, we have adopted a collaborative model in which faculty members assign the metaliteracy badging exercises in their courses and review the work of their own students. This model has enabled flexible applications of the metaliteracy content across various disciplinary contexts and has fostered meaningful faculty–librarian partnerships that include collaborative lesson-planning, co-teaching, and sustained conversations related to student research projects.

## Badges as Promotional Tools and Conversation Starters

The implementation of the metaliteracy content typically begins with a meeting between the faculty member and a librarian. Among its many applications, the Metaliteracy Badging System has served as a valuable marketing tool that provides an entry point to conversations about information literacy instruction. The faculty member often reaches out after learning about the badging system via promotional materials, for which the metaliteracy badges provide memorable logos, the Badges FAQ page on the Information Literacy department page, or simply by word of mouth. For instructors who are seeking information literacy instruction, initial planning meetings often naturally progress to the badges as a pertinent teaching resource.

The badge constellations, displayed on a large poster in my office, provide valuable talking points during instruction planning meetings, serving as a visual map of the metaliteracy principles and learning outcomes we have established for students. In effect, the badge graphics provide a preview and a summary of the instructional services that we offer. The constellations also illustrate relationships between fundamental concepts at the quest level, such as copyright—which faculty may be more accustomed to librarians teaching—that lead to more complex culminating concepts at the badge level, such as information ethics. This can be an illuminating discussion for instructors who are often unaware of the breadth of topics and competencies taught by librarians and the ways in which these concepts interweave with their own curricular agendas.

The metaliteracy objectives' alignment with disciplinary learning goals can bring structure to the concepts that faculty members are already teaching. Quests, which on average take about twenty to thirty minutes to complete, provide helpful thought exercises and precursors to research assignments, and can serve as formative assessments over the course of larger research projects. In the initial planning meetings, librarians work with faculty to decide how the metaliteracy assignments best fit into their curricula. The badge system content is flexible, so instructors may assign a selection of stand-alone quests that meet their particular instructional needs or a full series of exercises that lead to a culminating challenge capstone or badge.

The Metaliteracy Badging System uses binary assessment functionality, offering reviewers the option to mark submissions as *accept* or *resubmit*, so it is up to instructors to decide how much credit to assign for successful completion of a quest. Some instructors have assigned quests as extra credit, while one political science instructor designated badge assignments as 30 percent of the course grade. Due to the flexible nature of the assignments, students do not typically earn a master badge within one course but, rather, within several different courses over an extended period.

## Teaching with Metaliteracy Badges

Badge exercises are commonly assigned as prior learning assessments in conjunction with face-to-face library instruction. This flipped classroom model allows the instructor and librarian insight into student understanding and provides students with the opportunity to grapple with complex concepts on their own before applying what they have learned in more hands-on library sessions. Quests covering foundational concepts such as database searching allow librarians to forego bibliographic lectures for more nuanced classroom discussions.

Some of the most in-depth implementations of the badging content have been with the Writing and Critical Inquiry program, a required course for first-year students that prepares them for academic writing and research (University at Albany, SUNY, n.d.). As one particularly successful example, two librarians have collaborated with a WCI lecturer over the past two years to implement badging exercises in conjunction with five co-taught library sessions. The badge assignments serve as touchstones throughout the semester that we periodically refer to and reinforce in class, providing thematic undercurrents such as the growth mindset and research as a conversation. While students are often inclined to rush through research assignments, the badge system exercises prompt them to pause, reflect, and continually revise throughout the process. When students feel they have reached a dead end in their research, for example, metaliteracy concepts encourage them to persevere and try a different approach rather than simply switch topics.

The badging system has allowed for meaningful integration of metaliteracy learning objectives into a variety of courses, which places metaliteracy in context and allows students adequate time to grapple with important concepts that are difficult to cover in one-shot library sessions. Some instructors have invited the librarians to visit their classrooms as students present on final projects related to the metaliteracy content, which in some cases have involved students creating their own quests. The metaliteracy badges have thus provided a valuable framework and vehicle for creative, collaborative, and sustained instruction, opening doors for librarians to have significant input in the general curriculum.

## CHALLENGES AND LESSONS LEARNED

Feedback collected during the early stages of the Metaliteracy Badging System implementation, through conversations with instructors and informal, voluntary Google surveys, indicated that negative experiences with the system were mostly related to navigation issues. WordPress presented several challenges, because it is primarily a blogging platform, not intended to function as a learning management system (LMS). While the BadgeOS plug-in provided the core badging features, several additional plug-ins, such as LearnDash, were required to enable the private reviewing and submission of student work and the organization of users into private class sections. As the number of plug-ins increased, management of the system became more complicated and onerous, due to the constant upkeep and troubleshooting required when plug-ins became incompatible with each other upon completion of required updates. Consequentially, the system frequently experienced bugs or presented a broken interface. Additionally, quests assigned from various badges and for multiple courses often confused students who simply wanted to know what was required for a grade, and they lost the bigger picture of their progress toward earning a badge.

We have also learned that student reception of the badging system has little to do with their openness to badges and is largely dependent on how the instructor presents the assignments. Instructors who are enthusiastic about the metaliteracy content and communicate the purpose of the exercises to students tend to be much more successful than those who reluctantly assign the content to meet departmental information literacy requirements. This observation supports the value of collaborative lesson planning and has also highlighted a demand, particularly among graduate assistants, for more support in teaching and assessing the metaliteracy concepts, which we plan to address in the near future with faculty workshops and orientation materials.

## NEXT STEPS AND FUTURE GOALS

In order to address the technical and navigational issues experienced by users, we have been working to migrate the badging system to a new custom-built platform that will enhance students' experiences with personalized learner profiles and interactive progress maps. While many of the problems already described call for LMS functionality, Blackboard Learn, our institution's LMS platform, does not provide sufficient badging mechanisms to accommodate our tiered badge system design. Thus, with the help of a Web development company and an educational Web design consultant, the Metaliteracy Badging System has undergone a redesign and rebranding due to be launched in the fall of 2018.

Our central goal moving forward is to enhance the flexibility of the system for educators and students. To facilitate discipline-specific applications of the system, our current work involves the development of functionality that will allow faculty members to remix existing quests and create their own customized learning pathways. Ultimately, we hope to offer the Metaliteracy Badging System as an open educational resource that can be implemented at any institution and customized for specific programmatic and disciplinary contexts.

Eventually we may also extend customization capabilities to students. While the pathways leading to the metaliteracy badges are fairly prescriptive, we envision potential "desire paths" (Casilli 2013) that would allow students to establish personal learning goals and chart their own journeys as metaliterate learners. Additionally, we hope to incorporate social features into the system, fostering a cooperative learning community that replicates the team-based methods implemented in our classrooms and that embodies the collaborative goals of metaliteracy.

Lessons gleaned from the Metaliteracy Badging System about flexibility can also be applied to the implementation of badge programs in general. It is important to remember that a badge is only a tool and that students and instructors' use of the tool could digress from what designers originally intended. Ideally educators should design badge systems to accommodate various use cases and allow the system to morph and evolve according to user needs and applications.

As demonstrated at the University at Albany, digital badges can facilitate valuable conversations and instructional collaborations by framing critical competencies for disciplinary faculty and by fostering self-reflective learning in students. Badges have the potential to empower students, helping them find their voice and make a contribution. In Assessing Credibility, for instance, students are encouraged to apply what they have learned to edit an inaccurate Wikipedia entry; in the Speaking Out quest students prepare to present on a topic of interest to a public audience as they plan a hypothetical trip to Speakers' Corner in Hyde Park. In an increasingly tenuous information climate, we believe our students can make a difference not only as informed consumers but also as critical knowledge contributors and stewards of ethical information practices.

## REFERENCES

Blair, Lucas. 2016. "What Video Games Can Teach Us about Badges and Pathways." In *Digital Badges in Education: Trends, Issues, and Cases*, edited by Lin Y. Muilenburg and Zane L. Berge, 62–70. New York: Routledge.

Casilli, Carla. 2013. "Badge Pathways: Part 2, the 'Quel.'" *Persona* (blog), August 28, https://carlacasilli.wordpress.com/2013/04/28/badge-pathways-part-2-the-quel/.

Dweck, Carol S. 2006. *Mindset: The New Psychology of Success*. New York: Random House.

IITG. 2013. "Developing a SUNY–wide Transliteracy Learning Collaborative to Promote Information and Technology Collaboration." SUNY Co-laboratory on Immersive Virtual Environments for STEM Learning (website). http://commons.suny.edu/iitg/developing-a-suny-wide-transliteracy-learning-collaborative-to-promote-information-and-technology-collaboration/.

———. 2016. "Scaling the Metaliteracy Badging System for Open SUNY: Collaborative Customization for Teacher Education Programs." SUNY Co-laboratory on Immersive Virtual Environments for STEM Learning (website). http://commons.suny.edu/iitg/developing-a-suny-wide-transliteracy-learning-collaborative-to-promote-information-and-technology-collaboration/.

Mackey, Thomas P., and Trudi E. Jacobson. 2011. "Reframing Information Literacy as a Metaliteracy." *College & Research Libraries* 72 (1): 62–78. http://crl.acrl.org/index.php/crl/issue/archive.

———. 2014. *Metaliteracy: Reinventing Information Literacy to Empower Learners*. Chicago: ALA Neal-Schuman.

Mackey, Tom, and Trudi E. Jacobson, and Metaliteracy Learning Collaborative. 2018. "Goals and Learning Objectives." Draft revised April 11. *Metaliteracy* (blog). https://metaliteracy.org/learning-objectives/.

University at Albany, SUNY (State University of New York). N.d. "What Is WCI?" University at Albany (website). https://www.albany.edu/wci/about-wci.php.

———. N.d. "Who Studies at UAlbany?" University Libraries (website). https://www.albany.edu/admissions/who.php.

University Libraries, UAbany, SUNY (University at Albany, State University of New York) 2015. "Information Literacy Department Mission Statement." University Libraries (website). Last updated September 3. http://library.albany.edu/infolit/mission.

# Index

abilities: information literacy, 83, 86, 94, 100, 143, 185; integrated, 83; leadership, 22; showcasing student, 70; worker, 22, 124
accomplishments, value of, 77, 188
accreditation, traditional, 4
achievements: hidden, 37; markers of, 103, 162
ACRL. *See* Association of College and Research Libraries
ACRL Framework for Information Literacy for Higher Education, 10, 81–83, 86–87, 89, 114–15, 118–19, 126–27, 144, 167, 171–73, 184; customization and, 89; dispositions of, 81–82, 119, 172; effectiveness of, 10; shift from standards to, 81
ACRL Information Literacy Competency Standard, 89, 145
activities: badge, 7, 9, 156–57, 159, 163; co-curricular, 4; instructional, 12, 152; online, 159; practice, 121, 177
activity sequences, 102
adaptive learning systems, 51
adaptive learning techniques, 27, 136
administrators, 82, 94, 96, 99, 127, 185; challenges to, 33; communicating learning goals and, 96; conventional views of, 35; higher education, 21–22, 25, 27, 32, 35; marketing digital badges to, 47; mind-set of, 27; role of in higher education, 53; working with, 22
Adobe Captivate, 122
adopters: early, 35, 38; first, 127
adults, 17, 58, 181. S*ee also* learners, adult
Albany, University at. *See* University at Albany, SUNY
alternative credentialing, 4, 51–52, 55
alternative facts, 158
Alverno College, 133
American Educational Research Association, 4
American Evaluation Association, 49
annotated list, 172, 178
annotated research bibliography, 94
anti-intellectualism, general, 154
any-pace learning, 42
applications: college, 53, 71; employment, 70, 76; flexible, 193; gamified, 117; graduate school, 97; mobile, 98; potential, 16, 93–94
approaches: competency-based, 132, 147; concept-based, 81; cultural,

199

24; inquiry-based, 131; mastery-based, 136, 146; neoliberal, 147; personalized learning, 135; process-based, 132; progressive learning, 24; skills-based, 81; student-centered learning, 20; traditional, 165
APS. See Aurora Public Schools
Articulate Storyline 2, 122
ASPPH, 148. See Association for Schools and Programs of Public Health
assessment, 4, 7–8, 10, 33, 41, 48–49, 54, 100–101, 106, 109, 118, 132, 165, 168, 172–80; automated, 107; continual, 26; design of, 120–21; evaluation of, 99; formal, 114–15; formative, 4, 102, 109, 193; learning, 172, 190; learning goals and, 185; learning objectives and, 117, 121; learning outcomes and, 7, 169; performance-based, 100; prior learning, 194; summative, 102; tests and rubrics for, 171; traditional classroom, 103; Understanding by Design and, 91
assessment activities, formal, 8
assignments, 119–20, 122, 138, 149, 155, 158, 191, 193, 195; badge, 107, 194; completion of, 8, 88, 105, 117, 156, 171; course-specific, 89, 141, 149, 188; flexible, 194; mastery and, 191; multimodal, 43; prerequisite, 186; required, 116, 124, 156; research and writing, 149; Association for Schools and Programs of Public Health (ASPPH), 148
Association of College and Research Libraries: information literacy framework ACRL Framework for Information Literacy for Higher Education, 81, 89, 114; information literacy standards, 89
attendance, 4, 39, 51, 88, 117
Aurora History Museum, 75

Aurora Public Schools, 61–67, 70, 72; students of, 5, 7, 63, 79
autonomy, student, 19, 40, 105, 138

backward design, 10, 91–92, 103, 109, 121, 188
backward design: badges and, 91, 109; role of, 10
badge, purpose of, 93
Badge Alliance, 104, 107
badge clusters, 49–50
badge constellations, 39, 190–91, 193
badge earners, faculty as, 37
badge models, drawbacks of, 139
badge systems, 21, 32, 69–71, 73, 92, 95, 97, 102–6, 108, 190–91; basic, 102; choose-your-own-adventure-style, 105
BadgeOS plug-in, 186, 195
badges, 3–14, 16, 20–22, 24, 28, 31–56, 66–67, 69–79, 81–89, 91–105, 107–10, 116–18, 120–24, 126–32, 135–39, 141–44, 147–49, 152–54, 156–63, 167–72, 174–81, 183, 186, 190–91, 193–97; co-curricular, 16, 33; community level, 33; components of, 67; confirmatory, 84–85, 87; value of, 87; CORE, 135; creation of, 37, 69, 102, 149; credibility of, 21, 47, 94; criticism of, 7; culminating, 102–5, 161, 186, 194; customization of, 5; definition of, 5–7, 66, 91; efficacy of, 16, 88; faculty pilot program, 37; as feedback, 4, 33, 157; function of, 21, 170; honors level, 45, 186; implementation of, xix, 4, 6, 13, 16, 39, 71–73, 147, 154, 183; industry-granted, 50; locally relevant, 50; meaning of, 7, 92; open. See open badges OBs; originating values of, 108; physical, 75; purpose of, 93–94, 109; role of, 7–9, 12, 42, 94, 108, 147; scarce, 104; student value of, 40, 77; summative, 168–70;

# Index

supplemental, 149; transferability of, 73, 79, 94, 100; use of, 31–32, 85, 89, 97, 117, 154, 160, 162; validation of, 6, 70; value of, 5, 12, 21–22, 33, 40, 46, 49–50, 77, 94, 96–98, 153, 168–69; verification of, 32, 99, 108, 167–68; visual display of, 40; badging, 24, 38; competency-based education and, 131, 143, 167, 169; components of, 44; disruptive nature of, 15; purpose of, 92–94, 159; *See also* digital badging
badging environment, 1, 21, 136
badging goals, foundations of, 31
badging mechanisms, 102, 196
badging opportunities, 34, 37, 46, 53
badging pitfalls, 53
badging platforms, 48, 106, 110, 138; learning management systems and, 106–9; open, 51
badging program: focus of, 93; foundations of, 183
badging programs, 32, 93; arguments against, 170; career competency, 169, 180; creating, 36–38; development of, xix, 165; goals of, 31; implementation of, 35, 40; potential applications of, 93; rigor of, 38–40, 180; scaffolding of, 43; supplemental, 169; sustainable, 39; value of, 98; badging system: industry, 135; open. *See* open badges (OBs)
badging system design, 11; *See also* design
badging systems, xix, 9–10, 12, 21, 39, 88, 104, 106, 135, 162, 168, 193–95
badging ventures, finding value of, 33
Badgr, 98, 107
best practices, badging, 91–109
Beuth University of Applied Sciences, 27
Blackboard Learning Management System, 130, 196
blended learning, 24

Bloom's taxonomy, 41
Bradley Report. *See* Transforming Australia's Higher Education System
branding, 25, 42, 100, 168, 177, 184
businesses, 50, 53, 76–77, 177
buy-in: employer, 48–50; industry, 48–49; institutional, 52, 154; student, 73, 133; teacher, 71

California State University, Fullerton, 113–17, 121–22, 124, 127, 129–30
Camtasia, 123
Canvas Network, 25
capstones, 192, 194
career development, 123, 169
career exploration, 61–63, 69–71, 74–76, 98
career readiness, disparities, 44, 93
careers, 63, 70, 77, 79; academic, 66, 185
carpet badging, 48
CBE. *See* competency-based education
C-BEN. *See* Competency-Based Education Network
certificates, 3, 5, 25, 47–48, 50, 52, 64, 116
certification, 18, 26, 49, 52, 133
challenges: adult learner, 44; badge component, 85, 137–39, 141, 190; digital badge implementation, 33, 127, 144, 147, 154, 183, 195; faculty, 33, 143; motivational, 40, 136; stakeholder, 93; writing-related, 85; change, 15–29; culture, 129; technological, 16, 27
charts, 75, 77, 132, 177
CINDEr, 119–21
citations, 138, 143, 158
City University of New York system, 26
Class Hack, 48, 54
classes: 200-level, 159; 300-level, 156, 159; 400-level, 155–56; basic, 155; elective, 160; expectations about, 159–60; freshman, 116, 159; online, 153; social cohesion in, 160; student

development across, 46; video production, 61
classroom: challenges, 148; computer, 114; traditional, 33
co-curricular, 16, 46
codes: badge, 73; cheat, 85; claim, 73; teacher-supplied, 73
collaborations, 23, 26, 44, 51, 63, 148–49, 153–54, 170; instructional, 196
collaborative lesson-planning, 193
collaborative teaching model, implementation, 192–95
college, preparation for, 19, 63
college education, required, 50
College for America, Southern New Hampshire University, 134
college students, 32, 34, 40, 44; traditional, 19, 25, 44
colleges, 15, 18–19, 21, 25, 43, 50, 52, 56, 63, 77, 147–48, 169; public, 21; traditional, 17
Colorado Academic Standards, 66
Colorado Career Cluster Model, 78
Common Core, 158
Communities, Moodle, 128
community, 34, 37, 53, 64–65, 71, 76, 83, 93, 128, 166; digital badging and, 70–71; gaming, 187; global, 34, 46; open badging, xix
community colleges, 19, 48, 50, 55
community engagement, badges and, 46
companies, 22, 51, 64–65, 70, 76–77, 174, 177–78
competence, 23, 120, 132–33
competence development, 138
competencies, 26–27, 52, 97–98, 102–3, 132, 134–36, 139, 141–43, 171, 184, 193; accrediting agencies and, 147; achievement of, 135, 143–44; articulating, 105; assessment of, 22, 133; badge representation of, 92, 100, 135, 139; badges and, 20, 139; career, 167–69, 179–80; certification of, 133–34; critical, 95, 196; demonstration of, 27, 84, 104, 108–9, 132, 134, 138–39; evidence of, 28, 101; implementation of, 144; information literacy, 95, 107, 137, 143, 170; intercultural, 45; mastery of, 3, 39, 109, 136, 139; metaliteracy, 185, 193; overlap of, 143–44; specialized, 133, 143; transferability of, 100, 109; vocational, 170
competency-based education, 20, 130–37, 143–45, 169; badging and libraries, 131–46; challenges, 133–35
Competency-Based Education Network, 132, 134
competency-based learning, 39, 120–21, 130
competency-based recruitment and hiring, value of, 22
competition, 37, 77, 104
completion: badges as marker for, 7, 88; module, 113, 124
complexity, 15; badging level of, 10; minimizing, 36
compliance, OBI, 98, 135, 137
components, 44, 67, 185; workplace information literacy program, 171
computers, 74, 77–78
concept: badging as a, 15; micro-credentialing as, 4
concepts: advanced, 183, 191; complex, 104, 190, 194
Concordia University Wisconsin, 51
confusion: learner, 104; student, 153, 195
connections, community, 64–65
content: badge system, 188–89, 194; co-curricular, 21; course-specific, 89, 122, 137, 139, 154; delivery of, 107, 109, 170; ethical use of, 174; scaffolded, 136
content experts, faculty as, 15
context, information literacy influenced by, 166
conversation, digital badging, 154–63
conversation starters, badges as, 193–94
core badge curriculum, 149

core badge matrix, 150
corporations, 32, 76
costs: higher education, 18, 25–26, 131, 133, 169; tertiary education, 42; traditional textbook, 26
Coursera, 25
courses: accounting, 43; business, 37; community health, 149; design thinking, 138; elective, 149, 152, 160; first-year, 120; formal, xix, 5, 27, 51, 148, 154, 183; general education, 26; prerequisite, 154; public health, 148; required, 134; restructuring, 154; signature TST, 137, 144; speech communications, 137; technical education certification, 64; traditional, 19
coursework, 4, 42, 134
Creative Commons, 79, 191
creators, information, 84, 185
credentialing: alternative, 18, 27; badges as a form of, 103; costs of, 25; definition of, 3; standardization of, 52
credentialing bodies, traditional, 51
credentialing systems, 4, 52, 99
credentials, 18, 20, 31, 41, 43, 53, 61, 64–66, 71, 77, 79, 97, 100; access to, 78; badges as, 66, 94, 97–98, 100–101, 103; digital badge, 3, 47, 61, 66, 71–72, 75, 77–79; employers and, 47–48, 50, 64; evidence-based, 31, 46, 62, 71; mastery and, 4, 132; meaningful, 64, 108; professional, 99; quality of, 92, 99; stackable, 53; traditional, 27, 50, 93; validity of, 99; value of, 52, 79, 96
credibility, 7, 20–21, 39, 50
credit: academic, 87, 168; advanced placement, 64; extra, 31, 46, 194; lifelong learning, 17
credit hours, 137, 139
credit-bearing courses, 21, 87, 184
Credly, 46, 71–72, 74, 107, 123, 152–53, 155–56, 159, 190; badge design and, 45, 98; impediments to using, 153; Open Badge Interface and, 65, 75; teachers and, 72–73
Credly API, 186
Credly enterprise account, 66, 72
critical inquiry, badges and, 163
critical thinking, 8, 27, 41, 45, 63, 74, 96, 99, 143, 154, 166, 169, 172–73, 184; digital badges for creativity and, 148; fostering, 26; measuring, 170
critical thinking and persistence, 172–73
critical thinking skills, 148, 162
CSUF. *See* California State University, Fullerton
cultures, 3, 71; gaming, 3; innovation, 19
curricula, 8, 15, 147, 194
curricular design, 91, 132
curricular goals, defined, 108
curriculum: badge-based, 79, 103, 149, 153, 165, 168; campus, 96, 114–15, 120; competency-based education and, 132; excelling outside, 44; gamifying, 40; general education, 154, 195; information literacy, 118–20; information literacy and, 115, 119–20, 144, 169, 184; mapping of, 109, 147, 149, 165, 179, 190; metaliteracy, 189; technology and, 106; traditional college, 46
curriculum design, 7, 102, 183; scaffolded, 190
curriculum maps, badge systems as, 102–3
curriculum planning, 92; focus of, 92
curriculum vitae, 135, 162
customization, 5, 20, 41, 196; badges and, 89
CVs. *See* curriculum vitae
CyberPatriot club, 77–78

databases: effective use of, 117, 176; finding and identifying, 113, 119, 138, 170; degree: Transdisciplinary Studies in Technology (TST), 131–32, 137, 139; value of, 26

degree programs, 3, 114, 137, 144; competency based, 131, 139; online, 154
degrees, 42, 108, 131–32, 137, 139; applied studies, 45; associate's, 19, 63; college, 18, 21–22, 48, 52, 93, 147, 162; formal, 4, 167; four-year, 26; international comparability, 23, 27; low-cost, 25; non-four-year, 50; self-paced, 131; traditional, 18, 46, 52, 137; transdisciplinary, 144; value of, 26
demographics, changing, 18
demonstrations, hands-on, 70
departments (academic), 15, 37, 99, 131; partnering with, 100; role of, 93
design, 39, 97, 105, 107, 118, 183; badge, 6, 11, 38, 92, 94, 96, 98–101, 104–8, 171; badge system, 10, 92, 100, 103, 105–6, 196; curriculum, 147; decision-making through, 9; emancipatory, 10; metaliteracy learning objectives, 185; scaffolded, 186; technology use and, 27
design guidelines, 103
Design Lab, 137–38
design principles, 106, 136
Design Principles Documentation Project, 38, 48, 54–55, 95–96, 110
design process, 10–11, 92, 102, 106
design theory, 92
design thinking, 10, 131, 137
designation, accrediting body, 115
designers; graphic, 53, 108; instructional, 108, 119, 149, 185
Digication Help Desk, 46, 57
digital badge initiatives, 64, 66, 78
Digital Badge Program, Aurora Public Schools, 63, 66, 70–71, 77–79
digital badge systems, 66, 72, 113
digital badge tracking poster, 74
digital badges, 5–6, 11–13, 15–16, 18–23, 27, 31–34, 36–37, 39–40, 42–53, 61–62, 64–67, 69–71, 73–77, 79, 91, 94–95, 97–99, 113, 115–18, 120–23, 125–29, 135, 144, 147–48, 168–69; adopting, 36, 127; applications of, 135; architecture of, 65–66; Aurora Public Schools, 66–71; co-curricular programs and, 34, 117; credibility of, 50; definition of, 31, 66, 91, 120; deployment of, 121–22; disruption and, 53; earned, 62, 67, 69, 74, 128; employers and, 22, 48, 70; gamification and, 168; goals of using, 116; higher education community and, 37, 39; honors-level, 45; incentivizing learning and, 75; increased functionality of, 52; information literacy instruction and, 115, 117–18; integration of, 16, 95, 117, 129; lasting implications of, 5; lifelong learning and, 33; marketability and, 47, 147; mastery and, 47; meaning of, 12, 31, 40, 61; micro-achievements and, 42; micro-credentialing and, 5; motivation and, 11, 42, 118, 169; open. *See* open badges (OBs); portability of, 135; potential of, 20, 23, 42; professional associations and, 49; research competencies and, 165; skills and, 6, 73, 76; skills disparities and, 148; social justice and, 64; student strengths and, 66; as teaching learning and assessment tools, 6; value of, 39, 44, 70, 77, 98–99; verification of, 48; video games and, 116; *See also* badges
Digital Badges for Creativity and Critical Thinking, 148
digital badging, 15–16, 20, 22, 27, 32–35, 37–38, 40, 42–49, 51, 53, 64–65, 73, 76, 92, 108, 132, 185; adult learners and, 44; applications of, 37; components of, 38; deployment of, 49; emotions surrounding, 32; equitable access and, 64; future of in higher education, 51–53; higher education and, 27, 33, 42, 45;

Metaliteracy Learning Collaborative and, 185; motivation and, 35, 42; postgraduate, 45; technology and, 65, 132; transparency of, 48; *See also* badging

digital badging committees, digital badging, 38

digital badging program, implementation of, 16

digital badging programs, 27, 43, 45; administration of, 41; higher education, 47; industry buy-in, 48–49, 52; innovation and, 38; motivation and, 46; stakeholders and, 16, 47

digital portfolios. *See also* e-portfolios, 16, 20–21

diplomas, traditional, 42, 51, 57, 59

dispositions, learner, 185, 187

disruptive educational trend, lifelong learning, 18

disruptive technology, digital badging and, 53

diversity, 34, 50, 184

domains; disciplinary, 27, 121, 185; economic, 18; interrelated learning, 186

e-badges see badges. *See also* digital badges

ecosystems, learning, 6

ecredentials, 27–28. *See* badges

education, 50, 110, 147, 158–59, 169, 192; affordability of, 148; competency-based approaches to, 147; general, 149, 152, 169; goals of, 94; neoliberal view of, 169; public, 161; quality, 168, 170; role of, 26; traditional, 35, 169; transparency in, 98; value of, 161

education standards, 67

educational gaps, identifying, 93–94

educational opportunities, 24, 52

educational resources, open. *See* open educational resources (OERs)

educational setting, 6, 44, 137, 185

educational settings, traditional, 32

educational systems, 134, 144; non-traditional, 144

educators, 66, 91–93, 97, 108, 147, 172, 180; professional development of, 78, 102, 105; role of, 6, 13; Understanding by Design framework and, 91

employability, 16, 18, 21, 49, 169

employees, 32; achievements of, 38; prospective, 48–49; qualified, 50; skills of, 50; tertiary education system for, 32

employers, 21–22, 47, 78, 86, 168; badge verification of, 70, 167–68; badges and, 32, 47–48, 50–51, 53, 76–77, 79, 167–68; badging and, 47, 51, 167; career competencies and, 108, 168; education gaps identified by, 86; expectations of, 166; global, 53; information skills and, 172; libraries partnering with, 98; lifelong learning and, 16; local, 50; needs of, 50, 161, 163, 166; potential, 86, 101, 161, 170–71; "reputation economy" and, 167; skill-seeking of, 3, 21, 51, 63, 78; survey of, 22, 84; university collaboration with, 51

employment, 21, 27, 49, 57, 76, 97, 114, 169

employment opportunities, 48, 70, 169

empowerment: badges as tools for, 147–63; digital badging and, 42, 196; motivation and, 41–42

encouragement, 103, 137

endorsements: badge, 71, 100–101, 109; external, 6; issuer, 99; professional, 101

endorser workplaces, 70

endorsers, badge, 70–71, 78–79

engagement, 4, 88; civic, 46; co-curricular, 33; community-focused, 46; learning communities and, 104; metaliteracy and, 88; student, 34,

41, 87; technology and, 12; user-centered, 10
enrollments, 25–26, 128; traditional, 25
entrepreneurship, digital badging and, 51
environment; adaptive learning, 135; gaming, 104, 187; globalized information, 184; information rich, 23; K–12, 144; social online, 183, 185; virtual, 12
environments: higher education, 32, 39, 45; worklplace, 70, 167
e-portfolio systems. *See* e-portfolios
e-portfolios, 27, 45, 48, 50, 55, 92, 154, 156
equity and access, digital badging and, 63–64
evaluation: collaborative, 88; program, 45, 125; quality of, 85, 175
evaluators: certification of, 49; outside, 85, 92, 101
evidence, 8, 19, 21, 45, 47, 51, 71, 100–101, 105, 107, 174, 176; accessibility of, 96; assessment of, 107, 109; attaching to badges, 7, 45, 72; badge, 54, 100–101; badges and, 12, 45, 101; choices in submitting, 105; credentialling, 66; credentials as losing, 8; definition of, 100; determination of, 98; forms of, 37; identification of, 109; learning artifacts as, 101, 106; linked, 31, 99; metadata and, 108, 135; past performances as, 94, 100; supporting, 92, 99, 105; transcript as, 15
evidence types of, 107
exercises, 119, 192–95
expectations, 18, 141, 168; badge programs providing, 34; badging opportunities and, 53; instructor, 159; learner, 6, 91; learning, 132; stakeholder, 33, 93; student, 19, 73, 76, 142, 159–60; student goals and, 96
experience, 31, 45, 192; competency and, 101; digital badging project team, 154; documentation of, 34; educational, 169–70; information seeking and research, 81; job performance and, 21; negative, 39; student, 61–62, 75–76, 86
experiential learning, 15
expertise, 85; academic, 99; accessibility of, 86; assessments of, 101; benefits of badge program from, 108; employer neeeded, 50; establishing levels of, 49; information literacy, 81–82, 86; information literacy-related, 86; prior, 131; specific, 10; subject, 22, 41; training and, 48
experts, xix, 27, 65, 73, 83, 100–101, 107
extrinsic motivation, badges and, 137
extrinsic motivators, 35, 92, 137, 168

factors, motivational, 169
faculty, 15, 17, 19, 22, 33, 35, 37, 39, 43, 46, 96, 101, 107, 114, 116, 123–24, 126, 128, 152, 154, 165, 170, 179, 193, 196; advertising department, 171; campus, 35, 114, 129; college and university, 32; contingent, 154; copyright and, 193; digital badging by, 37, 39, 138; disciplinary, 82, 95, 101, 138, 170–71, 185, 196; FYE, 126; honors program, 45; individual, 154; lessons learned by, 138; librarians and, 127, 178, 183, 193; marketing to, 47, 125; objectives of, 35, 38; role of, 53; teaching, 149, 152–53
faculty members. *See* faculty
failure, 32, 40, 103, 186; fear of, 42, 192; technological, 153
failure wall, 192
fake news, 84, 158
families, 19, 64, 139–40, 142–43
feedback, 14, 175; badges as, 3–4, 33, 102, 159; continual, 191; design input and, 120; endorser, 70–71; millenials and, 43; negative, 157;

offering meaningful, 127; positive, 104, 115, 126, 157; real-time, 136; self-evaluation and, 186; student, 10, 79, 154; targeted, 136
feedback form, 124, 126
feedback mechanisms, 102, 104, 183, 188
FIPSE (Fund for the Improvement of Postsecondary Education), 133
first year experience, 124, 128
First Year Experience program, CSUF, 123
focus: learner, 6; user design, 10
formats: badge, 48; flexibility in badge evidence, 100; industry-standardized, 122; information, 84, 163
foundation, 31, 183; information literacy, 113, 116, 124; scaffolding and, 6
framework: ACRL (*see* ACRL Framework for Information Literacy for Higher Education); backward design as a, 92; badge integration, 6; college and career preparation, 63; competency-based, 119; Understanding by Design, 91
frameworks, badge, 135, 137, 143
freshmen, 115–16, 118–19, 123–24, 128–29, 155–57, 159
Fullerton. *See* California State University, Fullerton
fun, 117, 155; activities perceived as, 42; badges and, 160; intrinsically motivating and, 116; motivation and, 159
functionality, binary assessment, 194
functions, badge's main, 170
Fund for the Improvement of Postsecondary Education (FIPSE), 133
FYE. *See* first year experience

game designers, 108
game-changers, badges as, 42
gamers, 7, 85

games, 7, 85, 116, 121, 190; characteristics of, 116; design of, 103; goals in, 190; open universe, 85
gamification, 58, 116, 130, 168, 180; badges and, 105, 116; digital badging and, 43; effectiveness of, 116
gaming, badges and, 11
generation, millennial, 43
Generation Z, 43
generations, 40, 43, 53, 169, 185; college student, 40, 43; student, 185
Georgetown University, 52
Girl Scouts, 31, 59, 160
globalization, 16, 18, 22–23, 25–27
goal markers, digital badges as, 95, 98
goal setting, 33, 53, 58, 98
goals, 31, 185, 190; achievement of, 4–5, 10, 33, 42, 63, 84, 134, 186; campus, 96, 127; college degree as, 18; incremental, 102; mastery and, 37; meaningful, 104; metaliteracy framework, 187; objective-writing project, 115; personal motives and, 9; program, 73, 117; skill development and, 67; specific, 5, 39, 116; strategic plan, 63–64, 66
Google, 65, 71, 73, 97, 191
grades, 22, 35, 67, 69–70, 171; achievement and, 133; arguments against, 162; assignment, 96, 158; attendance and, 39; badges and, 39, 122, 158, 169–70, 180; course, 22, 175, 194; credentials and, 96; earning, 9, 12, 138; good, 175; learner orientation toward, 43; meaning of, 133; motivation and, 170; purpose of, 180; test, 174–75; test scores and, 71; traditional, 27, 74
grading, 39, 174, 193; test, 171
graduate assistants, xix, 108, 195
graduates, xix; competencies of, 92, 139; employability of, 16, 21; employment and, 21–22, 49; lifelong information skills and, 165
graduation, 77, 144, 169

grants, start-up funding and, 93
granularity: badges and, 39, 51, 73; badging and, 43, 51, 95, 142; learning pathways and, 52
groups: gamify your writing, 58; minority and low income, 17; working in, 139; writing, 37
growth mind-set, 192, 194
guidance, 26, 44, 65; librarian's, 127
guide: badge system mapping, 103; metaliteracy framework as, 188; one sentence badge definition as a, 71; guideposts, 104, 137, 185; guiding questions, following, 73

habits, 6, 11, 37, 43
Harvard University, 146
hierarchies, ideas organized into, 119
high school, 62, 76; credentials earned in, 61; digital badging and, 76–78; rote memorization and, 15, 20, 53, 147–48, 154, 157; theater equipment and, 62
higher education, 18, 21, 23, 36, 42, 45–46, 51, 82, 147, 161–62; access to, 19, 25, 162; adult learners and, 44; badge systems and, 32, 47; basic right of, 25; challenges facing, 17, 133; changes affecting, 15, 18, 23; critical thinking and, 162; definition of populations, 32; digital badges and, 16, 27, 31–32, 42, 185; factors affecting, 18; fragmented credentialling system in, 52; globalization and, 22; innovation in, 19; issues in, 154, 156; lack of flexibility of, 39; laws of supply and demand and, 49; neoliberal approaches to, 147; non-traditional institutions, 26; technology and, 16, 24, 39; traditional institutions, 15, 19, 26; transparency of, 23
Higher Education Act, 134
higher education experience, traditional, 25

higher learning, 13, 29, 54, 114, 145
hiring, 22, 28
hiring decisions, 22
hiring managers, 22, 99
honors, 52, 56
Honors Program, Illinois State University, 45, 56
Horizon Report, New Media Council, 18–19, 21, 24–25, 27–28, 145

Identities: digital, 31; online, 34
identity markers, badges as, 186–88
iGen, 43, 58
implementation: badge program, 71, 124, 137, 152–54; CBE badging program, 132, 137; planning and, 38, 92; Spark Tutorials, 124–25; technological, 154
implementation process, 36
IMS Global Learning Consortium, 98, 104, 135, 145
incentives, 34–35, 53, 130; grades as, 35; motivating, 35
inclusion, diversity and, 184
Indiana University, 110
indivdualized career and academic plan (ICAP), 63
individualized learning, 134
individuals, motivated, 26
industries, 32, 135, 177; appropriate skills and knowledge for, 78; local, 50; necessary skills for, 79; needs of, 51, 65; researching, 178; survey of, 50
industry certificates, 63
informal learning, 17, 134
information: analyzing, 141, 143; creation and sharing of, 23; creation of, 82, 173; creators and consumers of, 84; creators of, 184; documentation of, 143; ethics and, 176–77, 193; evaluation of, 82; finding, 143, 174, 180; reflective discovery of, 81, 83; retrieving, 84; sharing of, 185; sources of, 166, 173,

176, 178; synthesis of, 8, 143, 177; understanding of, 167; use of, 82–83, 138, 166–67, 175; value of, 82, 173
information competencies, 83, 87
information creators, 184, 191
information evaluation skills, 148
information landscape, 84, 184, 187
information literacy: badges and, 28, 81–89, 95, 138, 141, 148, 154, 168; badges and communication in, 86–87; badges and motivation in, 84–86; badges earned for, 45, 154; base level skills of, 157; capabilities of, 93; central concepts of, 82; competency based framework for, 117, 119; competency of, 143, 170; confirmation bias and, 84; critical competencies assessed in, 95; curriculum mapping of, 179; curriculum requirements, 138; definition of competency, 143; definitions of, 82–83; elevator speech explanation for, 86; foundation in, 113, 116, 118; general educational requriement encompassing, 184; importance of, 83–84, 179; integration in curriculua, 96; motivation and, 84–85, 87; non-expert meaning, 89; potential of, 83; required academic competency of, 137, 184; soft skill of, 167; standards-based, 81, 86; teaching of, 83, 89; traditional approach to, 165; unawareness of, 85; unfamiliar terminology, 96; value of, 83, 98, 138, 148, 179
information literacy competencies, 101, 143–44, 175, 184
information literacy education, 166
information literacy goals, 155
information literacy instruction, 86–87, 114; badges and, 81–89; basic, 116; collaboration to improve, 148; deploying, 118; first year experience program, 115; forms of, 87; instructors seeking, 193; integrating badges into, 88; librarians and, 41, 114; models of, 81, 87; public health, 148; role of, 84; role of badging and, 83; scaffolded, 116–17
information literacy instruction context, 83, 135
information literacy instruction programs, 117
information literacy instructors, 81–82, 88
information literacy programs, 87–88, 95–96, 99, 117
information literacy requirement, 114–15, 127
information literacy skills, 82, 124, 148, 154–55, 165
information literacy standards, 115, 185
Information Literacy Threshold Concepts, 81–82, 171, 175, 181
information literate, 81–82, 118, 169
information organization, 141
information practices, ethical, 196
information problems, 166–67, 178
information revolution, 23
information skills, 144, 172; lifelong, 165
information sources, 163, 177–78
information tasks, 167, 172, 175, 178
information technologies, 14, 17, 27, 56, 131, 135
information technology professionals, 65, 108
information tools, 167, 176–78
infrastructure, technical, 106, 160, 186
innovation: adopters of, 35; cultures of, 19; diffusion of, 35; Metaliteracy Badging System and, 183; opportunities for, 38; perceived characteristics of, 35; principles-based grounding and, 35; rewarding, 24; twenty-first-century skills and, 61; value of, 58, 95, 117
Innovative Instruction Technology Grant program, xx

innovators, 35, 38
in-person instruction sessions, 159
in-person learning, 17, 170
instituitons, higher education, 16, 18, 21, 23–24, 27, 32, 36, 38, 42, 44–46, 49, 51–53, 82
Institute for Credentialing Excellence, 13
Institutions: integration of badges in, 16; non-educational, 51; traditional education, 26, 51
instruction: alignment with assessment, 121; competency-based model of, 120; concept-based, 87; delivery of, 8, 131; design of, 106, 134; flipped, 115; in-person, 95, 159; integrated, 184; library, 115, 118, 127, 184; mapping to digital badge system, 72; multimodal, 43; online, 127, 159
instruction program, library, 114–15
instruction sessions, 124, 175; in-class library, 149; one-shot library, 114, 119
instructional design, 6, 9–10, 119; effective, 118
instructional design principles, 92
instructional programs, badge-equipped, 117
instructors, 89, 175, 188, 195; badging systems and, 194–95; course, 88–89; librarians and, 174, 193–94; MOOC, 25; one-shot sessions and, 124
insurgent credentials, digital badges as, 135
integration, 17, 38, 44, 194; badging and LMS environments, 106, 109; digital badging platform, 46; technology, 49
intellectual property, 138, 141
interactivity, 12, 129
interest: personal, 9, 17, 136; situational, 135–36, 144
interest in digital badging, learner, 32
International Baccalaureate Programs, 64
International Society for Technology in Education standards, 67

Internet, 3, 17, 25, 153
interns, 77
internships, 34, 70–71, 77, 79, 97, 168
interviews, 48, 70, 168
involvement, active learner, 10
issuance, badge, 54, 72, 113, 121
issuers: badge, 18, 32, 47, 100; division of labor among, 49; metadata about, 99

job candidates, badges and, 168
job interviews, badges and, 48, 92, 97
job market, 47, 49
job qualifications, badges and, 108
job searching, 70
job training, military, 44
jobs. *See* employment
jobs: badges and, 31, 71; entry-level, 70, 165, 171; higher-paying, 53; McDonald's, 76; paid, 77; requirements of, 21
job-seekers, 82
Joint Educational Project ,University of Southern California, 46
journey: badges and academic, 66; beginning of, 10; completion of, 10; iterative, 183; learner's, 7, 102; learning, 102; phrase leadership, 46; self-paced, 136
journey badges, 66, 69
journeys, metaliterate learner, 196

Khan Academy, 32
knowledge: adult learners and, 44; assessing, 27; certification of, 18; communication of, 43; demonstration of, 105, 132; diffusion of innovation theory and, 34–35; disparity in skills and, 154; new, 4, 10–11; prior, 118; skills and, 3, 6–8, 11, 21, 33, 44, 50–51, 84; student, 45, 97, 126
knowledge economy, 3, 23
knowledge practices, 81–82, 119
knowledge repositories, 95
knowledge transfer, 97

labor, 49, 57, 156; contingent. *See* faculty, contingent
labor markets, 17, 46, 52
labs, computer, 77–78
leaderboards, 104, 116
leaders, 27, 131
leadership, 23, 135
leaners, stakeholder, 32
LearnDash, 195
learner control, badge programs and, 11, 33
learner development, 43, 53
learners: adult, 43–44, 55; guidance for working with, 44; autonomy and, 105; badges and, 4–6, 9, 40, 94; co-development of badges with, 10; college-level, 43; community belonging and, 33; connect, 40, 97; demonstration of evidence, 98–101; demonstration of mastery by, 132; digital archive of, 73; disabled, 45; educational accomplishments, display of, 50; encouragement of, 104, 185; engagement of, 10, 41, 46, 104, 106; extrinsic, 42; intrinsic, 42; metaliterate, 186, 188, 196; millennial, 43; MOOC, 25; motivated, 9, 37, 40, 42, 45, 52, 104, 168; needs of, 20, 78; older, 25; opportunities for, 64, 106; personal interests of, 9; personal motives of, 9; preparation of, 91, 102; prior knowledge of, 118; prospective, 19; qualifications of, 49; roles assumed by, 188; self-directed, 9; self-efficacy and, 104; students as, 66, 69, 71, 183; support, 102, 183, 185; transformation of, 12; twenty-first-century, 185; value of badges for, 5, 91; values of, 92; learning: self-paced, 191; self-regulated, 58; web-based, 14, 56; learning activities, 17, 91, 101, 103, 175, 190–91: badges and, 175, 190; contextualizing, 98; scaffolding, 192

learning artifacts, 4, 7, 21, 75, 100–101, 106, 109, 133, 136, 138–39, 141, 143, 190–91
learning capstones, 183. *See also* capstones
learning catalysts, digital badges as, 6–7
learning communities, 36, 43, 104, 196
learning contexts, 12, 185
learning environments, 41, 55, 135, 144, 191
learning experience, 10, 12, 40, 43, 91–92, 97, 102, 105, 109, 187
learning experiences, badges and, 12–13
learning goals, 8, 91, 93, 96, 102–3, 106, 109, 155, 185–86, 189
learning management systems, 106–7, 121–22, 138, 195; administrators, 128; environments, 106; functionality, 196; module-based, 107
learning modules, 110, 177
learning objectives, 105, 109, 115, 117, 119, 121, 127, 129, 171: badges and, 91, 120; foundational, 118; information literacy, 118–20; mastery of, 121; measurable, 102, 119, 121; scaffolded, 120
learning outcomes, 119; ACRL framework and, 171; assessment of, 7, 134; associated, 149, 175, 177; badges and, 7, 97, 136, 141, 149, 161, 171–72; balance between assessment and, 169; described in terms of competencies, 23; information literacy, 117, 141; institutional competencies and, 46; specified, 38, 149; student, 171–72, 177–78
learning pathways, 9, 20, 41, 102; badges and, 9; customization of, 20, 41; customized, 196; flexible, 105–6; individualized, 5; personal, 21, 27; planning, 101–6
learning process, completion of, 23
learning processes, 4, 8–9, 12, 23, 43, 88, 98, 103, 106, 185–86, 188, 190–92; visualizing, 96

Learning Research Hub, 41, 56
learning services providers, 49, 51
learning system, 103–4
Learning Tools Interoperability (LTI), 106
lessons: activities and, 88; digital badges and, 73; small group, 74; student access to, 74
lessons learned, 79, 114, 195–96; faculty, 138; Spark Tutorials, 127–29; TST Badge Program, 143–44
levels, 9, 136, 158; competency, 135, 184; global, 47; granular, 67, 143; individual, 13, 35, 38; lower, 170, 190; lowest, 119, 191; personal, 20, 27, 134
levels of involvement, learner, 9
librarian: freshman program liaison, 124; FYE coordinator, 129; instructional design, 114
librarians, 93, 117, 119, 124, 127, 137–38, 194: academic, 114; assessment of badges by, 89, 99, 107; campus-wide information literacy challenges and, 93; CINDEr task force, 120; collaboration with, 101, 108, 115–16, 124, 148, 154, 174, 194; communication with, 172; co-teaching, 138; grading and, 174; guest lectures given by, 87; help from, 127, 153; as information literacy experts, 99; information literacy instruction and, 41, 83; information literacy language and, 171; input in general curriculum, 195; instruction, 114–15, 126; instructors and, 118; metaliteracy learning collaborative and, 183; misunderstandings about, 95; role of, 152; school, 158; subject, 120, 129, 165, 184; teaching and, 116; teaching faculty and, 149, 152–53; training, 129; TST faculty fellows, 138; tutorials used by, 127; university, 115–16
librarianship, academic, 90

libraries, 16, 82, 95, 116, 123, 131; academic, 41, 95–96, 117; alignment with campus curriculum, 96; collaborations with, 154; completed, 118; instruction programs of, 118, 120; lifelong learning and, 95; pilot programs and, 10; public school, 158; research, 13, 89, 130, 145, 180–81
library instruction, 115, 123–24, 126; face-to-face, 95, 194
library instruction program, 115–16, 118
library leadership, 126, 129
library research, 113, 116, 124
library research skills, 119
library skills, 117, 154; basic, 120
library tutorials, 115–16, 122, 126
LibWizard, 170, 177
lifelong learners, 17, 28, 33, 187; professional, 17
lifelong learning, 5, 14, 16–18, 20, 24, 26, 28, 33, 95, 123, 183
lifelong learning competition, 95
lifelong learning strategies, 95
LinkedIn, 58, 92
LinkedIn Boot Camp Badges, 34
LMS. *See* learning management systems
local industries, badges and, 50
locally, 50
LTI (Learning Tools Interoperability), 106
Lumina Foundation, 134, 145

MacArthur Foundation, 5, 14, 95
management, 49, 135, 146, 195
map: illustrative curriculum, 102; illustrative progress, 191; interactive progress, 196; visual, 193
mapping, 74, 102–3, 190
marketing, 36, 108, 116, 126, 171
marketing plan, 37
marketplace; economic, 161; global, 49, 54
massive open online courses. *See* MOOCs

mastery, 3, 7, 9, 19, 47, 121, 132, 136, 170, 175, 180, 191; badge acknowledgement of, 52; badge design incorporating, 39; badges and, 6–7, 39, 131, 136, 175, 191; certification of, 133; course concept, 11; demonstration of, 7, 23, 81, 109, 131–32, 138–39, 191; evidence of, 4, 19, 22; focus on, 131; measures of, 121; personalized learning and, 134
mastery. conceptual, 191
mastery learning, 103, 186
measures, 4, 121, 167
mentors; internship, 101; peer, 97
meta-badges, 7, 34, 102, 113, 123–25
metadata, 38, 52, 54; badge, 5, 7, 31, 47–51, 86, 100, 108, 122, 128, 135; badges and, 7, 48, 51, 54, 86–87, 122
meta-data, creating, 99
metadata: describing topic, 7, 87, 99; discoverability of, 47–48; inclusion of evidence in, 100; meaning of, 54; OBI standards and, 109; value of, 98
metadata fields, 98–99
metadata standards, 98
metaliteracy, 185–86, 192–96; information literacy and, 185; lifelong learning and, 183
metaliteracy badges, 187–90, 193–96; teaching with, 194–95
metaliteracy badging exercises, 193–94
metaliteracy badging program, xx, 185
Metaliteracy Badging System, xix, 88, 183, 186, 189, 192–97
metaliteracy concepts, 187, 190, 194–95
metaliteracy exercises, 192
metaliteracy framework, 183–88, 190
Metaliteracy Learning Collaborative, 183, 185, 187, 191, 197
metaliteracy learning objectives, 185–86, 189, 194
metaliteracy principles, 185, 193
micro-achievements, 42
micro-certification, 149

micro-credentialing, 5, 7, 9, 11, 13, 21, 40, 51–52, 55, 99, 129; history of, 3–4
micro-credentialling, badges and, 4, 51, 93
micro-credentials, 3–4, 14, 28–29, 42, 48, 51, 55–57, 78, 110, 170, 180–81; importance of, 4–5
micro-masters, 25, 42, 47
Microsoft, 22, 120
middle school, digital badging and, 75–76
milestones, 4, 42, 52, 84, 187
millenial learners, motivating, 42–44
millennials, 42–43, 57–59, 192
model, Colorado Career Cluster, 78
models: academic, 132; competency-based, 120–21; flipped, 88; flipped classroom, 170, 194; inclusive education, 24; traditional educational, 24, 133
modules, 113, 117, 120, 122–23, 125–26, 129, 171, 175, 177–78; first, 124–25; individual, 168, 172; special customized, 117
MOOCs (massive open online courses), 19, 25, 28, 42, 161
Moodle, 106, 113, 122–24, 126–28
Moodle profiles, 122–23
motivation, 9, 32–33, 40–41, 43, 53, 83–84, 87, 89, 116, 135–36, 145, 159–60, 168–69; badges and, 8, 35–36, 83–84, 87, 91, 96, 118, 136–37, 169; extrinsic, 42; goal-orientation, 136; intrinsic, 5, 97, 159, 168–69, 180; learner, 8, 11; student, 35–36, 42, 83, 117, 135–37, 144, 146
motivation displacement, 35
Mozilla, 47, 104, 128
Mozilla Backpack, 128
Mozilla Foundation, 5, 14, 98, 137, 145
Mozilla Open Badges Infrastructure, 137

nanodegrees, 42, 47, 57
National Council of Professors of Educational Administration, 51–52

National Novel Writing Month, 84–85
NCPEA. *See* National Council of Professors of Educational Administration
neoliberalism, badges and, 147–69
networks, informal, 175
NMC Horizon Report. *See* Horizon Report, New Media Council
Nova Southeastern University, 117

OBI. *See* Open Badges Infrastructure
OBs. *See* open badges
OERs. *See* open educational resources (OERs)
one-shot sessions, 81, 87–89, 95, 124, 126
online classes, 114, 127
online courses, 19, 107, 129; massive open. *See* Massive Open Online Courses (MOOCs)
online education, 26, 127
online learning, 20, 24–25, 121. *See also* learning, online
Online Learning International Symposium, 110
online profiles, badges and, 87, 122–23, 167
online training materials, creating, 66
online tutorials, 113, 127, 170–71, 177–78
open badges (OBs), 5, 33, 49, 71, 94–95, 98–99, 101, 128, 135, 137, 183, 186; certification process for, 49; definition of, 98; metadata standards of, 98
open badges ecosystem, 14, 94
Open Badges Infrastructure, 66, 98, 100, 109, 128, 137
open badging movement, 5, 95, 183
open educational resources (OERs), 26, 196
Open Praxis, 57
Open SUNY, 184, 197
Open University, 45
opportunitites, unlocking badge, 97–98

Organization Systems International (OSI), 135, 146
organizations, 3, 6, 20, 31–33, 45, 99, 117; accrediting, 15; badge creating, 32; external, 101
orientation, 43–44, 113, 123
orientation materials, 195
OSI. *See* Organization Systems International (OSI)
outcomes, 8, 12, 38, 103, 118, 136, 141, 149, 159, 170; mastery of, 132; overarching programmatic, 118
overconfidence, 85, 136

pace, 103, 131, 134, 190; personalized, 132; slow, 15
participation, 34, 40, 42, 88, 107
participation-based activities, 37
partnering, 37, 70, 98, 100, 144
partnerships, 51, 70, 101, 129, 193; co-teaching, 107
Path; career, 144; educational, 42, 139; individualized, 133; scaffolded, 118
pathways, 12, 52, 92, 105, 196–97; alternative, 5, 9; branched, 105
PebblePad, 154
pedagogy, 6, 10, 24, 32–33, 35; digital, 12; effective, 136
peer reflection, 8
peer review, 8
peer voices, 73
peers, student interaction with, 192
Penn State University, 32, 49, 100
perceptions: employer, 29, 130, 181; student, 28, 56
performance, 94, 104, 114, 122, 132, 135–36, 145, 167; demonstrated, 132; student, 39–40, 174; workplace, 70
performance assessments, 4, 131
performance goals, 106
performance objectives, 119
persistence, 137, 166–67, 172–73
personal identifiers, 97
personal learning, 17

personalization, 51, 105
personalized learning, 24, 27, 134
perspectives, 65, 173, 176; relevant educational, 40; student, xix, 34, 137; user's, 10; varied, 191
Pew Research Center, 17, 29
pilot programs, 10, 36–38, 45–46, 102
plaforms, choosing, 121–22
plagiarism, 173, 177
plan: academic, 63–64; lesson, 91, 119, 171, 175, 195; strategic, 63–64, 66
planning, 8, 11, 33, 42, 71, 92, 147, 149–52; strategic, 64
planning document, 71
platforms, 5, 36, 161; badge, 25, 98, 107, 121, 128, 133, 136; blogging, 195; customized, 186; digital tools and, 24; e-portfolio, 46; learning management system, 122, 126, 152, 196; researching, 65
Polaris, OSI, 135
Pollak Library, 113–14, 120, 124, 128
populations, 19, 37, 184; adult learner, 44; global, 46; immigrant, 63; specific student, 44–47; stakeholder, 32; student, 19, 44, 148; undergraduate, 184
portfolios, 19, 31, 51, 101, 103, 135
Portland State University, 117, 148, 153–56
positive reinforcement, 43, 104, 126, 191
positive reinforcement, digital badges and, 126
potential employees, 21–22, 48–49
practices: best, 21, 36, 38–40, 73, 92; ethical, 173; outdated, 100
prerequisites, 139, 156
preschool, 70, 74
prior learning: badges and, 44; demonstration of, 105
prior learning experiences, value of, 26
privacy, 4; ensured data, 65; student, 122
privileges, 36, 98, 104

problem solving, 40, 96, 99, 131, 166–67, 172, 192
problem-based inquiries, 175
process, decision-making, 9, 35
professional development, 17, 34, 44, 71, 78; badges and, 44, 49, 102
professions, 70, 171
proficiency, 31, 83, 139, 141–42, 175, 179
profiles, 85, 126, 153, 190–91, 196; digital badging, 46, 48; LinkedIn, 71, 179; professional, 34, 86, 92; public, 85, 87; social, 187; special, 84; student, 126; text-based, 92; user, 153
program, competency-based, 29, 117, 131, 133
programmers, computer, 122, 156
programming, educational, 50
programming expertise, 98
programming institutions, 24
programs: badge, 7, 11, 28, 34, 76, 78, 93–95, 98, 196; freshmen, 123–24
progress: learner, 6, 42; student, 74–75, 116, 118, 122, 128, 132, 152
progress markers, 183, 190
progression, 6, 143
project concept, 154
project goals, 23
project implementation, 147
Project Information Literacy, 86, 93
project managers, 64
project teams, 149, 154
projects: badging, 113, 115, 120, 122, 126, 149; curriculum mapping and instructional design, 149; final, 109, 194; informal student, 77; instructional design, 149; objective-writing, 115; proof-of-concept, 148
promotional tools, badges as, 96, 193–94
prospective students, 19, 50, 82
PSU. *See* Portland State University
public good, higher education as a, 147, 161

Purdue Polytechnic Institute (PPI), 131, 145
Purdue TST Program. *See* Transdisciplinary Studies in Technology (TST)
Purdue University, 32, 34, 58, 145
Purdue University's Passport, 38, 121

qualifications, 49, 101; individual, 53; library, 99
quality: badge, 6, 12, 92, 98–99, 168; education, 168, 170; program, 65; work, 85, 138
quality assurance, 39
quests, xix, 190–91, 193–96
quizzes, 105, 107, 113, 119, 138, 159, 191

reaccreditation, 114, 127
readiness, 133, 138
reauthorization, 134
recertification, 49
recognition, 18, 33, 42–43, 71, 77, 93, 108, 190; explicit, 179; formal, 3; gaining employer, 6; granular, 185
recommendation letters, 48
recommendations, expert, 100
records, 86–87, 133
repositories, badge, 94
reputation, 18, 28, 31, 42, 100; diminished, 168
reputation currency, 31
reputation economy, 167
requirements: general education, 124, 160, 184; information literacy, 113, 195; university's core curriculum, 138–39
research, 82–83, 149, 173, 175, 178, 194; advertising, 178; badging, 168; consumer, 177–78; evaluating, 175, 177; industry, 177; information literacy, 83; library-based academic, 81, 86; original, 43; student, 171–72, 175, 194
research as a conversation, 194

research as inquiry, 82, 172–73
research assignments, 86, 97, 119, 124, 178, 193–94
research process, 86, 89–90, 179, 192
research projects, 83, 87, 171, 191, 193
research skills, 8, 81, 126, 165, 168, 174
research strategies, 175
research-based process, systematic, 166
resistance, 86, 155
resources, 41, 93; access to, 10; annotated list of, 172, 178; best, 97; existing, 102; online, 184; scholarly, 109; shared, 191; supply of and demand for, 48
responsibilities; academic, 43; information consumer and creator, 84; institutional, 21; librarian, 107; student roles and, 34, 187–88
résumés, 22, 71, 97, 157, 162, 167, 179; online, 92; self-reported, 22; traditional, 22
reTHINK PSU, 148, 154
retroactive badge-granting, 44
rewards, 3, 14, 39, 116, 169; extrinsic, 168, 180
rigor, 3, 47–50, 53, 73, 168; badges and, 47–48, 73, 168, 172
role: badge coordinator, 122; digital badge partner, 65
role of badges, 8–9, 31, 33, 46, 83, 94, 147
roles: learner, 185, 188; stakeholder, 16, 23, 47, 53
rubric, scores of, 175
rubrics, 7, 36, 39, 88, 107, 171–72, 175–76; annotated, 101; benefits and drawbacks of, 39; scores of, 175

scaffolded design, 34, 183, 191
scaffolded learning, design of, 186–90
scaffolding, 6, 36, 41, 57–58, 102, 109; metaliteracy badging and, 183
scalability, 132
scale, 5, 9, 13, 37, 43, 115–16, 170, 193
scaling, 12, 115, 197

schools, 15, 32, 62, 72; badge branding and, 100; branding of, 168; elementary, 77; four-year, 19; graduate, 84, 94; public, 158; relevance of badging to, 41
science literacy, 154
search methods, 172, 178
search strategies, 176–77, 191
search tools, 119, 128, 177–78
searches, 41, 72, 83–84, 146, 172, 176–77; database, 122
self-determination, 135, 144
self-direction, 63, 137, 192
self-efficacy, 6, 11, 40, 58, 104, 135–36, 144, 187
self-esteem, 42
self-evaluation, 186
self-improvement, 5, 183
self-reflection, 8, 33, 196
seniors, 116, 118, 156, 159
services; instructional, 193; library, 113, 121
skill development, 41, 51, 70–71, 74, 76, 78
skill sets, 3, 6–8, 34, 39, 43, 48, 52, 99
skills, 3, 27, 50, 67, 84, 86–87, 101, 143, 166, 179; abstract, 41; articulation of, 139, 157; badges and, 31, 50–51, 67, 74, 76–78, 85–86, 149, 157, 162, 169; busywork and, 156; clinical, 45; communication, 23, 166; communication of, 149; competencies and, 26, 147, 179, 185; concepts and, 119–20; demand for, 48; demonstration of, 47, 66, 71–74, 78, 85, 139, 172, 179; development of, 8, 34, 42, 62, 66–67, 70, 73, 76, 78, 179, 184; employable, 157; employment opportunities and, 48; evaluation and assessment of, 17, 136; evaluative, 75; gauging competency of, 22; granular-level, 73; higher order, 41, 116; information literacy, 81, 83, 143, 155–56, 178–79; job, 17;

knowledge and, 4, 6, 8, 11, 18, 21, 27, 33, 44, 50–51, 100, 119, 132, 154; learning outcomes and, 161; lower-level, 41, 117; marketable, 43, 45, 49; metaliteracy, 22, 185; real-world, 20–21, 61; sharing, 52–53, 66; showcasing, 3; snapshot of, 5; specific, 51, 169; student, 63, 84, 147, 179; technical, 50, 77–78, 129; unrecognized, 33; value of, 83, 85; video game, 85; workforce, 51, 133; workplace use of, 70; writing, 143
skills development, badges and, 41, 76
skills gap, 29, 180
social media, 37, 71, 167
social system, 34–35
society, 5, 19, 23–24, 34, 56, 162–63; capitalist, 162–63; democratic, 147
soft skills, 22, 139, 167
sophomores, 116, 124, 156
sources: information, 82, 143; professional, 156, 159; relevant, 173, 176; research assignment, 86
Spark Tutorials, 113–29; evaluation of, 125, 127; implementation of, 124
stakeholders, 15, 32–33, 42, 82, 93, 143, 172; employer, 32–33, 39, 44, 47–51, 53; higher education, 16, 31–53; identifying, 122; institutional, 33–40; multiple, 101; potential, 83; relevant, 39, 52; school, 32; student, 36, 40–47, 49
standadization, badges and, 21, 23, 52, 89
standards, 4, 26, 39, 47, 50, 81, 89, 114–15, 141
State University of New York. *See* SUNY
Statista, 181
storyboarding, tutorial, 120
strategies, 4, 24, 41, 43, 49, 83–84, 166, 172, 174–76
structure, 26, 95, 138; competency, 144; design and, 11; digital badges and, 144; learning management system,

107; Metaliteracy Badging System, 186; program, 114–15, 129, 132; project, 23; scaffolded, 191
struggling students, digital badges and, 45
student behavior, 122–23, 126
student experience, value of, 62
student success, 24, 81, 93, 129, 137
student work, 127, 173, 179, 195
students: advertising, 165, 170, 181; at-risk, 44; commuter, 148; developmental, 44–45; freshmen, 120; graduate, xix, 107, 126, 184, 192; high school, 70, 77; honors, 44; middle school, 77; minority, 184; online, 127; preschool, 74; undergraduate, 148, 192; university, 45
sub-badges, 188–91
success: career, 169; digital badging initiative, 32–33; lack of, 133; learner, 6, 40, 43, 186; neoliberal, 169; path toward, 9, 12; program, 39, 128; project, 64, 153; self-motivation and, 12; skills for, 26; student, 73, 120
summative learning, 170
summit badges, 66–67, 69–70, 74–75, 102
SUNY (State University of New York), 19, 26, 29, 183–86, 192, 194, 197
sustainability, 63, 179
sustainable badging, 39, 107
syllabi, course, 86, 97, 117, 122, 124, 129, 149, 152, 155, 158, 162
synthesis, 6, 41, 141
synthesizing, 137, 143, 177
system: capitalist, 162; degree, 23; K–12, 138
systems. *See* badging systems

taxonomy, 119
teachers, 10, 15, 32, 41, 63, 65–67, 69, 71–73, 75–79, 103
teaching, 6, 11, 43, 57, 73, 81, 83, 95, 100, 107, 130, 148, 156, 159, 163, 192–95; lecture-based, 15; librarians and, 107; role of badges in, 8
teaching assistants, 152–53
team, badge leadership, 64–67, 69–71, 74, 78
team-based methods, 196
teams, 22, 64–65, 71, 119–20, 149, 155, 166, 185
teamwork, 27, 46
technology, 23, 39, 65, 160; access to, 17, 24, 72, 75; adaptive, 27; badging, 65, 117, 127, 149; challenges of, 156; changing expectations due to, 18; curriculum and, 106; disruptive, 53, 56, 134; education and, 23, 26; educational, 14, 24, 55–56, 58, 108, 133; emerging, 53, 95, 132; globalization and, 26; impact of, 12, 23–24; key trends in, 134; learning and, 12, 102; opportunities from, 16, 27; transformation through, 23
Temerlin Advertising Institute, 168
Temerlin Information Literacy Certificate Program, 170–80
tests, 22, 71, 109, 134, 138, 171–72, 174–75
tools, 19, 106, 196; assessment, 6, 107–8, 132; badges as, 31, 64, 82, 147, 196; badging, 87, 107, 156; branding, 96, 120; digital, 12, 24; educational, 83, 108, 183, 186; freely available, 102; innovative, 34, 148; motivational, 33, 118
tracking, badges and, 7, 38–39, 75, 98, 108, 116, 129, 153
tracking tools, badges as, 117
traditional educational models, disruptive effects on, 24
transcripts, 15, 38, 47, 51–52, 70, 86, 96, 99, 147; badging and, 5, 38; credentialling and, 18; evidence of learning and, 15; grades and, 22, 27
transdisciplinarity, 139
Transdisciplinary Studies in Technology (TST), 138–40, 142

## Index

transfer, 70, 94, 102, 121, 128, 166, 180
transfer students, 129
transferability, digital badges and, 128
transformational teaching, 11–12
transformations, 18, 24, 123, 183; cultural, 24–25
transformative learning, 34; badges and, 13, 34
transformative opportunities, 13
Transforming Australia's Higher Education System, 19
Trans-literacy Learning Collaborative to Promote Information and Technology Collaboration, 197
transparency, 23, 48–49, 96, 98, 102, 108, 135, 168
trends, key, 23–24, 134
troubleshooting, 75, 108, 117, 126, 195
trust, employer, 47, 50–51, 168
TST. *See* Transdisciplinary Studies in Technology (TST)
TST badge program: first revision, 139–42; second revision, 142–43
Tuning Educational Structures in Europe, 23, 29
Tuning Project. *See* Tuning Educational Structures in Europe
tutorials, 87, 89, 113, 115–16, 120–23, 125–29, 170; automated, 119, 127; design and development of, 116, 118, 121–23; interactive, 87, 89, 113, 115
twenty-first century skills, 61, 63, 66, 69–71, 74, 78
twenty-first-century learners, 184–86

UA. *See* University at Albany, SUNY
UAlbany. *See* University at Albany, SUNY
UbD. *See* Understanding by Design
Udacity, 25
undergraduate, xix, 148, 157, 184
Understanding by Design, 91–92, 94, 110, 130
Understanding by Design Framework, 110

universities, 23, 25, 45, 100; badging and, 18, 34; colleges and, 17–18, 21, 23, 25, 33, 49–53; employers and, 51; lifelong learning and, 26; MOOC model and, 25; private, 163; public, 158, 163; schools and, 41; workplace preparation and, 169
University at Albany (UA). *See* University at Albany, SUNY
University at Albany, SUNY, xix, 16, 184–85, 194, 196–97
University of Central Oklahoma (UCO), 34, 57
University of Michigan Library, 58
user design, 9–10, 13
user design research, 13
user engagement, 9–10
user-centered approach, 10, 65, 78
user-centered design, 9
users; badge, 3, 84–85; confidence of, 184; engagement and, 9; experiences of, 195; motivation of, 85; needs of, 196; new generation of, 53; organization of, 195

validation, 6, 65, 70, 100
validity, 3–4, 6–7, 53, 98–99, 101, 108
value, 6, 11–12, 21–22, 26, 33, 36, 39–40, 43–44, 47, 49, 62, 70, 77–79, 82–83, 87, 92, 94–95, 98–99, 108, 161, 168–69, 183, 188; articulation of, 12; badge, 22, 50, 91, 97, 108, 127, 153; co-curricular, 34; continued education and, 50; economic, 52; intrinsic, 42; loss of, 100; program, 179; skill set, 6; work, 157
value calculations, 135–36, 144
value of badges to employers, 47, 49
value of badging, communicated to students, 40
value of digital badges, 44
value of digital badging programs, 47
value of learning, articulating, 168

values: learning-related, 11; Open Badging movement, 95, 183; rubric, 36
veterans, 31, 44, 55–56
video, 61, 121, 127–28, 143, 155–56, 159, 191; embedded, 37, 127
video games, 85, 98, 116, 197

WCI. *See* Writing and Critical Inquiry
weaknesses, 49, 51, 88, 173, 175
websites, 122, 128, 171
WordPress, 121, 186, 195
work, 7, 10, 64, 85, 134, 153–54, 156, 160–61, 166, 196; assessment of, 38, 48, 88; assigned, 95; collaborative, 147; course, 16, 141; grades and, 138; group, 160–61, 170, 175; part-time, 126; program design, 117; research skills, 126; review of, 107–8, 193; sharing, 79; siloing and, 79; student, 77, 116, 136, 141, 143–44, 160, 171–72; student completion of, 7, 117; value of, 78; volunteer, 44, 46
workers, well-prepared, 20, 22, 26, 169
workflows, 5, 105, 152
workforce, 5, 10, 18, 21, 51–52, 133
workload, 38–39, 95
workplace, 24, 70, 78, 84, 90, 94, 98, 166–67, 169, 171, 180–81
workplace development, 21, 32
workplace information literacy, 165–67, 169–71, 175, 179, 181
workshops, 6, 38, 50, 100, 195
Writing and Critical Inquiry (WCI), 184, 192, 194
writing groups, campus, 37

younger grades, 69, 72, 74
YouTube, 114, 127, 191

# About the Editors and Contributors

## THE EDITORS

**Kelsey L. O'Brien** is an information literacy librarian at the University at Albany, SUNY. She has been involved with digital badges for the past several years, beginning in 2013 when she first started working on the Metaliteracy Badging System. Since then she has played a central role in its design and implementation and enthusiastically follows the latest badge-related literature and trends. Kelsey is co-convener of ACRL's Digital Badges Interest Group and an active member of SUNY's FACT2 Micro-credentialing Task Force. She has presented extensively on badges at her home institution and at national (ALA, LOEX) and international conferences (LILAC) and has also co-taught two metaliteracy MOOCs, one of which incorporated digital badges. Prior to her role as an academic librarian, Kelsey worked as a high school library media specialist and a youth services librarian. She serves as liaison for the Writing and Critical Inquiry program at the University at Albany, a required course for first year students, and enjoys helping students transition from high school to college research. Kelsey can be contacted at klobrien@albany.edu or via Twitter at @KelseyMoak.

**Trudi E. Jacobson** is head of the Information Literacy Department at the University at Albany and holds the rank of Distinguished Librarian. She has been deeply involved with information literacy throughout her career and thrives on finding new and engaging ways to teach students, both within courses and through less formal means. She has worked closely with Thomas Mackey for many years. Together they originated the metaliteracy framework to emphasize the metacognitive learner as producer and participant in dynamic information environments. They co-authored the first article to define this model with "Reframing Information Literacy as a Metaliteracy" (2011) and followed that piece with their book *Metaliteracy: Reinventing Information Literacy to Empower Learners* (2014). They co-authored the essay "Proposing a Metaliteracy Model to Redefine Information Literacy" (2013) and co-edited their most recent book, *Metaliteracy in Practice* (2016). Trudi has also written extensively on other topics. She co-chaired the Association of College & Research Libraries task force that created the Framework for Information Literacy for Higher Education. Trudi is a member of the editorial board of Communications in Information Literacy. She freelances as acquisitions editor for Rowman & Littlefield's Innovations in Information Literacy series. Trudi was the 2009 recipient of the Miriam Dudley Instruction Librarian Award. You can contact her at tjacobson@albany.edu.

## THE CONTRIBUTORS

**Laureen P. Cantwell** earned her MSLIS with a specialization in Academic Librarianship from Drexel University in 2011, after having spent several years in the field of non-profit fundraising. While attending Drexel she interned at the Van Pelt-Dietrich Library of the University of Pennsylvania, directed a toybrary, marketed cheese, conducted research for Rolex, and held several other exciting part-time jobs. She is currently Reference and Distance Services librarian at Colorado Mesa University (Grand Junction, CO); previously she worked at the University Libraries of the University of Memphis (Instructional Services librarian) and Grinnell College Libraries (Term Research and Instruction librarian). Her areas of research and publication include librarian engagement with institutional review boards, librarian outreach to STEM students and disciplines, MOOCs and librarianship, embedded librarianship, and librarians working with entrepreneurship programs. She is currently a Coleman Foundation Entrepreneurship Fellow, is layout editor for several librarianship scholarly journals, and continues to partake in odd jobs for the sheer fun of it. Laureen can be contacted via email at lcantwell@coloradomesa.edu or via Twitter at @LPC_reads_books.

**Emily Ford** is Urban and Public Affairs librarian at Portland State University, where she spearheaded the Digital Badges for Creativity and Critical Thinking project. In her instructional praxis she works to incorporate critical thinking into students' lived experiences. Emily may be reached at forder@pdx.edu.

**Michael Fosmire** is professor of Library Science and head of the Physical Sciences, Engineering, and Technology Division of the Purdue University Libraries. He has written over forty articles and chapters on the role of information in active-learning pedagogies and the integration of information literacy in STEM curricula, including co-editing *Integrating Information into the Engineering Design Process* (2014), authoring the *Sudden Selector's Guide to Physics Resources* (2013), and writing chapters on "Research in the Sciences" and "Engineering Research" in *Research within the Disciplines: Foundations for Reference and Library Instruction* (2014). His email address is fosmire@purdue.edu.

**Amanda Rose Fuller** has been working in the field of education for the last decade, starting in Tennessee, with a pit stop in Europe, finally landing in the Aurora Public Schools. Three years ago she made the move out of the classroom to join the exciting and innovative Digital Badge team. From planning professional development to coaching teachers to recognize the 21st Century Skill development in their instruction, Amanda Rose is dedicated to helping her district successfully implement the Digital Badge program to ensure all students are given access to credentials that open doors of opportunity. Amanda can be reached at amanda.rose.mclean@gmail.com or via Twitter at @EdTechARose.

**Megan Blauvelt Heuer** is head of Information Literacy and Communication Arts librarian at Southern Methodist University, where she leads efforts to build successful information literacy programming for the libraries and serves as liaison to advertising, journalism, communications, and arts management. She serves on the Communication Studies Committee for the ACRL Education and Behavioral Sciences Section, which is currently developing a discipline-specific version of the ACRL framework for journalism, as well as on the Instruction Section Communications Committee. Her research interests include the transfer of information literacy skills as well as workplace information literacy. She has an MLIS from the University of North Texas (2013) and an MM from Yale University (2002). Megan can be reached at mheuer@smu.edu.

**Allison Hosier** is Information Literacy Librarian at the University at Albany, SUNY. Her experience with badges includes creating content for the Metaliteracy Badging System and participating on the team that in 2015 launched two MOOCs based on these badges. In the past, she has published and presented on research related to practical applications of the ACRL *Framework* as part of information literacy instruction. Her current research is focused on exploring the metaconcept that research is both an activity and a subject of study and how the *Framework*'s acknowledgment of the contextual nature of research creates opportunities for introducing students to this metaconcept in the classroom. Allison can be reached at ahosier@albany.edu.

**Cinthya Ippoliti** is associate dean for Research and Learning Services at Oklahoma State University (OSU) where she provides administrative leadership for the library's academic liaison program as well as services for undergraduate and graduate students and community outreach. Previously she was head of Teaching and Learning Services at the University of Maryland, where she was in charge of the spaces, services, and programming offered by the Terrapin Learning Commons in addition to coordinating the libraries' First Year instruction program. She is past convener of the ACRL Digital Badges Interest Group and has developed digital badge programs for out of class learning and as part of the OSU Library's Graduate Digital Badge initiative. Cinthya can be reached at cinthya.ippoliti@okstate.edu.

**Betty Izumi** is associate professor in the School of Public Health at Portland State University. Her research and teaching focus on issues at the intersection of nutrition, agriculture, and health equity. Betty can be reached at izumibet@pdx.edu.

**Jost Lottes** is faculty at Portland State's Institute on Aging and School of Community Health. He teaches classes in gerontology, and his research interests include retirement planning, older worker issues, family caregiving, and creating age-friendly communities. Jost can be reached at jost@pdx.edu.

**Lindsay O'Neill** is Instructional Design Librarian at Pollak Library at California State University, Fullerton, where she designs and develops tutorials using Articulate Storyline, Adobe Captivate, and Camtasia. She is also a faculty member in CSUF's MS in Instructional Design and Technology program. Lindsay regularly consults on effective pedagogy, instructional design, educational technology, open licensing, and accessibility. Lindsay holds an MEd, specializing in Educational Technology/Instructional Design, as well as a MLIS. Lindsay can be reached at loneill@fullerton.edu.

**Dawn M. Richardson**'s primary focus is on advancing equity in public health by integrating and building on new knowledge, combining social determinants of health with the science of developmental origins of health and disease. Currently she is pursuing two areas of inquiry relevant to racial/ethnic health disparities: (1) understanding the intersection of place and health, specifically how neighborhood characteristics (e.g., race-based segregation, geographies of opportunity) shape health disparities, and (2) examining the impact of racism and discrimination on access to reproductive health services and birth outcomes. She is assistant professor in the School of Community Health in the College of Urban and Public Affairs at Portland State University. She was a Kellogg Health Scholar at the University of Michigan School of Public Health for two years after earning her DrPH from the University of California, Berkeley (2010). She completed her MPH in Global Health at Tulane School of Public Health and Tropical Medicine in 2002. Dawn can be reached at drichar2@pdx.edu.

**Kristyn K. Rose** earned her MEd in Instructional Technology, with a specialization in Distance Education, from Texas Tech University in 2004, while working as an instructional designer for Texas Tech's Outreach and Distance Education division. In 2007 she moved to Colorado Mesa University to help launch their distance learning program. That same year she joined the board of directors for the Association for Distance Education and Independent Learning (ADEIL). She chaired the Research Committee for ADEIL and has led the organization as president a total of three terms. She remains an active participant in the ADEIL board of directors. Since 2003 she has presented sessions at numerous national and international elearning conferences. She co-authored a research article about online learner interaction in 2007. Currently she is an instructional designer for ODU Online at Old Dominion University, in Norfolk, Virginia. Kristyn can be contacted via email at k1rose@odu.edu or via Twitter at @glitterstim.

**Amy S. Van Epps** is director of Science and Engineering Services in the Harvard Library. Prior to her move to Harvard, Amy was associate professor of Library Science and engineering librarian at Purdue University, with more than twenty years of experience as a subject librarian. Amy has extensive experience teaching engineering and technology students and in 2017 won the Purdue Libraries' Excellence in Teaching award. Her research has focused in part on developing effective methods for integrating information literacy into the undergraduate engineering curriculum, particularly on the use of information in design settings. Amy was an active member of the faculty team who developed a new competency-based degree at Purdue University, the Transdisciplinary Studies in Technology degree, offered by the Purdue Polytechnic Institute. Amy is a longtime active member of the Engineering Libraries Division to the American Society for Engineering Education and in 2014 won the Homer I. Bernhardt Distinguished Service Award from that organization. Amy has a BA from Lafayette College in Engineering Science, with a focus on mechanical engineering, an MSLS from Catholic University of America, and an M.Eng. in Industrial Engineering from Rensselaer Polytechnic Institute. She is currently a doctoral candidate in Engineering Education at Purdue. Amy can be reached at amy_vanepps@harvard.edu.